Palgrave Studies in Prisons and Penology

Series Editors
Ben Crewe
Institute of Criminology
University of Cambridge
Cambridge, UK

Yvonne Jewkes
Social & Policy Sciences
University of Bath
Bath, UK

Thomas Ugelvik
Faculty of Law
University of Oslo
Oslo, Norway

This is a unique and innovative series, the first of its kind dedicated entirely to prison scholarship. At a historical point in which the prison population has reached an all-time high, the series seeks to analyse the form, nature and consequences of incarceration and related forms of punishment. Palgrave Studies in Prisons and Penology provides an important forum for burgeoning prison research across the world.

Series Advisory Board:
Anna Eriksson (Monash University)
Andrew M. Jefferson (DIGNITY - Danish Institute Against Torture)
Shadd Maruna (Rutgers University)
Jonathon Simon (Berkeley Law, University of California)
Michael Welch (Rutgers University).

More information about this series at
https://link.springer.com/bookseries/14596

Ben Laws
Caged Emotions
Adaptation, Control and Solitude in Prison

Ben Laws
Department of Social Anthropology
University of Cambridge
Cambridge, UK

ISSN 2753-0604   ISSN 2753-0612   (electronic)
Palgrave Studies in Prisons and Penology
ISBN 978-3-030-96082-7   ISBN 978-3-030-96083-4   (eBook)
https://doi.org/10.1007/978-3-030-96083-4

© The Editor(s) (if applicable) and The Author(s), under exclusive licence to Springer Nature
Switzerland AG 2022
This work is subject to copyright. All rights are solely and exclusively licensed by the Publisher, whether
the whole or part of the material is concerned, specifically the rights of translation, reprinting, reuse of
illustrations, recitation, broadcasting, reproduction on microfilms or in any other physical way, and
transmission or information storage and retrieval, electronic adaptation, computer software, or by similar
or dissimilar methodology now known or hereafter developed.
The use of general descriptive names, registered names, trademarks, service marks, etc. in this publication
does not imply, even in the absence of a specific statement, that such names are exempt from the relevant
protective laws and regulations and therefore free for general use.
The publisher, the authors and the editors are safe to assume that the advice and information in this book
are believed to be true and accurate at the date of publication. Neither the publisher nor the authors or
the editors give a warranty, expressed or implied, with respect to the material contained herein or for any
errors or omissions that may have been made. The publisher remains neutral with regard to jurisdictional
claims in published maps and institutional affiliations.

Cover illustration: Chris Clor

This Palgrave Macmillan imprint is published by the registered company Springer Nature Switzerland AG.
The registered company address is: Gewerbestrasse 11, 6330 Cham, Switzerland

Azra and Dino

Acknowledgments

There are so many people to thank. Prof. Ben Crewe for his rigorous attention to detail, reliability and generous feedback through all the stages of this research have been incredibly humbling. Both projects would not have been possible without his wisdom, thank you so much. Prof. Alison Liebling helped to intellectually steer the second project at key moments—I am so grateful for her support.

I am further thankful to all the men and women in HMP Ranby, HMP Send and HMP Whitemoor who gave up their time and energy to take part in the interviews and shadowing. Thanks also to all the gatekeepers, staff members and officers who made me feel welcome and pointed me in the right direction with key information, and helped organise the practical and administrative components of my research.

I would like to acknowledge the ESRC for funding both projects, and the additional support I received from Wolfson College. A further thank you to the academics and friends in Cambridge who have helped this project, especially the inspiring people in the Prisons Research Centre: thank you Serena Wright, Elinor Lieber, Alice Ievins, Bethany Schmidt, Aiden Cope, Borah Kant, Julie Laursen, Anne Schliehe. And thank you to those academics outside the centre who have shaped my research,

viii   **Acknowledgments**

especially: Yvonne Jewkes, Thomas Ugelvik, Dominique Moran, all those in De Montfort Emotions and Criminal Justice Cluster, Victoria Knight, Prof. Derick Layder and Prof. Rob Canton. A special mention to Prof. Ian O'Donnell who went out of his way to offer feedback on my ideas.

Contents

Part I Emotions and Imprisonment	1
1 Introduction	3
2 Emotions Before Prison	13
3 Emotions and 'the Self' in Prison	25
4 Relational Emotions in Prison	59
5 Space and Emotions	107
Part II Solitude and Segregation	151
6 Motivation for Segregation	155
7 The Body and Solitary Confinement	179
8 Conclusions	201

x   Contents

Appendix A: Prisoner Artwork   235

Appendix B: Plutchik's Emotion Wheel   239

References   241

Index   267

List of Figures

Fig. 1.1   This piece shows the prisoner drowning in her emotions. Stressful thoughts are literally exploding out of her head   11

Fig. 3.1   The phoenix rising from the ashes is a powerful symbol of emotion and personal transformation   41

Fig. 4.1   The eyes, mouth and ears of the three women have been stitched closed. The woman who painted this image explained that it is very hard to help others in prison because of a lack of information, and misinterpreting the psychological pain and traumas that others' held inside: 'You're not hearing, you're not seeing, you're not getting at what's under the surface'   76

Part I

Emotions and Imprisonment

1

Introduction

Prison life brims with feelings and intense emotions. The three high-profile excerpts below give some indication of this. In order, they reveal profound anguish and sadness, the oscillation of emotions, and the importance of kindling hope and love:

> Once again our beloved mummy has been arrested and now she and daddy [the letter writer] are away in jail. My heart bleeds as I think of her sitting in some police cell far away from home, perhaps alone and without anybody to talk to, and with nothing to read. Twenty-four hours of the day longing for her little ones. It may be many months or even years before you see her again. For long you may live, like orphans, without your own home and parents, without the natural love, affection and protection mummy used to give you. Now you will get no birthday or Christmas parties, no presents or new dresses, no shoes or toys. Gone are the days when, after having a warm bath in the evening, you would sit at table with mummy and enjoy her good and simple food. (Mandela, 2014: 106)
>
> Wouldn't you just know it? You prepare yourself for a fight [in prison], then within seconds you're saturated with relief and it takes all your self-control not to burst into tears…His gesture was the best welcome I could have hoped for. (James, 2003: 57)

© The Author(s), under exclusive license to Springer Nature Switzerland AG 2022
B. Laws, *Caged Emotions*, Palgrave Studies in Prisons and Penology,
https://doi.org/10.1007/978-3-030-96083-4_1

When wisdom has been profitless to me, philosophy barren, and the proverbs and phrases of those who have sought to give me consolation as dust and ashes in my mouth, the memory of that little, lovely, silent act of love [a man who raised his hat to Wilde while he was handcuffed] has unsealed for me all the wells of pity: made the desert blossom like a rose, and brought me out of the bitterness of lonely exile into harmony with the wounded, broken, and great heart of the world. (Wilde, 2010: 85)

In spite of these explicit descriptions of feeling, academic accounts of imprisonment are prone to expunge rather than foreground emotionality. Paradoxically, emotions are both everywhere in prison writing yet also bereft from detailed analysis. Liebling (1999: 341) argues that much of the research on the effects of imprisonment is completely shorn of a 'sufficient affective dimension', and therefore key dynamics of prison life remain buried from view. Furthermore, the few existing studies of emotion in prison tend either to present a limited set of feeling states (narrowing the full spectrum of emotional experiences) or impose rather distortive preconceptions. Men's prisons for example, are typically described as volatile environments suffused with unrelenting aggression and violence. In this context, the argument continues, prisoners embody a hardened masculinity, emotional stoicism, and largely reject their 'soft' emotions. A similar 'skew' exists in accounts of women's prisons, where sexual relationships have been extensively studied but important emotions like anger are generally overlooked (Liebling, 2009). However, in both male and female prisons—which are rarely studied together—this is not the whole story.

There are three reasons that account for the distortive treatment of emotions in prison. First, large-scale research studies have often relied on clinical instruments to record a range of measures, including mood-based indicators (e.g. of depression and anxiety). But these tools typically fail to assess the 'subjective, cognitive, or affective contributions prisoners make to their own experiences of prison' (Liebling, 1999: 287). Second, there is a tendency to focus on incidents (riots, fights and deaths) over the daily prison routine. While this emphasis is understandable given the political and moral significance of these events, the spaces 'inbetween' acute incidents are also important to establish a more complete understanding of the prisoner experience. Third, prisons research is a product of wider criminological attitudes that have treated emotions with enduring suspicion. Indeed, criminological accounts have been criticised for presenting detached 'inhuman data' that is 'cold, calculated, [and] surgical' (Bosworth et al., 2005: 259), a practise Jewkes (2012: 72) describes as the 'extracting out of emotion and humanity from the research process'. These 'bloodless' approaches exclude the sensual, expressive and emotional dynamics that are intrinsic to offending behaviour (Ferrell, 1999). Emotions are not merely a supplement to criminological accounts, rather they play an essential role in shaping social life (Rustin, 2009), the dynamics of desistance and reform (Calverley & Farrall, 2011), informing decision making and a wide range of situational behaviours (Sapolsky, 2017).

In the field of prisons research there have been recent indications of change. A small but influential group of researchers have begun to highlight the affective texture, or 'emotional geography' of imprisonment (see Crewe et al., 2014). The growing field of carceral geography is particularly apposite here. For example, in her recent chapter titled 'The Emotional and Embodied Geographies of Prison Life', Moran (2015: 29) 'foregrounds the personal, emotional subject' and considers the 'ways in which individual spaces of the prison elicit and facilitate different emotional expression'. Meanwhile, Jewkes (2012) has drawn attention to the methodological dynamics of feeling states, calling for a culture shift among academics that have tended to purge their own emotions from the research process. Taken together, these various perspectives call for a re-examination of the role of emotions in prisons research.

First and foremost, then, this entails understanding the emotional realities of imprisonment grounded in the 'day-to-day' prisoner experience. This involves assessing the following fundamental questions: what kinds of emotions do people feel in prison? And what do they 'do' with these emotions? The answers to these questions will show that issues of emotionality are more complex and contested than suggested by previous accounts.

This book aims to tell the 'story' of emotions in prison by placing emotions at the centre of the analysis. The title, 'caged emotions', hints at a major theme of this book: that often imprisonment leads to the containment of emotion, or a least, a compression of the repertoire of feelings on display. This is a simplification, and the full argument goes far beyond this, but it remains a useful guiding principle.

This book is the product of two separate, but related, studies of emotion in prison and is therefore presented in two parts. The first study (Part 1) was a doctoral project (2014–2018) closely examining the experiences of 25 men and 25 women in two medium security prisons (HMP Ranby and HMP Send). The second study (Part 2) explored the emotions among 16 men in a segregation unit in HMP Whitemoor, a high security prison (2019–2021). The second study organically builds on the findings of the first study, both in terms content and concept. Both studies draw on ethnographic methods, mainly participant observations and interviews. Both are guided by a similar set of questions: what happens to a person's emotions under conditions of imprisonment? How exactly do prisoners regulate and express emotions in this closed world? Further, what are the social and spatial pressures that control, limit and constrain emotional expression in this environment? What role does gender play in the expression and control of emotion? In both studies, these questions were sometimes hard to stare at directly, and other questions had to be formulated and considered: what events shaped prisoners' emotions in their lives before imprisonment? What emotional experiences might lead prisoners to *seek out* solitary confinement and isolation?

Before outlining the coming chapters, it is necessary to briefly situate the approach to emotions in this book. As Chamberlen (2018) rightly argues, the meaning of studying emotion has a very different accent depending on the approach used Historical, sociological, psychological, anthropological, biological, and psychoanalytical perspectives have all contributed to the study of emotions in different ways. Selecting a particular approach among these can feel daunting. In this book, emotions are considered as powerful *energies in motion* that have personal depth (they have an individual history) but are shaped by the crucible of (anti) social life in the prisons studied. This approach gives much credence to psychoanalytical views of emotions and how these perspectives intersect with the biographical, social and spatial dynamics of imprisonment. This understanding of emotion was largely formed 'bottom-up' by the field-work findings but is surely also influenced by my own interests and biases. It is noteworthy that this approach is broad rather than narrow. Unlike many books on emotions there is no focus here on *particular emotions* as being primary in the narrative—and therefore worthy of being singled out above others. This may seem like avoidance. Indeed, it is possible to imagine approaches to imprisonment that differentiates chapters on 'anger', 'fear', 'sadness' as important focal points in of themselves. However, such a perspective jars with what I have come to see as the interconnectivity of emotions. Destructive and positive emotions often appear to emerge in sets that cannot be neatly disentangled. Beatty (2019) has been particularly formative here, with his insistence that we can learn much from paying detailed attention to emotional 'episodes', embedded in their local context, rather than decontextualised accounts of emotion as separate forces. In his words:

> Close focus reveals not only the diverse constitution of different kinds of emotions, but the problem of how emotions are bounded and located. I have set out the argument for a polythetic view in which no single element is necessary or sufficient. The approach taken is inclusive but also sceptical. In opting for 'emotional episodes' rather than emotions as-entities, we open up ethnography to unexpected junctures of thought, feeling, and action and widen the scope of comparison. (2019: 45)

Uncovering 'emotional episodes' requires extended time in the field and attention to small details. In this approach the significance of emotion is not observable a priori. By contrast, unpacking the intricacies in the field takes care to uncover 'the microscopic complexity of emotions' (Beatty, 2019: 95). But there are sizable barriers to asking questions about emotions in *any* form. Given that prior research has failed to adequately capture the affective dimensions of prison life, no clear methodological roadmap exists to effectively understand the 'emotional world' of imprisonment. Further, as Rustin (2009: 20) argues, 'one is more likely to learn about states of feeling and their complexity through engagement with works of art, than from study of the social sciences'. This is to say, there is a more established history in the arts and humanities of exploring affect. In a small number of places prisoner artwork has been introduced in this study to complement the text with visual aids. But the challenges of researching emotions remain noteworthy and are addressed in detail throughout the coming chapters as an ongoing thread of the analysis. There will be continued discussion about the ways in which emotions are elusive to measurement. Careful approaches *can* capture affective states to some degree but this is nebulous work. It involves engaging with further issues of authenticity and emotional literacy among prisoners, and how these issues create barriers to meaningful interpretation and analysis. A critical approach to emotions, and the challenges of researching them, is alive throughout the body of the book.

Part 1 introduces the comparative study of men's and women's emotions and the analysis is parsed at three levels, each with a separate chapter. It first considers emotion at the psychological level of 'the self' (Chap. 3); second, as existing between groups (Chap. 4); and, third, in relation to the physical environment (Chap. 5). This conceptual division is tentative and explorative, but hopefully usefully so. Much could be said about the overlapping of emotions across all of these domains—a point made in the conclusion—but holding them separate, even temporarily, has a place.

However, before these three substantive chapters, a brief biographical digression from imprisonment is included as a necessary supplement to understanding what follows (Chap. 2). This chapter starts by contextualising the lives of the men and women in this study before coming to prison, which were marked by a wide range of traumatic experiences. On the whole, participants in this study had had extremely unstable lives before coming to prison. These early experiences shaped many emotional dimensions of life before participants entered prison, especially: levels of emotional literacy, emotion regulation strategies, and the ability to express feelings. This background provides an important framing for all the subsequent chapters and is a reminder that we should be careful not to hastily attribute emotional responses to 'the prison' in a linear manner. Often, damage and trauma is echoed, reinforced and repeated by the experience of imprisonment. And the same is true for patterns of emotionality which can be said to repeat in predictable ways. But this

1 Introduction 9

argument is textured—sometimes prison is traumatising and not just retraumatising—and will be extrapolated further in coming chapters.

The next three chapters comprise the substantive body of the first study, following the conceptual categories ('self', 'social', and 'spatial') already outlined above. Chapter 3 begins this sequence by assessing prisoner emotion at the individual level. It introduces an original theoretical framework based on 'fluid-container' metaphors to describe how prisoners managed their emotions. More specifically, emotion management is placed into different thematic categories such as 'bottling up', 'diluting', 'distilling' and 'discharging' feeling. These strategies were often used in combination by prisoners and had a range of important protective functions. The context and motivation for exactly why prisoners adopted different strategies is discussed. The role of personal agency (and the extent to which prisoners felt emotion was something they could control) serves as an insightful explanatory function. The chapter findings suggest that the separation of prisoners into those considered emotionally 'rigid' and 'flexible' can shed light on emotional development in prison.

Chapter 4 shifts focus, to examine the social dynamics of emotion in prison. Relational emotions are introduced in two primary ways: first, through the significance of sharing of emotions within groups (e.g. with other prisoners, officers, and family members). Reaching out to others in this manner functioned as a way of giving and receiving support that helped prisoners ward off emotional extremes. Second, the chapter goes on to analyse emotions that *emerged in the social arena*. In general terms, small associations and friendship groups exhibited displays of care, affection and sporadic moments of joy. However, outside of these close-knit groups there was typically a harder edge to social emotions, which were marked by anger, hostility, distain, aggression, and fear. These contrasting perspectives on social emotions are structured around the theoretical concepts of 'social glue' (Planalp, 1999) and 'emotional contagion' (Hatfield, Cacioppo, & Rapson, 1993). In short, social emotions simultaneously bound prisoners to one another, while also serving important regulating and distancing functions. These conceptualisations of social emotions provide a way of moving beyond traditional dramaturgical metaphors of prison life that suggest prisoners display a staged version of themselves in public which is markedly different from their offstage, private selves (see Laws & Crewe, 2016, for example).

The final substantive chapter (Chap. 5) considers the spatial differentiation of emotions in prison. This account develops previous work on the emotional geography of prison life (Crewe et al., 2014), arguing that prison spaces can be grouped into three categories: living spaces, hostile zones and free spaces. Throughout, the chapter attempts to explain the spatial dynamics and forces that facilitated the display of particular emotions in these spaces. For example, the 'hostile zones' described in both prisons (where anger and fear was common) appeared to have a number of shared physical and social features. To steer this discussion, the chapter combines and extends theoretical approaches to 'liminality'. While prior research argues that prison spaces have important 'liminal' features (Moran, 2011), prisoners themselves can be said to navigate a kind of liminal experience of imprisonment, which involves moving through different internal stages (see Jewkes, 2005). In line with the latter idea, Turner's (1974) conceptualisation of liminality sheds light on prisoners' experiences of their cell spaces. Furthermore, Turner's (1974) development of 'communitas' provides a basis to understand the important features of free spaces and niches in the prison environment. These perspectives on liminality and communitas provide a useful explanatory frame for understanding the broader significance of the spatial dimensions of prisoner emotions (Fig. 1.1).

Part two of the book signals a shift in direction turning to the connected, but unique challenges, of managing emotions while in segregation. The brief introduction to Part Two describes the emergence of my interest in solitary confinement as being a direct outcome of the first study. More will be said, too, about Chaps. 6 and 7 that explore different aspects of solitary confinement in some depth.

Finally, Chapter 8 draws together the most significant findings from the individual chapters and discusses the wider implications of the

1 Introduction   11

Fig. 1.1 This piece shows the prisoner drowning in her emotions. Stressful thoughts are literally exploding out of her head

research. In the broadest terms, this concluding section argues that there is far more texture to emotions in prison than previous accounts suggest. But there is also an ongoing engagement with key themes in the existing literature. This is to say, what might emotions tell us about classic works on power, freedom, control and resistance in prison? Finally, the limits of the two projects are acknowledged and there is an attempt to situate this work between existing literatures on carceral geography and the psychology and sociology of imprisonment.

References

Bosworth, M., Campbell, D., Demby, B., Ferranti, S. M., & Santos, M. (2005). Doing prison research: Views from inside. *Qualitative Inquiry, 11*(2), 249–264.

Calverley, A., & Farrall, S. (2011). Introduction. In S. Karstedt, I. Loader, & H. Strang (Eds.), *Emotions, crime and justice*. Bloomsbury Publishing.

Chamberlen, A. (2018). *Embodying punishment: Emotions, identities, and lived experiences in women's prisons*. Oxford University Press.

Crewe, B., Warr, J., Bennett, P., & Smith, A. (2014). The emotional geography of prison life. *Theoretical Criminology, 18*(1), 56–74.

James, E. (2003). *A life inside: A prisoner's notebook*. Atlantic.

Jewkes, Y. (2005). Loss, liminality and the life sentence: Managing identity through a disrupted lifecourse. In A. Liebling & S. Maruna (Eds.), *The effects of imprisonment*. Routledge.

Jewkes, Y. (2012). Autoethnography and emotion as intellectual resources: Doing prison research differently. *Qualitative Inquiry, 18*(1), 63–75. https://doi.org/10.1177/1077800411428942

Laws, B., & Crewe, B. (2016). Emotion regulation among male prisoners. *Theoretical Criminology, 20*(4), 529–547. https://doi.org/10.1177/13624 80615622532

Liebling, A. (1999). Doing research in prison: Breaking the silence? *Theoretical Criminology, 3*(2), 147–173.

Liebling, A. (2009). Women in prison prefer legitimacy to sex. *British Society of Criminology Newsletter, 63*, 19–23.

Moran, D. (2011). Between outside and inside? Prison visiting rooms as liminal carceral spaces. *GeoJournal, 78*(2), 339–351. https://doi.org/10.1007/s10708-011-9442-6

Moran, D. (2015). *Carceral geography: Spaces and practices of incarceration*. Ashgate.

Planalp, S. (1999). *Communicating emotion: Social, moral, and cultural processes*. University Press.

Rustin, M. (2009). The missing dimension: Emotions in the social sciences. In S. D. Sclater, D. W. Jones, H. Price, & C. Yates (Eds.), *Emotion: New psychosocial perspectives*. Palgrave Geography.

Sapolsky, R. M. (2017). *Behave: The biology of humans at our best and worst*. Penguin.

Turner, V. W. (1974). *Dramas, fields and metaphors*. Cornell University Press.

Wilde, O. (2010). *De Profundis*. Modern Library.

2

Emotions Before Prison

In tiny surreptitious doses, anaesthesia is dripping into my heart—a formerly complacent heart that is slowly beginning to resemble my dreadful surroundings…Like an ancient tree—gnarled and wizened by time and nature's elements—my heart has grown rugged and callused…this setting helps drive people to anger, frustration, and despair.
—Hairgrove (A single unheard voice. In R. Johnson & H. Toch (Eds.), Crime and punishment inside views. *Roxbury Publishing Company, 2000: 147)*

Hairgrove's poetic testimony above highlights how imprisonment drives the suppression of some emotions (like anaesthesia for the heart) and increases the likelihood of others (anger, frustration and despair). Yet, while prisons research acknowledges the existence of 'masking' emotion in prison, the deeper processes that underpin this mechanism of emotional control, and the idea that it may be connected with behaviours at a later time, are not well-evidenced. This chapter shifts the emphasis from 'masking' as a surface-level social survival strategy to 'emotional suppression', arguing that the later term is better placed to explain the traumatic roots of this behaviour and the connections with subsequent destructive behaviours.

© The Author(s), under exclusive license to Springer Nature Switzerland AG 2022 **13**
B. Laws, *Caged Emotions*, Palgrave Studies in Prisons and Penology,
https://doi.org/10.1007/978-3-030-96083-4_2

14   B. Laws

To explore the emergence of this behaviour, however, it is necessary to glance backwards first. For these processes so readily seen in prison do not come out of a vacuum. There is an attempt to locate the foundations of suppression, which plays an importance role in the development and architecture of emotions. Patterns of emotional management are established long before most prisoners reach the front gate, rooted in childhood and adolescent development in the wider community and they continue to evolve over the lifespan (Cole et al., 2009). This chapter attempts to navigate some of the key dimensions of participants' emotional lives by piecing together their biographies, and by looking horizontally across these accounts to see what they have in common. This includes a detailed engagement with a dark triad of disadvantage, disconnection and trauma. This analysis is a necessary step to understanding the emotions of prison life in a meaningful way.

Troubled Lives

> I've not exactly had the best of lives. I've had no one I could trust. My mum left me and my sisters when I was five. My dad tried to kill himself and he beat me up for most of my life. All my missuses have cheated on me…All I have known is aggression and violence. (Mikey)

Mikey's life before prison—a cocktail of suffering and pain—draws together many of the experiences of the participants in this study: betrayal, trauma, violence, death, separation, and abandonment were all reoccurring themes. The purpose of introducing these accounts here is twofold. At one level, this is a descriptive exercise providing important background information about the lives and prior experiences of the participants. Second, it is an analytical exercise, exploring the possibility that these experiences constitute a kind of 'emotional disposition' that orientates how emotions are handled in prison. Exploring prisoners' biographies, then, can clarify the extent to which particular emotion management strategies appear to reflect a continuation or extension of behaviours acquired before prison (for example, by growing up in care homes or through exposure to physical aggression at home). Conversely, it also sheds light on the way in which living in imprisonment can be a unique experience. That is, it reveals the particular environmental constraints that force prisoners to adapt, expand or suppress their emotional repertoires in ways that do not necessarily correspond with pervious experiences.

There is, of course, an established pool of 'importation' research that studies aspects of offenders' lives before prison to deduce factors that may affect subsequent behaviours in it (see Delisi et al., 2004 for example). This research has mainly drawn on large-scale quantitative data sets, which provide an unsatisfactory framework for the close analysis of affective states. However, Irwin and Cressey (1962) emphasise a more interactive process where the 'external behaviour patterns' of prisoners influence their situational conduct (145). That is, responses to problems of imprisonment are not found solely 'within the prison' but rely on pre-existing orientations 'as determinants of the solutions' (Irwin & Cressey, 1962: 145). For current purposes, this perspective provides a 'crucial ideological bridge between internal and external behaviour' (Crewe, 2009: 150) that can help explain the use of particular affective strategies in prison. The overall argument is inspired by psychosocial perspectives (see Frosh, 2003) emphasize a balance between past history and present reality, focusing on both the inner and outer forces that shape emotional life, without prioritising either aspect in particular.

Most of the study participants summarised that they had had 'horrific childhood experiences' (Haley) and related stories that involved multiple traumatic events. At times, prisoners explained that the chaotic nature of their stories made them hard to verbalise: 'I couldn't even put it in a box, it was one extreme to the other' (Lacey). These accounts were united by the overall level of instability that was being conveyed. Put in a different way, while there was wide variance in their individual circumstances and life experiences, *volatility* consistently emerged as a motif. Often this was manifested in the form of turbulent living situations, which involved being taken from primary caregivers and placed in the care system or foster homes. In the former case, this provided a first exposure to institutional life. Similarly, many prisoners had unstable learning experiences, ranging from reallocation ('I couldn't cope with managing at school so they put me in another one'—Wayne) to complete termination ('Kicked out of school at 14, so education pretty much stopped'—Katherine). These experiences may be symptoms rather than the root cause of the problems described—that is, something must have necessitated the removal from home and school environments. However, it was clear that these incidents were extremely impactful life events that intensified or reinforced existing problems: 'When my mum put me into foster care that made me tenfold worse. I felt like I was pushed from pillar to post' (Molly).

Often, destabilisation was triggered by parental neglect, or by 'caregivers' who abused drugs and instilled feelings of helplessness in their children ('Both my parents were alkies [alcoholics] and my dad left before I could even recognize him'—Neil). Some participants related specific instances or key turning points when they had become conscious of feeling unworthy. For Dean, this moment arose when he found out he had been adopted by his parents: 'They [his family members] told me he's not your real dad. You're feeling unloved'. Paul described a particularly stark moment of childhood abandonment: 'I came back from school one day and my mum had left with my twin brother. I was 15 and it completely burned my head out'. For others, these realisations were not moments of epiphany but rather more measured assessments of their lives. Irene explained that, having lived in over 50 foster homes and secure units, she never felt like 'part of a family, I couldn't attach myself to anything'. In all of these accounts, intense feelings of isolation, hurt and a longing for genuine connection were being communicated.

Some interviewees explained that their isolation was the product of unfathomable levels of childhood suffering and encounters with death:

> My real dad killed himself, and my stepdad hung himself, and I found him when I was ten. And obviously my mum died. And I actually know that life is important, but sometimes you feel what is the point? (Stacey)

Such tragic events created profound grief and existential pain that lingered for many years: 'Do I get haunted by it? Sometimes…I've got so many unanswered questions about my dad's death' (Blanche). Such circumstances made some prisoners cynical about whether they possessed the capacity to feel affection: 'I loved once, and I saw him murdered in front of me, and every bit of life I had left in me went' (Gabriella). Experiencing the death of a loved one signalled a turning point in the behaviours of some interviewees. Billy, for example, reflected on losing his father: 'Ever since then, if anybody ever said anything that made me angry, I would just attack them. Before that I had never been violent in my life with anyone'.

It was common to hear accounts of exposure to domestic violence ('My dad used to batter my mother'—Irene) and, less frequently, that participants had been the direct target of such abuse. One prisoner explained, however, that the physical abuse he incurred from his stepdad paled in comparison to the profound sense of injustice he felt at his mother's response:

> I had welts on my face, you could see the belt marks on my face. I told my mum and she just said "why would he do that to you?"…I had no one to turn to. The only person you feel you can trust, your mum, you confide in her and she shuts you down. (Liam)

A Cycle of Trauma

As noted above, prisoners who had undergone traumatic childhoods articulated how their orientation to the world and their attitude towards relationships changed fundamentally as a result of such experiences. This process was particularly salient in prisoners' accounts of gang activity. Indeed, entering into 'gang stuff' (Katherine) was seen as a remedy to the rejection experienced at home and school. However, rather than a conscious act of rebellion, this was described as a gradual process of exploring alternative lifestyles. That is, participants described getting 'caught-up' in gang cultures (Howard), or simply seeking out those who were like-minded ('I didn't know how to deal with my emotional state at the time. I turned to other young lads that didn't know how to deal with their emotional states'—Dean). In a different vein, Rebecka expressed a fundamental need for affection: 'I was lonely and insecure and I had to be in a gang to keep me loved'. Indeed, in these groups, a person could find unwavering loyalty and:

> …unconditional love, they would ride to the death for me, and I would for them. They would never leave me and I would never leave them…We were kids that came from pain, and to kind of soothe that pain we stuck together. (Liam)

These intimate descriptions of fraternity in gang life are an inversion of stereotypical portrayals of these groups in popular culture. In these affiliations 'trials of strength and character' existed alongside 'forms of social and emotional support that had been absent' from their other relationships (Crewe, 2009: 204). In these relations, the abandonment and pain experienced in the home could be soothed, and a newfound sense of purpose and identity could be established. A second theme that arose from traumatic experiences, especially for the men in this study, was learning a 'language' of violence from a young age. These participants explained that exposure to physical aggression strongly shaped how they viewed the world. First, using violence was a way of temporarily extinguishing deep feelings of shame:

> Someone called me a tramp and five or six guys were giggling at me. That was a time when you start realising material possessions and different levels. He's laughing at me and I just went up to him and knocked him out. You could look at it as he deserved it, or you could look at it as me coming from a violent household, and that violence was a way to mete out any disagreements in the world. You humiliated me, now I beat you and now you're humiliated. (Liam)

As Gilligan (2003: 1162) argues, 'people resort to violence when they feel they can wipe out shame only by shaming those who they feel shamed them'. Second, participants believed that fighting back was an effective way of securing personal safety and standing up for oneself:

> I ended up biting the lad's ear off. After that, I never had no trouble at all…You learn rules from the way life is. The way I thought life was, was if you want someone to do something for you and they won't, you use violence and aggression. (Dean)

Engaging in violence was complex: in one sense, it was a kind of 'currency' that could help one to survive, but it was also viewed with a sense of inevitability by these men. More simply, violence was one of the 'rules' of the social world they inhabited. The need to comprehend these rules— and the monomaniacal compulsion to follow them—explained why some prisoners were drawn into revenge plots in their adolescent years that would re-orientate the course of their lives: 'My brother got shot. So I was kind of forced into a situation' (Howard). Importantly, however, far from resulting in stigmatisation and social rejection, violence enabled these men to carve out an identity and experience acceptance. For example, Neil gained esteem and social approval through his role as an 'enforcer': 'I started getting a name for myself; I was fighting in night-clubs and stuff, I thought I had friends and I'd never had friends before...If you kick off with someone, stand behind me and I'll leather them for you'. However, others reflected that even though benefits were conferred by violence, it was essentially a communication of inner pain: 'Why did I feel the need to be an arsehole and fight? Because I was hurting and I didn't know how to get it out' (Wayne). Similarly, Nia attributed 'outbursts of anger' to her inability to express feelings 'in a good way'. There are further connections here with Crewe (2009: 205) who describes how displays of violence are often deeply rooted in emotional pain, especially experiences of rejection and abandonment. Indeed, De Zulueta (1993: xi) explains one pathway through which 'trauma can be processed into rage':

> When cultural and parental conditions fail to give us a sense of worth, the self knows only how to survive. The 'other' must become the 'object' of a self that needs to be in control. Reminders of inner weakness and pain must be banished, even at the cost of destruction of the self or dehumanisation of the other. (de Zulueta, 1993: 35)

A third rule that was learned was the 'virtue' of emotional suppression. Indeed, many prisoners were taught from an early age that emotions should be kept to oneself. One prisoner described a fraught home environment that gave no opportunity to ventilate emotions in general: 'Family very much was where is the elephant in the room? Let's not discuss things and they'll go away' (Danielle). At times, specific emotions, especially sadness, were circumscribed: 'I've never really been one to cry, my dad has always told me not to cry and suck it in' (Mikey). Moreover, when difficult feelings actually did bubble to the surface, they were met with derision:

I was really upset and I didn't know how to handle it. I didn't have anyone to talk to. My family would say "why are you crying, stop crying!" We just don't talk about those things. I struggled a lot because I am the person who likes to talk, I do cry, even when I get angry I do cry. (Francesca)

Outpourings of emotion were sometimes met with indifference in the school environment, as well as the family: 'I blurted everything out about it [the story of being physically abused] in school but nothing actually happened' (Liam). The study participants thereby learned that emotions were unwelcome intrusions in social life and that the consequences of sharing feelings were often negative. Because there was little viable outlet for inner pain, participants could be left with a deep sense of affective dissonance, a process that van der Kolk (2014: 272) argues leads to either emotional 'numbing' or 'compensatory sensation seeking'.

The *way* in which prisoners delivered these testimonies was also striking. That is, extremely difficult life experiences were expressed with disarming openness and understatement ('I had a bit of trouble, my work partner committed suicide'—Alan). This may be indicative of both the frequency and 'normalization' of such stark events in the lives of these participants. Furthermore, there was a sense of generational circularity in these accounts. That is, prisoners spoke of living in a 'vicious circle' (Molly) and following in the footsteps of parental figures either to custody ('My dad has been in prison since I was six'—Ula) or addiction: 'Remember, your life is a circle, some people go around and around and around. I am one of them. My mum was an alcoholic. I am an alcoholic too' (Irene). Freddy, for example, explained that he was a natural product of his life circumstances:

Obviously being from the environment I'm from people don't always know how to get out of the situations they're in…because of other people, I was forced into a certain situation where I had to defend myself. That brought the sentence on me. Circle of life I suppose. (Freddy)

It is notable that only one participant spoke in positive terms about his upbringing and could not point towards any traumatic incidents. To some degree, prisoners probably engaged in 're-biographing' when sharing their stories: downplaying their own accountability while casting blame on external forces. Almost in anticipation of such a criticism, Mikey reflected: 'I can't blame my life. I've made the choices I've made'. That prisoners themselves often espoused a sense of personal responsibility places important limits on any neat deterministic interpretation of these accounts. Nonetheless, it is apparent that life events can, for many individuals, create traumatic fissures that at least partially constrain and mould their patterns of emotional response.

Crossing the Bridge: Emotions Before and During Prison

As the coming chapters will show, emotional difficulties were also perpetuated or amplified by the prison environment. On some occasions, prisoners explicitly outlined the connections between their past lives and their current circumstances. For example, while discussing the numbing of her emotions in prison, Katherine stated: 'I'm so used to doing it, that's the way I grew up in my house; we don't cry, we don't show emotions, so being like that in here is normal for me'. Female prisoners explained that communicating emotion had a similar quality: for example, it was claimed that 'just like outside' (Molly) women were inclined to be more indirect; capable of being 'friendly to your face and bitchy behind your back' (Molly). In a different manner, those who suffered severe traumas before custody struggled to stave off re-experiencing these unpleasant memories and were periodically triggered by the environment. Chantal explained her attempts to manage her PTSD: 'I keep reminding myself that this is now, this is now, you're in the prison. I'm here. I'm grounded, I'm not there. It will literally take you back if you don't know what you're doing'. As well as the evocation of past trauma, however, prison could also contribute to trauma in harrowing ways. Two participants described the disturbing experience of witnessing suicide in prison: 'I've seen his legs dangling on the pipe…I've heard him die and everything' (Dean).

In these sections, some of the broad forces that shaped prisoners' lives have been traced. In terms of specific emotions, fear, frustration, anger, and sadness take centre stage. The absence of more positive affective states in this narrative—with the exception of affection and care felt towards gang affiliates—is notable, and may indicate the extent of the damage to this socially marginalised group. However, other interpretations are possible: first, when reflecting on the past (as participants were requested to do), people are often led towards remembering negative over positive events (Gray et al., 2008). Secondly, because many participants felt that they had undergone a transformation over the course of their prison sentence, emphasising the adversity of their past life could provide a stronger point of contrast. Ultimately, however, the variety and sheer consistency of turbulent life experiences shared by these participants is stark and sets an important backdrop for understanding their affective states in prison.

Implications

The coming chapters will have much to say about the importance of emotional suppression in prison. This biographical analysis of participants' emotional lives makes three important implications to these discussions. First, the idea that suppression is as a product of rugged masculinity alone is considered as a limited argument in light of the accounts above. Men and women were both seen to be burying their feelings. Second, masking has most commonly been described as a situational strategy, adopted due to the demands of prison culture, but the emphasis given to traumatic life experiences before prison provides an important context to understand it more fully. Third, suppression is typically seen as an end in itself, or as a discrete behaviour, rather than being closely tied with other behaviours—making it appear to be a more adaptive than it is. The threads of these three arguments will be followed and lead directly into the next chapter.

References

Cole, P. M., Dennis, T. A., Smith-Simon, K. E., & Cohen, L. H. (2009). Preschoolers' emotion regulation strategy understanding: Relations with emotion socialization and child self-regulation. *Social Development, 18*(2), 324–352.

Crewe, B. (2009). *The prisoner society: Power, adaptation and social life in an English prison.* Oxford University Press.

de Zulueta, F. (1993). *From pain to violence: The traumatic roots of destructiveness.* Whurr Publishers.

Delisi, M., Berg, M. T., & Hochstetler, A. (2004). Gang members, career criminals and prison violence: Further specification of the importation model of inmate behavior. *Criminal Justice Studies, 17*(4), 369–383.

Frosh, S. (2003). Psychosocial studies and psychology: Is a critical approach emerging? *Human Relations, 56*(12), 1545–1567.

Gilligan, J. (2003). Shame, guilt, and violence. *Social Research, 70*(4), 1149–1180.

Gray, E., Jackson, J., & Farrall, S. (2008). Researching everyday emotions: Towards a multi-disciplinary investigation of the fear of crime. *Journal of Chemical Information and Modeling, 53*, 1689–1699. https://doi.org/10.1017/CBO9781107415324.004

Irwin, J., & Cressey, D. R. (1962). Thieves, convicts and the inmate culture. *Social Problems, 10*(2), 142–155.

van der Kolk, B. (2014). *The body keeps the score.* Viking.

3

Emotions and 'the Self' in Prison

It's every kind of emotion you could ever experience. (Neil)

The hardest thing really is being with myself. (Gabriella)

This chapter sets out to examine emotions at the 'person level', that is, the affective states occurring within individual prisoners. As the statements above suggest, imprisonment is often a deeply emotional experience in terms of both the frequency and intensity of the affective states that are evoked, and navigating these states is an important, highly personal, aspect of the sentence. For many offenders, then, prison initiates an emotionally charged confrontation with the self. How prisoners react to this circumstance forms the substance of the chapter. That is, the various possible responses to emotions (called 'emotion regulation strategies' here) will be considered in some depth alongside an attempt to address the function and distinguishing features of these strategies. In general terms, prisoners' responses to emotion are broad-ranging: from attempts to actively transform difficult feelings (termed 'reappraisal strategies') at one end to a complete rejection or stifling of emotions at the other (called 'emotional suppression'). However, it is not the case that prisoners existed

© The Author(s), under exclusive license to Springer Nature Switzerland AG 2022   **25**
B. Laws, *Caged Emotions*, Palgrave Studies in Prisons and Penology,
https://doi.org/10.1007/978-3-030-96083-4_3

as static points on a regulatory spectrum; rather they often integrated a number of different approaches, depending on the situation at hand and as they adapted during their sentence. One striking feature of the accounts introduced here is the relative concordance between the experiences of male and female participants. In light of this, these groups are largely integrated in the analysis.[1] However, on a few occasions gendered differences were clearly salient, and these instances are clearly distinguished in the text.

Clearly, learning to deal with emotions is not a challenge unique to the prison environment. Foundations are rooted in childhood and adolescent development in the wider community and continue to evolve over the lifespan (Cole et al., 2009). Understanding life experiences before imprisonment helps to contextualise and inform the types of emotion regulation strategies adopted within prison. It is to these biographical concerns that we first turn. Following this, the discussion moves on to specific emotion regulation strategies that prisoners implemented. Finally, the key concept of 'control' is introduced, which provides a further perspective on why prisoners select particular approaches to regulating their emotions.

Emotion Regulation and Imprisonment

The remainder of this chapter assesses the patterns of emotion regulation among prisoners. At one level, this section describes the different ways prisoners attempted to increase, decrease or maintain emotional states. But further, it tries to address the benefits, limitations, and motivations for each of these strategies. To guide this analysis, the chapter introduces a framework based around 'hydraulics' and fluidity. This 'fluid and container' imagery is found across many different cultures to conceptualise emotions, which can be thought of as liquids which fill or exit the body (Stanghellini & Rosfort, 2013). These metaphors have currency in prison and offer a useful way to visualise emotions communicated at the individual level, as in the phrases: 'letting-off steam', 'filled with joy/sadness',

---

[1] Gender divisions are far more apparent in the next chapter (relational emotions between prisoners).

'he makes my blood boil', or 'blowing my lid'. For current purposes though, this frame of reference is primarily used to demarcate the different subheadings of the analysis (for example, 'bottling feelings' inside or 'diluting emotions' through distractions). The account below integrates psychological terminology alongside this imagery in the body of the analysis.[2]

'Bottling-up'

> I bottle it up, bottle it up, bottle it up until it spills over and then I talk about what's on the surface but never actually get in too deep. And then you skim the top away and then you go again. And then when it runs over, you do the same thing, but you never actually empty that bottle. (Chantal)

Most participants (over two thirds) explained that, to some degree, they suppressed their emotions in prison. A distinction is drawn here between suppression and repression: although both processes involve the removal of mental content from one's awareness, the former is a conscious activity, whereas the latter operates at an unconscious level. This separation has been critiqued by some scholars (see Boag, 2010), while others have used the words interchangeably (Burgo, 2012)—in reality, these processes may overlap or reinforce one another. However, the methodological design employed here was primarily tailored towards understanding processes of emotion regulation that prisoners could actively articulate.

Prisoners employed a variety of imagery to explain how they 'pushed down' their feelings, including fluid containment ('You're almost like a kettle, you're waiting to boil, but you're suppressing everything' - Danielle) and dissociative experiences: '[you] just do the zombie thing and go through the motions…rather than dealing with the actual emotions' (Katherine). Essentially, suppression entailed locking off from or 'bottling up' (Alan) one's 'true emotions' (Molly). A key part of this process was a feeling that one could only 'touch briefly on the surface' (Nia) of feelings without delving any deeper. A small number of prisoners

---

[2] Psychological terminology alone can arguably obfuscate rather than clarify the understanding of affective states.

explained that drugs could be used 'as a blocker' (Paul) to assist in this process because they could numb sensitivity to powerful emotions (especially using opioids such as methadone, heroin and Subutex). However, as Paula explained, blunting one's affect could have undesirable consequences: 'I realised when I came to prison that cannabis suppresses the emotions. And while you might want it to suppress bad emotions, it suppresses good emotions too'. Even without the addition of illicit substances, suppression could involve shutting off any affective state in prison, including joy and love. A number of participants acknowledged that there were negative side effects to suppressing feelings: 'I know I'm not dealing with things by putting it to the back of my head' (Mikey). Taken together, these perspectives beg the question as to why a strategy characterised by avoidance was so prevalent in both prisons.

A number of factors seem relevant here. First, the suppression of emotions was often connected to specific gender expectations in prison, at least at first glance. Among male participants, this surfaced through the pride of being a 'strong' man, defined by self-reliance: 'I've never asked for help before, and I'm not going to ask for it now...I've never wanted to put my family under strain' (Alan). Further, the repercussions for not displaying such masculine 'virtues' could be severe in prison, including the risk of exploitation and public shaming from other prisoners (Jewkes, 2005). As Paulie explained: 'If you start coming out [of your cell] crying and getting upset, people will call you a pussy'. Dean used animalistic imagery to summarise this atmosphere:

> Say you've got a bunch of wildebeest, and you've got one outside on the edges talking about emotions and that. As men, normal people, some look at that as weakness. You've got a pack of wolves, all gathering for these fucking wildebeest here. They're looking and they're thinking that's the weak one there. Every one of them will go for the weak one. That's prison man. That's why you keep it bottled up. That's why violence and aggression is needed in these places. I don't like using it myself, obviously I have done it. But violence and aggression is needed for you to be kept safe. (Dean)

It was noteworthy, then, that because withholding emotions was encouraged and open expression could be penalised, there was a double incentive to suppress. This is strongly redolent of broader accounts of masculinity in prison that describe an atmosphere of fierce dominance and a rejection of all emotions apart from anger (See de Viggiani, 2012, for example). Suppression was more prevalent and somewhat more explicit in the men's prison. Interestingly, however, similar accounts were shared by women in this study: according to Rebecka 'people will kick you when you're down', and Pia further explained that 'if you show your emotions, people think you're weak…then people start bullying you and taking liberties'. That these narratives existed in the women's prison too hint that they are not the sole province of 'masculine' conditioning, and are perhaps indicative of a more universal prisoner experience. Given that women and girls are routinely 'sanctioned in their families…and discursively policed by a language which focuses on their sexuality' (Howe, 1994: 183), female prisoners may already be adept at controlling emotions, but for a different set of reasons than men. That is, women are subject to a range of 'disciplinary regimes' and 'control mechanisms' both within and without the prison (Howe, 1994: 129), which place limits on their personalities and emotional expressions (Carlen, 1983).

Second, a number of participants explained that there were negative institutional repercussions that reduced the incentive to share feelings. One of these concerned the perception that *all behavioural displays* were closely scrutinised. Prisoners felt that any aberration from the norm would result in 'people writing reports on us' and 'if they [officers and staff] see you're not stable then you're not getting out' (Pia, both quotations). This concern appeared to be more acutely felt by prisoners serving long sentences. While prisoners might desperately want support, institutional responses often left them feeling 'under the spotlight' (Danielle) and ostracised, rather than assisted. There are strong resonances here with Crewe's (2011) concept of 'tightness', a form of penal power characterised by 'the sense of not knowing which way to move'(522), and a 'highly adhesive' (518) culture of report writing (and record keeping) that can leave prisoners feeling suffocated. Engaging with the ACCT (Assessment, Care in Custody and Teamwork) planning system was a pertinent example of this in Send.[3] Going on an ACCT was perceived as a hindrance

---

[3] This process is used to identify and manage prisoners at risk of self-harm or suicide.

and something that prisoners would come to 'regret straightaway' (Lacey). Danielle further explained that her resentment was rooted in the perceived inequity over the level of behavioural examination:

> They think you can't cope and that by showing emotions when you get into the world again you're not going to be able to cope. But people out there cry, people out their show emotions, but in prison you seem not to be allowed to. (Danielle)

Going on an ACCT document could also stain a prisoner's parole report years after an emotional episode had passed; lifers were particularly sensitive about not having such 'baggage' on their record. Reaching out for help in prison then could have long term ramifications that were better off avoided. In a similar vein, Zoe explained that this degree of behavioural scrutiny also applied to expressions of anger:

> I can't voice my opinions to them [officers] because you're not allowed. If you do decide to voice your opinion, you're being aggressive. Because I'm not allowed to voice my opinion I keep it in, and then when I keep it in I get angry and I get frustrated...I just start screaming because I don't know what to do. (Zoe)

Some participants felt that expressing emotional states such as joy and happiness was also penalised.

> I was dancing around, proper dancing around the prison, letting other people listen to the music. The next day I'm doing an MDT [mandatory drug test]. I was like what is this for, they said "suspicion". Suspicion of what? They said "well you've been very happy lately". (Zoe)

Craig further explained that for a number of reasons 'you can't be happy, you can't be shining in here', because officers will 'try and rock your world'. This could lead not only to more drugs tests but also an increased frequency of 'pad spins'[4] and frisk searches. In sum, then, the environmental conditions were shaping prisoners' affective responses by

---

[4] Searching prisoner cells for drugs and other illegal contraband.

making certain kinds of emotional expressions more or less permissible. Penalising emotions like anger, joy or sadness effectively tightened and funnelled the repertoire of 'acceptable' feelings that prisoners could display.

Positive emotions could also risk unsettling other prisoners. This was most apparent in relation to sentencing decisions. Expressing jubilance about an upcoming release date was disturbing for others serving long, or indeterminate, sentences: 'Being too happy can have a negative effect on people...I have to downplay it' (Ula). A final concern related not so much to being reprimanded by officers *per se* but rather that their response would be underwhelming. That is, prisoners felt that staff did not have the correct resources to assist with their problems or did not want to provide this assistance: 'When you try to speak about it, you don't get help' (Elliot). For some, this was not simply a product of cynicism about officers' capabilities. Prisoners with PTSD diagnoses had highly complex issues that officers had not been trained to support. Finally, there was discord about the social distance between prisoners and officers: 'It's hard to cry to someone who you don't know' (Pia). For all of these reasons, many prisoners felt they had no viable outlet for their emotions. When they tried to express them, it repeatedly brought them the wrong kind of attention and left them feeling trapped.

The third rationale for suppressing emotions—especially salient among the female prisoners—was a deep fear that one might deteriorate if feelings were explored: 'It's like the past and maybe I shouldn't go there, because God knows what going to happen' (Nia). Pia speculated that looking inside could induce a downward spiral of uncertainty about 'what would happen next? Will it be anger? Will I want to commit suicide?' Clearly, then, the prospect of creating irreversible states of suffering led to existential angst for these participants. A small number of prisoners perceived that even acknowledging pain and sadness was akin to admitting defeat: 'What do you do? Just give up and sit in your room depressed?' (Francesca). Prisoners who had relied on medication and drugs to deal with their emotions described an unsettling process of re-experiencing difficult affective states when going clean. Paula was haunted by reoccurring nightmares and 'an overwhelming anxiety' after giving up cannabis (which she claimed suppressed the recall of unpleasant memories), while

Elliot explained that 'it all came to a breakdown' when he realised that drugs had helped to block out his emotions. Overall then, emotional suppression served a range of diverse and important protective functions for prisoners—including both external concerns (avoiding exploitation from other prisoners, keeping a clean record for parole, protection against behavioural scrutiny from officers) and internal factors (buffering fears of breakdown and self-capitulation). However, while some degree of 'bottling up' might be necessary and beneficial, when relied upon extensively this strategy had pernicious side-effects, as discussed in the section that follows.

'Pressurised Explosions' and Losing Control

> In tiny surreptitious doses, anaesthesia is dripping into my heart—a formerly complacent heart that is slowly beginning to resemble my dreadful surroundings...Like an ancient tree—gnarled and wizened by time and nature's elements—my heart has grown rugged and callused...this setting helps drive people to anger, frustration, and despair. (Hairgrove, 2000: 147)

> If I'm feeling angry sometimes I just keep quiet. But then it's like a pressure cooker and I let it out. (Tamara)

As suggested by Hairgrove (2000) and Tamara's commentary, Prisoners who regularly 'locked off' their feelings suffered from a kind of boomerang effect, which suggested that emotional suppression was part of a cycle, or oscillation, between avoiding emotions and feeling overwhelmed by them. This was readily acknowledged by some participants: 'I am an emotional person, but trying to hide your feelings all the time, it does make it worse and I can get quite angry' (Rebecka). Zoe further explained:

> I try my best, but it accumulates and builds up and builds up. I just keep suppressing my feelings and suppressing my feelings, that's me, I suppress my feeling so much that when it does come out it's like people say "we've never seen you like this before!" (Zoe)

3 Emotions and 'the Self' in Prison   33

Unlike Zoe, not all participants lucidly identified a link between their behaviours. However, almost all of those who blocked their emotions regularly could articulate times when they had been suddenly overcome with rage or sadness. These episodes were defined by the following features. First, there was a loss of temporal agency in these moments ('It all comes out at the wrong times' - Lacey) and prisoners felt that their behaviours were 'very unpredictable' (Molly). Second, these outbursts occurred in an altered state of awareness that felt alien. This included feeling dissociated from one's mind ('It wasn't a conscious thing that I did' - Jerry), physiological reactions ('I felt like I was betraying myself by crying. Normally I don't cry for anything' - Amber), or a complete separation from the body itself ('My head went' - Zak). Third, losing control over emotions could lead to extreme outcomes that were described as 'nervous breakdowns' (Bernie) or 'meltdowns' where one completely 'lost the plot' (Stacey, both quotations). One way this manifested itself was through explosive confrontations with officers:

> Listen, I went ballistic, I went crazy, and I open the door and I said 'how dare you, are you fucking crazy? Do I look like a dog?' I said 'this is madness, do I look like a dog? You don't even do that to a child that is rude!' (Zoe)

For some, such explosions were channelled inwards through suicide attempts or extreme self-harm: 'I tried to light myself on fire' (Gabriella). It is worth reiterating that the onset of these behaviours was, to some degree, shaped and intensified by institutional factors.[5] Liebling (2001: 35) notes that the 'helpless and sometimes angry reaction of staff' to self-harm and suicide incidents that can lead to further feelings of social isolation. For current purposes, such reactions serve to perpetuate emotional suppression by ratcheting up the pressure on prisoners to dull their affective states, or only display those that are institutionally acceptable.

It appeared, then, that these prisoners were stuck in a toxic cycle of suppression and explosion—stifling their emotions entirely or being

---

[5] Though, of course, prison suicide is 'not a single problem with a single profile' and is best understood as having 'different causal pathways and different relationships with the prison environment' (Liebling, 2001: 36).

34   B. Laws

completely overpowered by them. De Zulueta (1993: 169) explains this as a typical 'biphasic response' brought on by traumatic experiences, involving 'numbness or a reduced responsiveness to the outside world' alternating with 'the reliving of the traumatic events'. That is, according to the author, victims of unresolved trauma oscillate between these two phases. This cycle of extremes is strongly redolent of Maté's (2003) argument that 'repression and discharge are two sides of the same coin. Both represent fear and anxiety, and for that reason, both trigger physiological stress responses' (272). Maté further argues that because both processes put the body under such acute stress, they are 'examples of the abnormal release of emotions that is at the root of disease' (270). While it is beyond the scope of this research to consider the impacts of emotional stress and long-term health outcomes, the participants in this study who were caught in this cycle did appear to be more unsettled, both physiologically and psychologically, than others. Further, there was evidence here that losing control often led to short-term injuries, including skin lacerations, muscle tears and bone fractures. These injuries were typically sustained through self-harm,[6] punching walls, engaging in fights, or being restrained by officers. By way of contrast, there was some sentiment that losing control, or at least pretending to do so, was an effective means of achieving goals in prison. That is, in an environment where staff resources were limited and needs could easily be overlooked, shouting loudly and acting out could at least provide some guarantee of being dealt with. In some respects then, the institutional climate could reinforce this destructive response strategy.

'Diluting' Emotions

> The way I managed my emotions from day dot was to be proactive and keep busy. (Paula)

---

[6] The picture is rather more complex for self-harm, that may serve a myriad of important coping functions for prisoners. The point being argued here is that self-harm incidents functioned as an 'explosive' outlet for pent-up emotions.

3 Emotions and 'the Self' in Prison   35

Although the majority of prisoners in this study expressed the need to suppress some of their emotions, for most this strategy was not used in isolation. In fact, at least half of the participants explained that they found different ways to 'dilute' unwanted emotions. This section, then, considers the ways in which prisoners found outlets for their feelings and how doing so provided a degree of balance and stability. What is notable about these accounts is the relatively passive (and indirect) nature of the distractions that were employed. This is to say, rather than confront emotions head-on, this strategy entailed sidestepping them.

In broad terms, these prisoners explained that it was necessary to stay busy and 'fill your time' (Rebecka). Instead of viewing the prison sentence as one undifferentiated mass, this approach could help to 'break it up into little sections' (Alan) that were more manageable. Having a stable routine in place 'is what gets you through time…you hear people saying your time will fly, but you don't realise that your time will actually start flying' (Jerry). The most effective routines incorporated *a large quantity* of activities to use time constructively ('I was trying to engage with as many things as possible straightaway' Paula) combined with *a broad variety* of pursuits. Often, this included a 'great balance' (Ellie) of both physically and mentally engaging activities on one hand and a mixture of time spent alone and in the company of associates on the other.

Distraction was further enhanced by *spatial variety*, and prisoners highlighted the importance of 'getting off the wings' (Kyle) during the day. When prisoners spoke of these routines, it was not uncommon to hear a tone of reverence for the mastery over their sentence that they had wrought into reality: 'I know where I'm at and where I need to be and I'm ready. I'm not rushing. I'm not woken up by the officer coming in' (Kyle). Val further explained that his schedule was especially 'joyful' because it enabled him to almost transcend the pains of imprisonment: 'It's like you're not in here. It's a feeling you shouldn't have in here'. It was clear in these accounts how routine offered a kind of 'refuge', or 'skeleton to support each day' (O'Donnell, 2014: 198-199), which enabled prisoners to ease 'into the groove of prison life and alleviating the sources of stress, anxiety, and discomfort' (230). Perhaps ironically then, when these prisoners fully engaged with all the activities provided in prison (programmes, work, education and physical exercise) they felt more 'free' from institutional control.

However, distraction seemed less about institutional compliance and more about cultivating a mental haven where the vagaries of the thinking mind could be diffused and more difficult emotions could be avoided. The polar explorer Richard Byrd (as cited in Cohen & Taylor, 1972: 92) describes a need to 'extract every ounce of diversion and creativeness' out of the immediate surroundings, and to 'routine things more systematically', in order to cut off thoughts about the past. Put simply, these accounts of 'escapism' are firmly concerned with freeing oneself from mental traps that could sabotage wellness. The most important thing was to refocus this potentially destructive mental energy and keep the 'mind occupied' (Verity) by creating enough external stimulation (or physical tiredness) so that 'you don't really think about what's going on' (Andrew). Through engaging in this process, prisoners could bypass the bleak realities of their situation: 'It stops you from remembering that you're constantly in prison' (Amber), and 'you just feel like a weight has been lifted' (Haley).

Although distraction was mainly articulated as a general strategy, it was also used by some to gain equilibrium after particularly acute emotions had been evoked:

> If something has happened to piss me off and I feel like I could get into a fight, I go behind my door [into the cell] and I'll grab my piece of art and start drawing. Before I know it, I think it's not even worth it, it just brings you back down…you might not forget about it but it brings your stress levels right down. (Craig)

Distraction also provided a way of staving off boredom and the temptations of illicit substances, which provided a more exotic but riskier form of diversion. Elliot explained that:

> it is boredom that drives you towards these things [Spice]. If you've got things to occupy your mind, you don't need drugs. Everybody's just trying to escape reality, but then they have to face it again, which is just more stress. (Elliot)

3 Emotions and 'the Self' in Prison   37

Boredom was reported to be one of the most unwelcome affective states that could be felt in prison, and could become a gateway to depression. Descriptions of Send that emphasised inertia and decay were typical: 'It's like an old age home in here' (Gabriella). Indeed, the static prisoner population, dense concentration of lifers, and remote location of the prison contributed to these perceptions. Molly described a process of having to combat the onset of apathetic states:

> Whenever I was feeling negative, I would wake up in the morning feeling like I don't want to go anywhere today. I had to force myself to get up. Staying in bed all day will only make yourself worse. Get up, go out, do something, and focus on something else. (Molly)

While these punchy imperatives to action had benefits, adopting diversion strategies had a number of drawbacks. First, rather than encouraging prisoners to refrain from drug use, distraction could become the precise rationale for seeking them out. Prisoners who literally got 'off their heads' (Karl) on strong psychoactive drugs—especially the various synthetic cannabinoid blends and research chemicals that comprise Spice—temporarily escaped their problems by entering a different sphere of consciousness. Indeed, these substances were often described as providing a 'day out' of prison. As Jewkes (2002: 102) explains, rather than merely tranquillising the prisoner, hallucinogens create separation from the 'physical environment and they "readjust" the temporal flow, releasing the user from the seemingly endless mass of formless time'. Clearly though, some forms of distraction came with higher stakes than others, and prisoners who used drugs risked facing stringent penalties, and risks to their health.

Second, those who relied upon distraction were vulnerable to sudden changes in the prison regime. This vulnerability surfaced when staff shortages led to the cancellation of particular activities (association, gym sessions), security lock-downs, or official changes to the prison timetable. In some ways, far from being liberated from the institutional grip, prisoners who used distraction were at times at the mercy of it: '[when it changes] it's very unpredictable, it's very nervy' (Freddy). In a related way, some prisoners recognised other problems with their dependence: 'I am embedded in a routine, and I really hope I'm not institutionalised from the sentence, I really do' (Lacey). Further, Bernie felt the collective sentiment to stay busy was absurd and unnecessary: 'There seems to be this thing in jail that you've always got to be doing something, but why? Nobody does that outside so why have we got to be constantly doing something in here?'

Finally, because distraction avoids looking for the root of emotional difficulties, it is a perpetual project. At times, then, prisoners expressed strong sentiments that revealed not only that they wanted to stay busy, but that they simply *had* to: 'I don't do relaxing' (Danielle). If such prisoners stopped, even temporarily, their underlying issues would defiantly re-emerge. Indeed, some recognised that they were diluting their problems ('You still think about it, just not as much' - Andrew) but doing nothing to process them: 'But all day, every day, those emotions were still there' (Molly). Ultimately, distraction is a passive and inflexible approach to long-term emotion management. It was best utilised alongside other strategies as sole reliance on it could leave prisoners vulnerable to sudden regime disruptions and the sense that they were merely evading their underlying emotions. On balance, however, distraction was a relatively successful strategy in the short term, enabling prisoners to reduce the potency of unsettling feelings, even if it did not eradicate them entirely.

'Alchemy' and Emotion Transformation

Unlike the strategies considered above, 'transforming' emotions involves a direct engagement with affective states. This strategy aims to completely alter the impact and diffuse the intensity of emotional states. The figurative appeal to alchemy, which is defined here as the attempt 'to transform one chemical element into another' (New Dictionary of Cultural Literacy, 2005) emphasises the creative, generative aspects of this emotion regulation strategy. This process, then, which is referred to as 'emotion reappraisal' or 'cognitive change' in psychological literature, can lead to a complete change of mood 'without negative effects on physiology or memory' (Ehring et al., 2010: 563). Reappraisal was a common approach for around a third of the prisoners in this study, who appeared to reap positive effects from it. This mindset was most typically described in

3 Emotions and 'the Self' in Prison   39

terms of choosing to focus on the positive aspects of a given situation, or as Chantal put it, to 'always see the good out of the bad'.

Within this broad strategy there were a number of different approaches. Some prisoners evoked spiritual philosophies to make sense of their sentence. Indeed it was not uncommon, especially amongst long term prisoners, to hear accounts that reframed the prison experience in terms of 'the grand scheme' (Simon) of things:

> How can prison be the best thing that can happen to someone? For me and where I was, it's the best thing. I was on a chaotic roller coaster for too long…I believe in fate. I try to tell myself that the sequence of events inevitably had to happen. (Paula)

Olivia discovered a similar route through meditation and mindfulness:

> If you can make yourself aware that there is something bigger than you in all of this then it's not as bad. If you can try and find a spiritual resolution…you see it like a test as to how far you have come and if you can stay grounded and balanced, without allowing their mood to affect yours. (Olivia)

Hitting 'rock bottom' was mentally recast as the solid foundation that allowed one to rebuild: 'Out of the tragedy has come something good' (Ellie). Participants claimed that a long prison sentence was absolutely necessary to disrupt their pernicious thought patterns and emotional responses, and that a shorter sentence might have left them unreformed.

> The more I think about it, I got sent down for murder to prove to me that you're not the person you think you are and you've got to change. The more time I spend in prison I think that is true, because I am changing almost weekly or monthly. (Karl)

Prison was thus interpreted as a kind of heroic journey, or bildungsroman,[7] and a powerful test of resilience: 'I keep reminding

---

[7] A genre of literature that focuses on the main character's formative years, especially the time of spiritual and moral education.

myself that prison hasn't broke you so far, don't let it break you now'
(Molly). It is noteworthy that prisoners who spent longer periods of time
in custody were more likely to frame their sentence in these kinds of spiritual terms (Fig. 3.1).

Cognitive change also involved forms of 'bigger picture' thinking
without any spiritual dimension. For example, during particularly testing
situations, daily life could be seen as *positive-by-comparison*. That is, those
with mid-length sentences pointed out that at least they were not doing
a life sentence, and those who disliked prison conditions expressed gratitude that they were in a British prison and not some forgotten gulag. It
was common to hear these sentiments distilled into slogans and mantras,
such as: 'Things could always be worse' (Verity). A further mental crutch
during testing moments involved reminding oneself of cherished family
members or loved ones: 'My kids need me and I need my kids' (Mikey).[8]
Thinking about the future and upcoming release dates could also provide
hope: they were reminders that this time in their life was 'only for the
moment' (Katherine) and not a permanent or static state. At the affective
level, these reappraisal strategies replaced anxiety and fear with feelings of
comfort and serenity, functioning like a kind of psychological escape route.

Somewhat distinct from these broad level strategies, reappraisal was
also used in relation to specific events in prison. Often, this involved
placing a positive spin on the aggressive behaviour of others. For example, Amber explained her thought process when faced with confronta-
tional prisoners: 'I don't know what it is but something just says to me
"maybe they've had a bad day"…maybe it's not that person's fault. Maybe
they're going through something and they're just taking it out on me'. By
contrast, prisoners serving life sentences reminded themselves that the
stakes for fighting and conflict engagement were particularly high for
them: 'I can't afford to get angry in here, I've just got to keep that focus
in my head daily' (Oscar). These prisoners realised that 'violence and
aggression are often met with similar or the same outcome. It's destructive, you can't win anything' (Olivia). These interpretations allowed prisoners to take the 'high road' and save face when walking away from

---

[8] The significance of family and 'emotion work' achieved through relationships is a key theme of the
next chapter and is therefore not developed at length here.

3 Emotions and 'the Self' in Prison

Fig. 3.1 The phoenix rising from the ashes is a powerful symbol of emotion and personal transformation

potential conflicts. In a different sense, the pain of not hearing from (or being able to contact) family members was sometimes assuaged by reminding oneself that 'they are busy with their lives, they do care about me but they probably have other stuff going on' (Andrew). Finally, while the environment stripped individuals of many privileges, pleasure could still be found in the small things: 'I can go and get a nice meal from the servery and I can think yeah, I'm happy now. I don't need the big satisfactions' (Bernie).

Taken together, these accounts show prisoners actively taking control over and transforming emotional stimuli. An important feature of reframing is that prisoners seemed able to forge a more positive reality for themselves. While this strategy is a close bedfellow to denial, it is distinct in the respect that it does not involve the passive rejection of uncomfortable emotion states. Put succinctly, while reframing involves some degree of distortion or selectivity, the uplifting effect on prisoners' moods was undeniable. Further, reappraisal does not exclude or reject the presence of uncomfortable feelings or stimuli, rather it tries to reshape these feelings by taking a different perspective. Ultimately, then, because prisoners were not avoiding their emotions, they benefitted from trying to see the 'silver lining' in their circumstances.

'Distilling' and Emotional Processing

> The first rule of any handbook on survival: *understand what is happening to you.* (Cohen & Taylor, 1972, 138, emphasis in original)
> Now I am dealing—without alcohol—with the highs and lows of prison: happiness, anger, frustration, every emotion. I'm learning ways and techniques to deal with them. (Karl)

Distillation is introduced here as 'the extraction of the essential meaning or most important aspects of something' (OED, 2009). In this manner, a subset of prisoners (around a third) explained that they were able to use various 'distillation methods' to explore their emotions and gain deeper understanding in the process. To return to the metaphor of 'fluids', rather than purging or filling their metaphorical containers, distillation entailed examining what was *within* these containers and exploring its 'fluid form' in a particular way. More specifically, this entails working on the essence of emotion states to concentrate a particular meaning, or cultivate insight from them.

However, facing difficult emotions head-on was not without risk; there was a sizeable fear that such thinking might lead to rumination. This emerged strongly among the female participants, who explained that engaging with feelings was easy to start but difficult to finish. Tamara had ambivalent thoughts about the experience: 'You got so much time to think, which is good. But when you start thinking you go deeper and deeper, and then obviously that's when you start feeling more depressed'. Prisoners were outlining fears about obsession and getting bogged down in 'a merry go round of the same thoughts and the same visions' (Amber). This process could have a significant impact on health and sleeping patterns: 'I'd look at the time and I had been awake all night. Sitting thinking and getting wound up, regurgitating crap' (Olivia).

Part of the reason such thoughts became cyclical is that prisoners were often powerless to act on their problems or implement solutions. For example, there was little that prisoners could do to solve issues with their loved ones: 'I always sorted everything out in my family, so now when things go on and there's arguments, there's nothing I can do, and it makes me feel really anxious and angry. I can't cope' (Francesca). A key turning point for some prisoners, before they could consider 'distilling' their feelings, was coming to accept the reality of their relative powerlessness: 'I can't help them, not until I get outside and sorted out…it's better for me to keep my head in the jail' (Tamara). Some prisoners explained that it was useful to set time limits on their grief:

> So you have to deal with that shit [being left by a partner], it hurt for a day but then I moved on from it, don't dwell. Deal with whatever emotions you're experiencing and then put it in the drawer. (Neil)

A second temporal strategy was to postpone—but not suppress—difficult feelings. For example, Yvonne explained that finding the 'right' time for emotions was an important personal development:

> If I've got a problem, or if something is annoying me, I don't deal with it straight way. I'd rather leave it and come back to it when I feel comfortable and confident…before I didn't have no thought process, I would just act on impulse. (Yvonne)

Exploring feelings some time removed from their elicitation allows for a reduction in physical sensations that may hijack judgment in the moment. Instead of acting impulsively then, this approach could enable participants to 'weigh up the pros and cons' (Ellie) of particular actions. These accounts are strongly redolent of Frankl's (1946: 86) notion that 'even in terrible conditions of psychic and physical stress' there is still the internal mental freedom 'to choose one's own way'. While there may be limits to the 'choices' that can be made in prison, uncovering a capacity for a degree of freedom over when to experience—and how to act on—emotions was a liberating discovery. Placing these kinds of temporary limits on affective states struck an important balance between denial and fixation, both of which could be damaging.

The above caveats aside, analysing emotions could be an empowering and stabilising activity for prisoners. Distilling took on a number of different forms. At a fundamental level, it was an attempt to pinpoint a particular feeling and extract the most important insight:

> I just go back to my cell and I just think…I don't think it through to "right, I'm going to go and do something now". I just think it through, and in the end, *I just label it*. (Bernie, emphasis added)

Billy explained that he had developed an ability to identify his emotions ('I know how I work and how I feel') and was able to connect the arousal of particular states with his physical sensations ('If I'm embarrassed I feel myself getting hot') or even specific locations of the body ('Anger? I feel it here [points to his stomach]). Another strategy was to use positive 'self-talk' (in the form of post-it notes or daily mental reminders) to help cultivate awareness of *underlying* feelings and ensure that one was not 'making molehills into mountains' (Katherine). A small number of prisoners had clearly benefitted from therapeutic courses and insights to help uncover key emotions:

> I do an inventory every night on myself; *I can look underneath at what's really going on*. So if I've got resentment throughout the day, I look at why I'm resentful. I look at the cause of it and then I think what part of me has been affected. Is it my ambition to get something? It is my self-esteem? Is

3 Emotions and 'the Self' in Prison   45

it my pride? Is it my emotional security or my financial security?...Then I look at the parts I have to play in their problems, am I being selfish or dishonest to them? And what is the fear underneath it?... And usually there's another fear underneath it, so what is the core fear and how am I feeding it? (Janice, emphasis added)

Putting labels on feelings in these different ways enabled prisoners to locate the root cause of difficult emotions, which could lead to greater understanding and acceptance of internal states. This distillation process helped prisoners to garner perspective on their emotions rather than feel at their mercy. Put differently, analysing emotions was also, somewhat paradoxically, a way to gain distance from them. Such metaphorical 'distance' helped prisoners think about how exactly to act on their emotions, or it provided a way of understanding the 'message' that these emotions were communicating.

At this juncture, a distinction is drawn between distilling and processing emotions. While the former attempts to tunnel down into the essential aspects of the experience, the latter is understood here as a more prolonged, and explorative, series of actions to diffuse feeling states. For example, a small group of prisoners used writing in this manner. Those who penned letters after an altercation explained that the writing process was more important than sending the letters: 'I will sit down and write them a letter, but I won't post it' (Paul). That is, although many letters were not actually delivered to their targets, having 'full on rants' (Nia) was still cathartic and clarifying: 'It calms my thinking down, and before you know it I'm calm' (Wayne). These accounts suggest that writing could be a reliable perspective-enhancing activity: 'As soon as something bad happens I put it on paper; once I read it back I can see it in a different light. I am getting it off my chest straightaway' (Molly). As Billy put it: 'Once I've wrote it down I can sort of end that chapter'. O'Donnell (2014) explains that:

The scratching of a pencil on a page, the reviewing and revising, the deletions and annotations, the marginalia; all force clarity on thoughts that might otherwise have continued to career across an anxious mind, with potentially ruinous consequences. The discipline required to bring words together into sentences which can be enjoined into paragraphs helps to draw coherence from chaos and offers some clear reference points in a new and bewildering territory. (248)

Importantly, and unlike distillation, this did not involve identifying the key components of emotion states initially but, rather, allowed prisoners to establish distance from their feelings and construct new meanings. That is, difficult emotions were being externalised into diaries and letters and slowly reconfigured. This process of 'repositioning' released prisoners from feeling trapped in the cycle of difficult emotional states.

In a similar vein, a number of prisoners used more artistic methods to process their feelings. Making time for artwork was crucial for some participants ('My emotions speak through my art...this is my heartbeat' - Danielle). Danielle further explained that there was an ambiguous quality to this kind of internal navigation: 'You're reaching out to the emotions but not realising what you're doing'. Feelings could bubble to the surface spontaneously through the images selected and choice of colour. It was only retrospectively that prisoners gained deeper insight about their meaning:

I found that I repeat the same things when I go through certain emotions. When I'm in a certain mood I do certain drawings and stuff. I do channel my anger and sadness into my artwork. It took me a while to recognize it. (Katherine)

Music was generally discussed less in this context, but for a small number of prisoners it too could serve as a sounding-board for their affective states:

When I get angry I play grime all the time. If I'm sad or feeling a bit loveydovey it will be slow jams. So yeah, I play music to match my mood but half the time I didn't know I was doing it. It was unconscious. But now I'm aware of it, so as soon as I put music on I know what mood I'm in. (Molly)

Jewkes (2002: 90) notes that prisoners use media in 'highly reflexive ways to move through moods and reconfigure themselves'. It was important that some prisoners explored their 'emotions and feelings with colours' (Nia) and music precisely because they found more traditional forms of expression difficult: 'It's a good way of venting without speaking to people, I struggle to communicate to some people' (Katherine). Two prisoners complained about the accessibility of art materials ('You can't have stuff sent in no more' [Nia]) and the struggle to get into prison art classes. This placed limits on their ability to channel their expression in a preferred way. Letter writing and artistic pursuits could serve as a proxy for more direct forms of confrontation and enabled prisoners to maintain a degree of emotional privacy. That is, strong feelings did not have to be publicly declared, and emotional messages disguised within artwork did not have to be explained.

Taken as a whole, these methods of distilling and processing feeling appeared to be reliable strategies for establishing emotional balance. This process closely relates to what Cohen and Taylor (1972: 138) term practices of 'self-observation' and 'mind-building'. According to Bluhm (1948: 103), self-observation indicates an important 'turn from passive suffering to an active undertaking' which allows prisoners to regain a sense of control. At the affective level, this brought stability to prisoners' feelings, helping them to navigate the middle ground between rejecting their emotions and being totally overwhelmed by them. While tempering the extremes of absence and excess did not come easily to all prisoners in this study—leading some to destructive rumination—those who did appeared physically and psychologically healthier and exerted more control over their prison lives.

Letting It Flow: Expressing Emotions

> The E-Wing prisoners simply do not hide their feelings and thoughts, if anything, the opposite is true and there is very little pretence. (Cohen & Taylor, 1972: 136)
>
> I don't have a lot to hold in. If I'm angry you hear my mouth, if I'm happy you hear my mouth. (Verity)

Up to this point, the 'fluid-container' framework has largely emphasised how emotions have been controlled or pushed inside. Yet, emotions were not always tightly regulated and some prisoners felt able to discharge feelings in an unfiltered manner. As the next chapter describes in detail, this form of emotional expression typically had a range of important social features. For example, displaying feelings directly allowed prisoners to communicate to others and quickly attend to relational problems: 'Most of the time I just voice it to them, [I will say] "I feel really angry about this"' (Janice). Further, Ula explained that it was unnatural for her to hold herself back: 'I can't hide how I feel at any time. If I'm sad you're going to know it, if I'm happy you're going to know it…If the feeling is in me, I never swallow it'. While this approach might be considered hostile in an environment that is already prone to tension, Ula stated that the opposite was true:

> Can we just try and clear this feeling up so we can move on?…I like harmony. People say you should think before you talk and be careful what you say. But I believe that the more you try and hide away your feelings and emotions the more you're building those dark holes inside of you. (Ula)

According to this account, displaying emotions directly could extinguish problems before they festered and avoid more destructive confrontations down the line. It is noteworthy that these sentiments were articulated more often in the women's prison than the men's prison. Verbal altercations were common in Send but, unlike in Ranby, these confrontations were less likely to erupt into physical violence. Put short, displaying emotions openly in Send was less risky and could help prisoners navigate relations in the moment.

While emotional expression is often tied primarily to social relationships it did have some significant implications at the level of the self. First, both male and female prisoners expressed a view that it was important periodically to have a 'good cry' while alone in their cells. This provided a way to release backlogs of emotion, or siphon off feelings, without necessarily having to cultivate deeper insights. A number of prisoners reported feeling more stable after these episodes. Similarly, exercise provided rebalancing effects and was a further channel for prisoners to expunge frustration and aggression. The haptic sensation of throwing barbells on the ground, and the clanging sound of dumbbells, provided an escape valve for many male prisoners who used the gym. Both of these examples (crying and exercise) are reminiscent of Scheff's (1979) conceptualisation of 'positive catharsis', wherein the discharge of emotion leads to increased 'clarity or thought and perception' and powerful 'relief from tension' (53).

However, for some prisoners, such open expressions had a darker side. For example, some found that crying had an almost 'haemophilic' quality: 'When you finish crying you still think there's more to come out, it could be anger, frustration, confusion. You're just feeling dark, frozen, cold' (Tamara). At times then, expressing emotions only appeared to intensify rather than resolve inner pain. Dean stated: 'My life is ruined with this sentence. I might as well just fucking end it. All I have got to look forward to is more years of this'. Another prisoner, who was severely traumatised from having witnessed a suicide in his prison cell, appeared to be extremely disturbed in the interview while expressing himself, being on the precipice of tears throughout. Open expression, then, may be useful for a certain kind of prisoner whose problems are of a lesser magnitude. But for those who had severe issues and traumas, therapeutic support was clearly needed to work through these emotions.

In sum, emotional expressivity was most typically associated with social dynamics of prison life that are beyond the scope of this account (but are fully explored in the next chapter). In some instances, displaying emotions directly was a route to catharsis which brought about a temporary suspension of unsettling feelings states. The direct discharge of emotions is an important addition to the fluid-container model that could otherwise suggest that feelings are always tightly controlled or regulated.

Controlling Emotions: Flexibility and Rigidity

The fluid-container framework introduced here provides a preliminary description of the different emotion regulation strategies used by prisoners and the personal and institutional factors that motivated them. This model can help describe how emotions are experienced and managed in prison at the individual level. Yet, important questions remain about the broader significance of this framework to the psychology and sociology of prison life. The section that follows does not attempt to fully resolve these questions, but instead argues, that emotional regulation strategies point toward the existence of different states, or patterns, of feeling among prisoners. Calverley and Farrall's (2011:82) discussion of emotions in the desistance process is particularly instructive here. The authors argue that emotions are not just 'by-products of criminality' but instead constitute the 'causal factors that drive and sustain crime'. Building on this claim, the authors examine the emotional states of offenders at different points in the desistance process, organised by a primary phase characterised by 'early hopes for a new life'; intermediate stages marked by feelings of shame and guilt, and finally the emotions trust and pride that are associated with a return to 'normalcy' (Calverley & Farrall, 2011, pp. 82-83). For current purposes, rather than focusing on desistance or specific feelings, two preliminary states of emotion regulation are identified in prison: 'emotional rigidity' and 'emotional flexibility'. These categorisations begin a discussion of patterns of emotional development in prison, and more tentatively, suggest this can relate to pathways out of crime.

While most prisoners used a variety of regulation strategies, there was a clear separation between those who 'bottled up' their emotions and those who reframed them. This separation is significant because a growing pool of evidence in psychological literature places these two strategies at the opposite end of the spectrum of health and well-being outcomes (John & Gross, 2004). More specifically, suppression has been linked to less social closeness and a range of deleterious psychological and physiological effects (Maté, 2003), whereas reappraisal is associated with far 'healthier patterns of affect, social functioning and well-being' (John & Gross, 2004: 1301). However, rather than reflect on the validity of these differential health outcomes for prisoners in this study (which were not measured systematically) the focus, here, is on the differential patterns of emotional agency among those participants who might be considered either 'suppressers' or 'reframers'. The contention advanced is that prisoners who suppress emotion held 'rigid' attitudes about their perceived ability to control their affective states, whereas those who reframe evidenced far more 'flexibility'.

Emotional Rigidity

Prisoners who suppressed their emotions had an extreme understanding of their 'locus of control' (Rotter, 1966).[9] They cast themselves either as the architects of change (*active*) or, by contrast, as passengers of emotional forces outside of themselves (*passive*). However, these seemingly different positions both reflected a rather fixed approach to emotionality. Indeed, all of these prisoners were prone to making absolute statements about their feeling states. The 'passive' group stated that they felt powerless with regard to their emotions: 'You don't have any control, which makes you anxious, and makes you want to get control, but you can't get it' (Francesca). They explained they were caught in the waves of their emotions ('It's crazy…one day you can be like happy, the next day you are just low. It's ups and downs all the time' Haley) and felt unable to avoid troubling states altogether: 'I've got triggers that will set off my emotions, and I can't manage the triggers' (Rebecka). Further, these prisoners communicated that any sense of 'choice' in prison was illusory:

> Even right down to your sentence plan that chooses what course you should do. It's up to you whether you do them or not, but if you don't do them you won't get out. Where is the choice? Okay, you choose what you eat, but it's been the same menu for the last 10 years. Okay, so you've got a choice of what you eat, but not what is healthy and not what you want. (Danielle)

These prisoners felt infantilised and micromanaged ('Bloody hell, you can't even brush your teeth without permission' [Haley]). With regard to their general custodial situation, they felt that information was withheld, that they were given inadequate explanations for decisions, or sent contradictory messages ('It's as if they're telling me to move on but also saying you can't move on' [Ian]). Further, they felt officers mistrusted them ('I'm sick to death of being called a liar' [Zak]) and constantly made them wait. Some perceived that all of this was indicative of broad systemic

---

[9] Locus of control is a concept developed by Rotter to understand the extent to which a person perceives they have control over their behaviour. It is typically separated into 'internal' (a person feels in control of events) and 'external' (a person feels that outside forces control events) categories.

failures that they were powerless to change: 'You're looking behind the curtain…and there's nothing there' (Bernie). In short, these prisoners felt suffocated by institutional 'tightness' (Crewe, 2011), by forces that 'operates both closely and anonymously, working like an invisible harness on the self.' (522).

By contrast, the 'active' group stated that outside influences were moot and that 'it's all down to the person' (Katherine). They claimed that prisoners alone had autonomy over their sentences: 'If you choose for it [prison] to make you, then positive things can come out of it. If you choose for it break you, then negative things will come out of it' (Amber). They spoke in clinical terms about their emotions: arguments and confrontations had logical solutions: 'You don't want to speak to that person again, alright so why don't you just ignore them!' (Amber). Ricky explained that cutting off all ties with his daughter, partner and friends 'might sound concerning' but was a way of 'controlling the situation' and deciding not to cause unnecessary pain to others or himself. Apparently, then, emotions could be experienced on their own terms.

Importantly, seeing oneself as the source of change could build resilience and it enabled these prisoners to separate themselves from emotionally volatile situations and daily entanglements of the environment. In this sense, this active subset of prisoners had a more developed awareness of where and how negative emotions emerged (and the need to control them) than the passive group above. Indeed, Harvey (2005: 249) found that young adults 'who were more internal in their locus of control reported lower levels of psychological distress…As they feel they are able to control the environment, the environment has less control over them'. However, although these prisoners reported to be coping well in general, at the affective level their absolute stance made them particularly vulnerable to backlogs and 'pressurised explosions' (discussed above) where emotions suddenly erupted and caught them off guard.

Taken together, these prisoners described a fixed approach to handling their emotions. This is redolent of Calverley and Farrall's 'first phase' participants who 'were found to express a narrower range of emotions' than those in later phases of desistance (Calverley & Farrall, 2011:84). There are further resonances with Crewe et al. (2017) analysis of long-term prisoners in the early stage of their tariffs who were 'in effect treading water, being carried by the tide of the sentence or…seeking to swim against it' (21). These rigid approaches to emotion regulation were characterised by decreased awareness and emotional literacy which left prisoners caught in negative cycles of emotion.

Emotional Flexibility

The prisoners who reframed their emotions fell between the two poles of control articulated above. They often sought compromise, balancing a desire to assert their will with a realisation that this was not always possible. Of particular importance here was the cultivation of acceptance:

> You have to accept you can't do anything about your situation…you're not going to be able to move out of the prison any time soon. Acceptance of people's behaviour, having to live in close proximity to people. Mainly with people who you wouldn't associate with normally. (Lacey)

Not everything in prison could be changed, and it would not serve prisoners well, they argued, to spend time reeling against institutional realities. When these prisoners discussed the importance of control, it was not in an absolute sense: 'Don't let this place dictate to you or control you. You've got to control your sentence…obviously with their help' (Blanche). That is, their accounts were often characterised by collaboration. Indeed, whereas the rigid group were often focused on their individual entanglements, these prisoners were more 'other focused'. Most of the participants who reframed their emotions held positions of responsibility around the prison, working as Listeners, mentors, mental health 'buddies', and prison information desk workers. Again, Calverley and Farrall's (2011) work is instructive, arguing that later stage desisters in their study moved into a 'building bridges' phase, characterised by increased trust and improved social relations (90).

Instead of grappling against the confines of the system, these prisoners found ways to co-opt it. This did not mean that they were immune from challenges and confrontations; rather they were usually able to find balanced ways to navigate them: 'I'll say what I've got to say in an assertive manner, but keeping my body language calm. And then just keep it moving' (Oscar). These prisoners were versatile with their feelings states, being able to mobilise a range of processing strategies alongside reframing depending upon the circumstance. While they had regular routines, they were not dependent on them. They were far less avoidant of difficult emotions—being willing to explore their sadness and frustrations—without being ensnared in them or plunging into rumination. Possessing the adaptability to take setbacks in their stride, while asserting one's agency when needed, promoted their welfare and endowed them more choices. These prisoners resembled the more experienced half of Crewe et al's long-term prisoners who 'were swimming with the tide, rather than against it, using its energy to their advantage' (21-22). Similarly, most of these flexible prisoners had had significant experience in prison (over five years), and many had been through various therapeutic programmes—these factors enabled them to cultivate a more adaptable set of emotion strategies to navigate their imprisonment. The fact that they held positions of responsibility in prison, especially roles that involved social collaboration (e.g. mentoring roles), suggested that these prisoners might be in a better position to reintegrate into the community after their sentences.

Taken as a whole, this final section of the chapter has described two phases of 'rigid' and 'flexible' emotion regulation. A key distinction between these groups is the extent to which prisoners felt they could control their feeling states. These categorisations are preliminary and non-exhaustive. The account above focuses on the distinctions between two emotion regulation strategies (suppression and reappraisal), excluding the other ways of managing emotion from this framework. Further attention could be given to the important role played by sentencing conditions, prior experiences of imprisonment, and the age and maturity of prisoners that could further elaborate on these differences. Nonetheless, examining these phases of emotion regulation highlights important emotional patterns among prisoners. Identifying these different feeling groupings has the potential to advance the study of affective states beyond purely descriptive accounts of individual differences.

Conclusion

In the broader literature, the emotional dimensions of prison life are often compressed and typically emphasise negative affective states. This sentiment is reflected by Scraton et al. (1991: 17) description of anger, aggression and 'festering sores' in prison. But as Jewkes (2002: 99) notes, imprisonment entails 'periods of conflicting emotions, containing both good and bad'. This chapter, and the ones that follow, attempt to unpack these different emotion states in order to capture the affective texture of prisoners' worlds. A fluid-container framework was introduced here to examine a range of emotion regulation strategies at the 'person level', and shed light on the various strengths and drawbacks of these strategies. Put short, prisoners regulate and express their emotions in complex ways. Most prisoners used a combination of different strategies rather than a single approach, depending upon the context. The prevalence of emotional suppression is unsurprising given the range of existing literature that emphasises the need for prisoners to construct a 'mask', or put up a masculine 'front', to defend against intrusions from other prisoners (de Viggiani, 2012; Jewkes, 2005). However, this chapter has gone further, pursuing the idea that emotional suppression is both a psychological process, and a force driven by broader institutional culture and policy. On one hand, the participants' biographies, introduced in the previous chapter, reveal a degree of continuity between ways of dealing with emotions outside prison and their behaviours inside it. Indeed, prior experiences of trauma may create heightened sensitivities to institutional life, and many prisoners in this study were already well versed in numbing their emotions (van der Kolk, 2014), or dissociating from emotional pain (De Zulueta, 1993). On the other hand, these processes were perpetuated and amplified by institutional 'tightness' that left some prisoners feeling particularly suffocated and spotlighted, unsure of where to put their feelings and not knowing which way to turn for help. Specific emotions, including sadness, anger and joy, were penalised and discouraged, creating a pressurised climate in which prisoners were expected to closely control their feelings.

The fluid-container metaphor introduced here is in dialogue with other frameworks of prison adaptation (especially Cohen & Taylor, 1972; O'Donnell, 2014; Toch, 1992). But unlike models that emphasise 'survival' or 'coping', the placement of emotions at the centre of this framework constitutes a shift of focus. Highlighting prisoners' responses to pain and negative affectations is important, but taken alone it risks denuding other key dimensions of the prisoner experience. The discussion of 'reframing' and emotional 'processing' has brought some of these alternative scripts into relief. For example, some prisoners experienced profound spiritual transformations and identity changes that left them brimming with *joy* and *hope*; others found that art or writing was a way to disentangle their affective states and cultivate *serenity*. This is not to claim that prior frameworks of adaptation pay no attention to positive accounts and feelings, only that by focusing on emotions these narratives are made clearer and are easier to trace (Laws & Crewe, 2016).

This chapter began with the idea that imprisonment can be understood as an emotional confrontation with the self. The various 'resolutions' and attempts to manage this conflict could be healing, destructive, or some combination of both. However, prisoners who struggled with their emotions were not always condemned to face their challenges in isolation. Nor did those who handled their feelings competently exist like 'islands' apart from the prison. This is to say, dealing with feelings internally is one means to regulating affective states, but it is not exclusive. Indeed, relational aspects of imprisonment in particular—including ties with family members, other prisoners, officers and vocational staff—have much to contribute to an understanding of prisoners' emotional worlds. It is to these concerns that we now turn.

References

Bluhm, H. O. (1948). How did they survive? Mechanisms of defense in Nazi concentration camps. *American Journal of Psychotherapy, 2*, 3–32.

Boag, S. (2010). Repression, suppression, and conscious awareness. *Psychoanalytic Psychology, 27*(2), 164–181. https://doi.org/10.1037/a0019416

3 Emotions and 'the Self' in Prison   57

Burgo, J. (2012). *Why do I do that? Psychological defence mechanisms*. New Rise Press.

Calverley, A., & Farrall, S. (2011). Introduction. In S. Karstedt, I. Loader, & H. Strang (Eds.), *Emotions, crime and justice*. Bloomsbury Publishing.

Carlen, P. (1983). *Women's imprisonment: A study in social control*. Routledge & Kegan Paul.

Cohen, S., & Taylor, L. (1972). *Psychological survival: The experience of long-term imprisonment*. Penguin.

Cole, P. M., Dennis, T. A., Smith-Simon, K. E., & Cohen, L. H. (2009). Preschoolers' emotion regulation strategy understanding: Relations with emotion socialization and child self-regulation. *Social Development, 18*(2), 324–352.

De Viggiani, N. (2012). Trying to be something you are not: Masculine performances within a prison setting. *Men and Masculinities, 15*(3), 271–291.

de Zulueta, F. (1993). *From pain to violence: The traumatic roots of destructiveness*. Whurr Publishers.

Ehring, T., Tuschen-Caffier, B., Schnülle, J., Fischer, S., & Gross, J. J. (2010). Emotion regulation and vulnerability to depression: Spontaneous versus instructed use of emotion suppression and reappraisal. *Emotion, 10*(4), 563.

Hairgrove, D. D. (2000). A single unheard voice. In R. Johnson & H. Toch (Eds.), *Crime and punishment inside views*. Roxbury Publishing Company.

Harvey, J. (2005). Crossing the boundary: The transition of young adults into prison. In A. Liebling & S. Maruna (Eds.), *The effects of imprisonment*. Routledge.

Jewkes, Y. (2002). *Captive audience: Media, masculinity and power in prisons*. Willian Publishing.

Jewkes, Y. (2005). Men behind bars 'doing' masculinity as an adaptation to imprisonment. *Men and Masculinities, 8*(1), 44–63.

John, O. P., & Gross, J. J. (2004). Healthy and unhealthy emotion regulation: Personality processes, individual differences, and life span development. *Journal of Personality, 72*(6), 1301–1334.

Laws, B., & Crewe, B. (2016). Emotion regulation among male prisoners. *Theoretical Criminology, 20*(4), 529–547. https://doi.org/10.1177/1362480615622532

Maté, G. (2003). *When the body says no: Exploring the stress disease connection*. Wiley & Sons.

O'Donnell, I. (2014). *Prisoners, solitude, and time*. Oxford University Press.

Rotter, J. B. (1966). Generalized expectancies for internal versus external control of reinforcement. *Psychological Monographs: General and Applied, 80*(1), 1.

Scheff, T. J. (1979). *Catharsis in healing, ritual, and drama*. University of California Press.

Scraton, P., Sim, J., & Skidmore, P. (1991). *Prisons under protest*. Open University Press.

Stanghellini, G., & Rosfort, R. (2013). *Emotions and personhood: Exploring fragility-making sense of vulnerability*. University Press.

Toch, H. (1992). *Living in prison: The ecology of survival*. The Free Press.

van der Kolk, B. (2014). *The body keeps the score*. Viking.

4

Relational Emotions in Prison

This chapter focuses on the social aspects of emotions, and their influence on power relationships, order and control in prison. The social here is conceptualised as being one level 'above' the level of the self—though in some ways this distinction is nebulous. It is widely acknowledged that the most common cause of emotion is social interaction, and 'no matter how deeply personal an emotion seems, we embark on a timeless drama not of our own making' (Cochran & Claspell, 1987, p. 157). In this sense, this chapter extends the last one rather than introducing a completely different level of analysis. This argument will focus on a reciprocal process considering how social processes *shape* emotions and, at the same time, are 'shaped by emotions' (Hareli & Parkinson, 2008, p. 131). As Planalp (1999, p. 135) explains, 'many of our emotions promote and regulate social and communicative connections'. This perspective has particular significance for the prison context. For current purposes, the idea that emotions function as 'social glue' (Fischer & Manstead, 2008) is introduced to conceptualise important aspects of prisoner relationships. This 'adhesive' function emerges clearly through the 'social sharing' of emotions in prison. In the first half of the chapter, the concept of social sharing is developed by explaining how feelings are *regulated through the social audience*. That is,

© The Author(s), under exclusive license to Springer Nature Switzerland AG 2022   **59**
B. Laws, *Caged Emotions*, Palgrave Studies in Prisons and Penology,
https://doi.org/10.1007/978-3-030-96083-4_4

social sharing facilitates the outward movement of emotions from individuals to their confidants. The three primary outlets for sharing are other prisoners, officers, and family members outside prison. These different associations are explored in turn—each had different qualities, implications and risks. Social sharing highlights the importance of establishing trust, intimacy, and communicating key information to others through emotional expressions, all of which reveals the significance of affective states in establishing and stabilising prisoners' relationships.

The second half of this chapter considers emotions that *emerged in the social arena* as a by-product of relational interactions. This first segment considers small prisoner groups, while the second section examines the wider prisoner population. There was a significant distinction between expressions of care and affection in these small collectives on the one hand, and the displays of fear, anger, embarrassment and shame that characterised the wider prisoner atmosphere on the other. These contrasting relations are explored in some detail, and are guided by the idea of emotional 'contagion' (Hatfield et al., 1993). Emotional contagion involves the 'transmission of moods as akin to the transmission of social viruses' (183). Specifically, this section details the mechanisms of this emotional 'contamination' and examines how prisoners attempted to avoid certain feelings states altogether. For example, prisoners were particularly keen to ward off toxic displays of sadness and anger that they claimed had a powerful momentum or emotional charge.

The chapter concludes by seeking to evaluate the key intersections between gender and emotions in dialogue with the wider literature. Gender was a significant variable, shedding light on different patterns of emotionality in these prisons. In many ways, Send and Ranby represented different relational worlds. While there were some similarities in these establishments, there were marked differences in the expressivity, intensity, and repertoire of emotions on display, most of which were more pronounced in the women's prison. This is not to say that Ranby was devoid of social emotions, but rather that emotions typically emerged in less explicit ways. The chapter concludes by attempting to examine the connections between social emotions, power, order and control in prison. The argument is guided by Layder's (2004) notion that power and emotion are inseparable phenomenon that are always found together in social life.

The Social Exchange of Emotions

> There's obviously a point where you need to talk and get your emotions out there and put them on the table. It's good to talk, it's good to think that someone's listening to you. It's good to hear other people's problems and perspectives on life. Situations they're going through. It's good to engage with other people. (Freddy)

Rimé (2007) argues that the need to talk after experiencing an emotion is pervasive, applying not only to traumatic events but equally to everyday emotions, both positive and negative. While it was common to hear maxims in prison that ostensibly refuted this need ('do your own time', 'keep your head down'), in reality almost all the participants engaged in some form of emotion sharing. This practice manifested itself in a number of different ways and served a range of needs, as highlighted by Freddy's introductory quotation above. More specifically, social sharing between prisoners was typically a reciprocal process that provided a platform to ventilate feelings, problem solve (or 'perspective widen') and strengthen affiliative bonds through increasing intimacy. By managing their emotions in concert with others, prisoners were often able to achieve a degree of 'emotional convergence' (Fischer & Manstead, 2008, p. 459). Put short, sharing and processing affective states helped realign and harmonise prisoner relations. But sharing feelings was not straightforward and finding the 'right' social outlets entailed weighing up a number of risks. The three principal groups for sharing included prison officers, family members and other prisoners—this final group was the most common, and least problematic, outlet for exchanging emotions. These three subgroups are evaluated in turn.

Sharing with Officers and Staff

Prisoners had strong, often polarised, opinions about sharing emotions with officers. It was typical to hear that there was a minority of highly skilled officers who really 'understood' them, but that most showed little compassion or concern. While most interactions with staff on the wings and house blocks were brief and practically orientated, a small number of prisoners felt comfortable opening-up to officers at length: 'I find it easier to talk to a uniform' (Bernie). For these prisoners, no topics were off limits: 'We can talk about anything from football, to going on holiday, or if I need to speak about my troubles or my son back home' (Jerry). For these prisoners, officers provided an avenue to offload pent up emotion. Dean explained that venting to psychological support staff was a valuable outlet ('it's been helping me keep my head down'), but he worried what would happen when he completed his clinical course ('who am I going to vent at when they're gone?'). Unlike prisoners then, who were readily accessible, skilled staff members were a less available and a more unstable resource.

These well-liked staff members were regarded as possessing emotional intelligence, and understood when prisoners were distressed. A few participants recalled situations where they had shown flexibility: 'They give you a little bit of space. And then they say "When you're ready and if you want to, come talk to me"' (Nia). Further, these relationships with staff were particularly fruitful because they facilitated direct access to resources that alleviated the sources of emotional distress. This included assistance in solving problems or processing applications ('If I need to make a call, they will do it for me. They sort of understand' Jerry) or providing emotional support and advice. In a different manner, Val explained how female officers had a unique capital in Ranby, providing a 'girl's perspective' on relationship problems. Such advice and understanding was highly prized and could, by definition, not be ascertained from the prisoner population.

A crucial aspect of these relationships that facilitated emotion sharing was the presence of mutual respect and humanity: 'It's not us and them. He's a human being, I'm a human being' (Kyle). Such individuals resemble Ben-David and Silfen's (1994) description of 'integrative or personal' officers who are 'flexible, adaptable' and who evince an 'egalitarian orientation'. These officers were praised for not 'just using their job as power' (Val), or compounding the pains of imprisonment by punishing prisoners excessively. Some officers displayed their compassion openly, which left an indelible mark on nearby prisoners: 'Someone died in prison and the officer cried over his body' (Bernie). Karl explained two further moments when he realised that some officers genuinely cared for their work:

> One officer came to the spur other day, and he had a badge on his tie which said 'Prison me! No way!'[1] I said "what's that badge all about?" He said "it's a charity I work for. I go to schools and tell kids about prison. I tell them that I'm an officer and I tell them what prison is really like, and tell them not to go there". I never looked at him in that way. I said to him "I respect you for that, it means a lot". It is not just another shirt that comes to lock my door. He actually cares about people coming to prison. He actually cares that this is a good place.
>
> Me and a few lads had jokes with different officers, one of the lads were saying "you don't care about us, you just bang us up". And he said "that's not true, anybody could end up in prison". And when an officer speaks like that you start to think to yourself, ah he doesn't just want to bang us up, he actually does care. (Karl)

Such 'mutual identification' could 'lead to a sympathetic view by prisoners of the prison staff condition' (Liebling & Arnold, 2004). Indeed, prisoners felt affection for officers who 'actually love what they do' (Gabriella) and did not shy away from challenges: 'They're helping in any way they can' (Kyle). Nicknames and playful colloquialisms used by officers indicated that affection flowed in both directions: 'They all call me 'Trouble'... One officer told me "if we had a prison full of women like you, we'd look forward to getting out of bed"' (Chantal). While these amicable relationships established a foundation for real emotional exchange they were the exception rather than the rule. Further, prisoners who 'benefited' from these relations complained that there was a notable drawback. Namely, other prisoners resented this preferential treatment ('If you play with one, why not with the other?' [Danielle]) and labelled these prisoners as snitches: 'They start spreading rumours....then by the end of the day you have to be watching your back' (Andrew). While there was value in sharing emotions with some officers, the speculation and judgment of the prisoner population was a powerful deterrent against doing so.

---

[1] 'Prison Me! No Way!' is a charity that aims to raise awareness among young people about the causes and consequences of crime.

Prisoners pointed to a number of other reasons why it was not expedient to share emotions with staff. First, they claimed that skilled officers were in the minority, and it was far more typical to hear uniformed staff described as cold, mechanical, unsympathetic and completely devoid of humanity: 'They're not a human person' (Amber). Interacting with them, it was claimed, was 'like talking to a pre-determined response robot' (Alan). These relationships were unsatisfactory because of a perceived lack of sensitivity: common complaints were that officers were either inactive, dismissive ('they just don't listen' Oscar), punishment-focused, antagonistic or some combination of these factors. It was also customary to hear frustrations that officers rushed in to 'solve' problems without having full understanding. This was described as dealing with only the symptoms without 'getting to the root of the problem' (Blanche) or 'helping a person to look at what's really going on' (Janice). Some prisoners felt that these (over)reactions made it impossible for them discharge emotions like anger in the proximity of officers without receiving unwanted institutional consequences.

> If I went into my room and punched a wall, oh my god, alarm bells would be ringing. They freak out. Straightaway an officer will come up to you and say "this isn't healthy, this is a form of self-harm, we need to open an ACCT document." (Molly)

Paul wanted to talk through his emotions but felt pathologised by the mental health team: 'Throughout the conversation I felt absolutely embarrassed'. Further problems emerged when officers mistook idiosyncratic personalities of some prisoners as violent.

> I've seen a person talk to a member of staff, he waved his arms a bit and had a frown on his face, and the member of staff took it as him being threatening, abusive and aggressive. But he just doesn't know how to articulate himself, he does the same things around his mates as he does staff. (Niel)

In a similar vein, prisoners claimed that cultural practices among were misinterpreted by staff. Lively verbal exchanges and gesticulating were sometimes perceived as hostile: 'They like to say that black people are aggressive but it's just the way we express ourselves, we are passionate, when we stand for something we go hard' (Ula). Rebecka felt the prison needed 'more black or ethnic minority officers' to close this cultural distance. When officers provided emotional 'support' it was often claimed to be inauthentic: 'the minute you start showing emotion they will act out of duty of care, not because they actually care' (Danielle). Craig explained that when speaking to officers 'some say "yes, yes, that's alright" like they're listening but they're not really...you can tell from their body language and eye contact'. Further, in Ranby when prisoners were angry they felt that female officers were used instrumentally, as a buffer: 'Time after time I've seen people get mad, so they go and get the woman officer to calm the situation. A lot of blokes will calm to a woman, they are not going to hit a woman' (Paul). In Send, a similar situation manifested when prisoners cried in front of male officers: 'they can't cope with a woman crying or a woman wanting to sit down and talk with them...so they'll go find a female officer' (Ellie). Prisoners wanted to feel as though they were being attended to authentically, rather than being offloaded or manipulated. Taken together, these accounts indicate a lack of understanding in these relationships that created significant barriers to sharing emotions.

The trust deficit in these relationships flowed in both directions. Some officers were sceptical about prisoners' motives when they claimed to be experiencing emotional or physical pain. Similarly, prisoners mistrusted staff with their private information because they felt 'it's not confidential' (Stacey). Some participants pointed towards specific instances when their medical records had been disclosed in public, or where mental health staff had embarrassed them by approaching them in the middle of busy association periods. A further aspect of this problem was the lack of privacy: 'You can't go anywhere. If you come to my room to talk to me about something everybody would know about it. If you're being bullied you can't go down to the office because everyone is in there' (Stacey). Again, the seemingly omniscient surveillance of the wider prisoner population magnified the difficulties of emotion sharing.

Finally, some prisoners felt that, because officers had not themselves experienced imprisonment, first-hand sharing was impossible: 'they don't know where you're coming from, they don't get banged up or hear the bolts going off and on, and they don't hear people shouting at you for work' (Tamara). Yet, at times, prisoners' assessments of officers lacked a nuanced acknowledgement of their operational pressures and responsibilities. Many officers were observed in a near constant state of activity, dealing with a broad range of prisoners' concerns and requests. Furthermore, institutional policies that regularly rotated staff members to different house blocks created relational impediments that were beyond the control of individual officers.

In sum, most prisoners thought officers did not provide a viable outlet for their emotions. One prisoner concluded that reaching out to officers left you 'feeling abandoned' (Paul), because they did not invest time into prisoners' emotional needs or did so reluctantly. This sentiment harked back to the toxic life experiences of participants before imprisonment. Indeed, in some instances officers' behaviour perpetuated the abuse of power, emotional neglect, manipulation, insensitive treatment, and heavy-handed approaches that had already left imprints on prisoners' lives. Under these conditions, typically only the most destructive emotions were being exchanged between prisoners and officers, the consequence of which was pronounced 'social distancing' (Fischer & Manstead, 2008, p. 460). Put short, regular displays by prisoners of frustration and anger signalled a 'reverse relational movement' which ensured that 'distance from others' was established (460). This affective distancing was not unique to relations with officers, it also emerged in the broader relations between prisoners outlined in the second half of the chapter. Ultimately then, because the tone of officer prisoner interactions was generally marked by frustration, misunderstanding, and a deficit of trust, most prisoners looked in other directions for emotional support.

Intimate Relationships and Family

An alternative source of emotional support was found in familial relations. A small number of prisoners explained that their primary outlet for emotion was 'loved ones outside' (Freddy). These prisoners had longstanding relationships with partners or family members who knew them intimately: 'Mum always knows from my voice if something is wrong'

(Karl). These relations were reinforced by regular visits, phone calls, letters and pictures. An important aspect of these bonds was that the confidant was a trusted person outside the prison regime, not contaminated by the pressures of the environment, and could therefore open a comforting window back to the world outside. Confiding in others was not limited to sharing problems, but included positive emotions too: 'If I am having a bad day or a good day I will ring home and talk about whatever's happened' (Amber). These outside relationships also provided a channel for romantic or erotic energy that was otherwise stifled in the men's prison: 'I reboot my batteries…when I write a nice dirty fantasy letter to my missus' (Wayne).

However, these perspectives were not ubiquitous. Indeed, while the majority of participants maintained important relationships with loved ones, these relationships were rarely *emotionally open* and were often far from straightforward. Most prisoners explained that they did not want to burden loved ones with difficult emotions: 'I try not to show any weakness to my partner at all. I don't want her to become concerned about my well-being because it's already a hard job for her' (Simon). Prisoners felt this pressure acutely on visits where family members had travelled all day to see them, often relying on expensive public transport and missing time off work. One prisoner, who collapsed during a visit due to a debilitating illness, explained that this was the first time his girlfriend discovered he was unwell. Some participants felt it was wise to avoid contact completely if they did not feel capable of maintaining this positive façade: 'I won't ring if I'm upset, they don't deal with that very well' (Victoria). Many prisoners felt compelled to protect their children from learning about their imprisonment too: 'you have to tell them white lies, like I'm at work' (Val). These relationships were clearly significant for prisoners, and they drew strength from communicating and receiving messages of love. However, because they wanted to protect these bonds, emotional authenticity was often absent in these connections.

For other prisoners, contacting loved ones was the source of—rather than the remedy for—emotional pain. In these conversations, prisoners were forced to confront the collateral damage of their imprisonment: 'My youngest son said, "Dad I've forgot what you look like"' (Kyle). Similarly, women prisoners felt they had failed in their maternal roles 'My daughter said to me "Mummy we've never been apart this long". That put a big hole in my heart' (Zoe). There was an underlying fear being described here that prisoners were being erased and forgotten: 'Contacts with the outside world are painful reminders that while people they care about are changing, the prisoner is not' (O'Donnell, 2014, p. 223). Other participants experienced the hypocrisy of trying to discipline their children while being imprisoned: 'The other day my son got in a fight at college and he said "I learned from you"' (Howard). More generally, participants experienced guilt when they considered how their absence was straining family bonds, as their partners struggled to raise children alone. In light of this, it was particularly hard for prisoners to share their own affective states and problems.

A few prisoners felt they were at the mercy of volatile and unpredictable partners: 'The one thing that made me cry in here was when my daughter's mother wouldn't let me speak to her' (Tommas). In these turbulent relationships, insecurities flourished about being replaced or cheated on: 'It's always in the back of your mind' (Simon). Prisoners frequently heard stories about disintegrating relationships, and it was easy to feel 'a bit paranoid' (Andrew) that theirs would be next. Liam felt his relationship was being sabotaged by the prison regime:

> Jail is not built for relationships, everything it entails is made to damage relationships. You can't keep in contact with letters. Everyone is listening to your phone calls. Your missus is frustrated and all they have to go on is your word. (Liam)

Taken as a whole then, there were many barriers that impeded prisoners from establishing authentic relationships with their loved ones. Contacting family members outside was a useful channel for a small number of prisoners. In these relations, there were opportunities to offload, process and reframe emotions. But for most prisoners, sharing was laden with difficulties and resulted in only partial disclosures of affective states. At worst, these relationships perpetuated detrimental forms of emotional suppression that were explored in the previous chapter. While prisoners often cared deeply for those outside there were institutional barriers that made it difficult to establish intimacy, especially the rigid

4 Relational Emotions in Prison 69

structure of prison visits and the long distances families had to travel (explored further in Chap. 6); the expense of making regular phone calls; and the sluggishness of the prison mail system. The inherent difficulties of these outside relationships compelled prisoners to search for support elsewhere, most often this entailed turning to the prisoner population.

Sharing Emotions with Prisoners

> Over a long period of time you get to know people a bit better. It is strange because even with my friends on the outside, I'm not with them every day for a year. Every single day. Every day you see them. (Jerry)

The most common avenue for sharing emotions was through seeking the counsel of other prisoners. In part, this was because they were the most available population. But further, given their mutual experience of incarceration, other prisoners were seen as having an authentic understanding of the challenges that were being faced: 'We're all going through similar things' (Katherine) and 'They just know where you're coming from' (Olivia). It was through these relationships that feelings were primarily discharged. At one level, this extends the emotion regulation strategies framework set out in the preceding chapter to the social world. At another level, emotions between small prisoner groups functioned like a form of 'social glue' (Planalp, 1999), bonding prisoners together and increasing intimacy. However, this did not mean that sharing took place indiscriminately; indeed, most prisoners were highly selective about who they disclosed information to.

Sharing emotions took on a number of forms. Broadly, there was a strong desire to talk and to be heard: 'I have to talk about it, otherwise I'll go mental' (Ula). Finding someone who was willing to 'lend an ear' (Ricky) conferred an important affective benefit to the sharer: namely, the opportunity to offload emotions. For example, this could include pouring out emotions like guilt in the company of others:

I was just crying my eyes out and I was telling them my whole life story and really expressing how guilty I felt. I think I needed to feel guilty, I think I just needed to be guilty and express how sad I felt. (Paula)

Anger, was discharged in a similar way: 'I vent at them...to get all my anger out' (Dean). One of the fundamental services other prisoners provided, then, was acting as a sounding board for emotions, or a kind of receptacle for feelings. It follows that taking the role of listener was perceived as a virtuous and non-judgmental way to support the welfare of other prisoners, to help facilitate this cathartic release: 'Listening is the most important part. Often you're trying to act and help someone, when you just need to listen' (Val). Further, the existence of 'Listener' programmes in both prisons illustrates the demand for open channels to offload emotion without judgement.[2] One prisoner who had been trained as a Listener explained: 'With the Listener role you're very much empathetic towards them [clients], you're seeing everything from their point of view as opposed to you telling them about a time you experienced something similar' (Amber). The mere act of listening to prisoners, whether informally or in Listeners programmes, appeared to provide a fundamental reduction in affective tensions and could help prisoners down regulate their emotions: 'Sitting with somebody and sharing...it's like a weight off your shoulders' (Paul).

For some prisoners however, simply being listened to did not constitute emotional support. For example, while the aforementioned Listeners scheme was largely valued by prisoners some criticised the professional role limitations that proscribed advice giving:

Some people don't wanna go to Listeners or Samaritans. They don't give you any feedback. They sit there and they listen, but sometimes as a human being you want feedback, but they are not allowed to give it, which is wrong. If I'm gonna come and share my thoughts, you're meant to say something to me. At least say to me this is the way you should go about that...give me some positive advice. (Zoe)

---

[2] Distressed prisoners could ask to speak with a Listener at any time of the day or night with relative anonymity by leaving a small sign under their cell doors for officers to collect.

Listening was most effective when it was undertaken using active techniques. That is, good support involved asking probing questions, clarifying information and communicating a form of engaged presence. This enabled participants to explore and view their emotions from a different perspective—many problems could be effectively resolved in this manner ('I'll dig deeper into what they are going through, and they normally come up with their solution' Haley). Some prisoners needed support to initiate sharing, and adept listeners understood that sometimes hard defensive shields needed to be softened:

> I just talk to them and say "are you alright?" They say "yeah" but deep down you know that they're not. So that's not the end, and I won't leave it there, I'll push a bit more. (Billy)

Most importantly, prisoners wanted to receive compassion and understanding for their emotions. This need was validated when prisoners offered one another verbal reassurance ('He had the most down look on his face and I was trying to say "look it will be okay when you get outside to sort things out"' [Jerry]) or physically comfort: 'Sometimes we don't need a psychologist, all we need is an arm around our shoulder' (Ricky). According to some prisoners, then, a sensitive and non-judgemental approach was required in these interactions: 'I have to be very compassionate towards what she is going through on a day-to-day basis…because I know her journey' (Ula). In a related manner, Karl explained that during his most difficult moment in prison—when he broke down in tears in front of his friends—he was met with acceptance rather than judgement: 'After I finished talking, one my friends said "When emotion gets you there's just nothing you can do", and that made me feel a lot better'.

The features of emotion sharing also varied across the two establishments. In Send, there were multiple outlets where emotions could be voiced to a receptive audience. Indeed, the range of therapeutic spaces, especially the PIPE and the Therapeutic Community, provided formal venues that actively encouraged prisoners to ventilate their emotions. Janice explained that her alcohol recovery meeting was one such 'forum where people are talking that kind of language'. Further, there was a pronounced collective effort to assist women who were struggling: 'We could have had an argument five minutes ago, but if you hear some bad news everyone is hugging and crying and saying sorry to hear that' (Ula). These efforts were often characterised by touching and affectionate language: 'If they're upset I'll give them a hug or sit down and talk with them... I'll send little notes saying I love you' (Rebecka). At times, this support involved reminding others about the strength of existing bonds:

> Somebody wrote me a letter the other day because they know I'm having a bad time. I'm going through a divorce and it's been difficult. They wrote me a letter saying how much I meant to them as a friend, and how much they're gonna miss me because I'm leaving. It moves me you know, it changed how I perceived the rest of the day. (Olivia)

Across these women's accounts, there is an explicit flow of emotional language: feelings are labelled and the nature of relationships is openly commented on. By contrast, in the men's prison, while there were affectionate conversations, they were usually less visible or veiled in symbolic language. Showing care for those in need was often channelled into guidance or material support: 'Lads in prison, we don't just sit there putting arms around each other's backs. We give advice' (Karl). Male participants often looked for ways to fix their problems rather than exploring the accompanying feelings: 'If something deep down is troubling you, they may give you information that you haven't heard before' (Billy). There was a distinction here, then, between forms of 'informational' support and more explicit emotional support. This 'information' sharing involved conveying the nuances of the prison regime, sign-posting sources of support, and explaining the pathways to enhanced resources:

> I've seen them [new prisoners] come in here and cry... I'll inform them. We have a PID [prisoner information desk] worker and here's how it helps. If you need to speak to someone I'm a Listener. I tell them I'll have a word with staff to get them on House block 7 or 6 [favourable accommodation]. (Kyle)

Although this approach appeared to be more 'solution orientated' than 'feeling focused', this advice was often accompanied by notes of empathy and care—even if they were not explicitly articulated. This resonates strongly with Tait's (2011, p. 446) conceptualisation of 'old school' prison officers who provide 'limited emotional support' but whose 'responsiveness and straightforward approach' signalled a 'genuine commitment to helping prisoners' (446). In short, giving information was a form of care and a way of communicating empathy. Karl explained how this process worked with his peers:

> I've been in seven years and my close friend has been in 13 years. So when I told him that my Dad had cancer and there's nothing we can do, he says he was in a bad situation a few years ago. He's saying "I went through it and this is what happened". And then you know that he knows how you're feeling. He's not just sat there listening. He's thinking. He knows how you're feeling. So then he's saying "this is what I did, and this is how I dealt with it, I spoke to this person and then I did this". (Karl)

Beyond giving advice, male prisoners shaped others' emotions through material support and other proxies. For example, some provided financial assistance to prisoners who received no money from outside sources, or shared their canteen items ('I might have the last biscuit in my cupboard and I'll ask them if they want it' Andrew). Others performed selfless acts that could reduce suffering: 'There was somebody in the phone queue who's desperate to get on the phone to his partner I said "go ahead on the phone before me", otherwise he's going to be banged up all night worrying' (Simon). Finally, some participants explained how they helped prisoners overcome inertia and fear by introducing them to exercise and fitness, or less frequently, by supporting them with hygiene needs. These acts were proxies in the sense that they communicated care through action, without being explicitly expressed openly in these terms.

Taken together, these testimonies reveal that emotions were shared, and responded to, in distinct ways among male and female prisoners—these gender differences are further explored in the second part of this chapter. But these accounts also shared a key feature: exchanging emotions was integral to the initiation and maintenance of prisoner relationships.

Emotions as Social 'Glue'

> When you do something nice for somebody... Without realising it, it makes you feel nice. A lot of people don't understand that, but they understand the feeling. (Paul)

Up to this point, little has been said about the perspective of the 'helper' and why prisoners bothered to assist those in need. At one level, these prisoners empathised with the suffering they saw around them: 'It hurts me to see all these guys coming to jail...it upsets me a lot' (Andrew), or as Olivia put it, 'You can feel different girls going through their thing'. Rebecka was more sceptical, suggesting that empathy was to some extent enforced by the environment: 'In here it's so closed you see everyone's face [when they're upset] all the time'. However, empathy was not evenly distributed, and prisoners favoured friends or associates in their 'circle'.[3] This point is crucial and reveals that the emotional dimensions of prisoner interactions functioned like social glue contributing to 'the intimacy and harmony of the relationship' (Fischer & Manstead, 2008, p. 459).

First, speaker-listener interactions were fluid. That is, these were not one-way interactions, and prisoners described ongoing relationships characterised by the reciprocal offloading of emotions: 'I will say something that's stressing me out, they will say something that's stressing them out, it will be a to and fro kind of thing' (Jerry). For these relationships to function, prisoners had to heed this principle of reciprocity: 'you don't put too much on other people because he's got his own stressors... you have to respect other people's feelings and understand that they need to let things out as well' (Val). These sharing and helping cycles mutually reinforced social bonds between prisoners, increasing intimacy, cooperation and trust.

Sharers benefited from receiving empathy, because other prisoners could relate precisely to their challenges and validate their problems. On the other hand, helping others was described as an investment, ensuring that there would be a support network in place when needed. As Ula

---

[3] Little empathy was extended to prisoners who were in debt, addicted to drugs, bullies, or those who were suspected of having committed a sex offence or other offences against children.

explained, despite feeling irritated with others, 'there is going to be a time when you have problems and you want someone to listen...so you always have to have your door half open'.

As depicted in the artwork above (Fig. 4.1), sharing and giving empathy was not always straightforward in prison. For Danielle, the process was particularly complex: empathising with others served as an important form of concealment:

> By nurturing somebody else's emotions I can cry for someone else, but I could be crying for myself. I can use it as an excuse to cry for someone else... Staff can see me cry but they won't actually know what's inside. (Danielle)

Given that female prisoners felt unfairly 'spotlighted' or punished for displaying particular emotions, channelling them through other prisoners' feelings could circumvent these consequences. But further, prisoner accounts often blurred the lines between helper and helped—interactions were mutually reinforcing exchanges that strengthened affiliative relations. For example, attending to others' emotions could reduce the tension of living in tight quarters for everyone. This was particularly important for prisoners sharing a cell: 'When I talk to him [when his cellmate is angry], I'm trying to give him other options, I'm trying to change his thinking, and in doing so it helps me' (Paul). This is consistent with the process that Fischer and Manstead (2008, p. 459) describe as 'emotional convergence', achieved through the patterned expression and experience of emotion in communal relations.

In a quite different manner, the information gained during affective exchanges allowed other prisoners to 'actually see things differently' (Haley). As Rimé (2007) argues:

> [The] propagation of emotional information...means that members of a community keep track of the emotional experiences affecting their peers. It also means that in a group, the shared social knowledge about emotional events and emotional reactions is continuously updated as a function of new individual experiences. As emotions generally occur when events are unexpected or unpredicted and as such events generally require rapid and

Fig. 4.1 The eyes, mouth and ears of the three women have been stitched closed. The woman who painted this image explained that it is very hard to help others in prison because of a lack of information, and misinterpreting the psychological pain and traumas that others' held inside: 'You're not hearing, you're not seeing, you're not getting at what's under the surface'

appropriate responding, the spreading of information about emotional situations and responses in a social group appears as a particularly efficient prevention tool with regard to future emotion-eliciting situations. (478)

Through learning about environmental challenges, prisoners who took time to listen could increase a shared knowledge base, helping to ward off future problems. Phil explained this process: 'It makes me more aware of

4 Relational Emotions in Prison   77

how to deal with my own personal problems. It makes you think, how would I deal with this before? And, how would I deal with it now?' As Planalp (1999, p. 139) puts it: 'If one person runs into danger, expresses fear, and alerts everyone else, the whole group benefits'. This was strongly reminiscent of the events that took place following a one-sided fight in Ranby where a prisoner had knocked another unconscious with a single punch. Prisoners who saw the incident functioned like human 'broadcasters' (Harber & Pennebaker, 1992, p. 382), engaging in a form of 'secondary social sharing' (Planalp, 1999, p. 139) that spread the information around the prison rapidly 'alert[ing] the whole community to the danger' (139). Given the sometimes volatile nature of the prison environment, accounts that were full of strong emotions circulated key information to social groups.

Helping others had a mood enhancing quality, which was an end in itself for some prisoners ('It makes me feel better' Kyle). Performing these acts, and the gratitude received as a result, was a way to find meaning in one's punishment: 'it's like helping everyone else makes me feel much more like I'm in prison for a reason' (Chantal). It also provided a rare opportunity to experience pride in prison: 'I helped that guy and look at me now, that makes me giddy, it makes me feel proud' (Billy). While these prisoners did not seek out favours in return, they were more likely than others to benefit from mutual generosity—for example, being able to borrow items without interest, or receiving free haircuts. That, in turn, encouraged more generosity: 'Now I will go above and beyond to help that person' (Paul). Finally, helping others also reflected a form of relational intimacy that was gained from being privy to highly sensitive information:

> I was chatting with someone yesterday, a big strong man, and I was really surprised because he opened up about things that I never thought he'd want to chat with me about. I felt privileged. He was strong enough to speak about it and he trusted me. I felt good about that. (Ricky)

The first half of this chapter has explained the various routes to sharing emotions and the reasons why most prisoners found this difficult with officers and family members. These relationships highlighted the importance of finding a willing listener, receiving advice, and locating sources of understanding and compassion—all of which could help prisoners alleviate their difficult emotional states. Put simply, the prisoner population was the most available and empathetic group that provided a range of opportunities to offload feelings and reframe the significance of these states. This account has further drawn attention to the various 'adhesive' features of sharing emotions that benefitted dyads and groups of prisoners, returning a degree of affective harmony to these relations.

Emotions and the Social Arena

Up to this point, this account has largely discussed social emotions from the perspective of individuals who sought to release and process their own feelings in concert with others. However, this is only one way in which emotions can be considered to be 'social'. This section considers the various ways in which emotions *sprang out of* the social arena. The focus here then is on the emergence of emotions in the social sphere and the social regulation of those emotions. This first section considers small groups of prisoners, while the second expands outwards to examine emotions in the wider prisoner population. According to Kovecses (2000), the most fundamental underlying metaphor of feelings is that *emotion functions as a kind of force*. This suggestion has already been hinted at through discussions of 'pressure', 'outbursts' and 'flows' of emotion that featured in the previous chapter. The following discussion develops this idea, arguing that relational emotions in prison are illuminated by the idea of a force that sprawls outwards. More specifically, the chapter draws upon Hatfield et al.'s (1993) conceptualisation of 'emotional contagion', defined as the spread of emotions from one individual to another, to explain why most prisoners feared mixing with the wider prisoner community and preferred their small groups affiliations instead. In these smaller prisoner constellations, there was typically a positive attunement of collective emotions.

Going with the Flow: Care, Affection and Humour

While prisons can be volatile places, their quotidian feel was for the most part defined by routine and relative relaxation. The general 'baseline' level of interactions in both prisons was characterised by a steady flow of relational emotions that drew groups of prisoners together. There was a predictable rhythm to these exchanges in which it was common to observe displays of care and affection. Yet, the precise nature and pattern of these affective streams marked a key difference between these two research sites. As has already been suggested, in the women's prison, displays of emotion were both more open and more expressively intimate. That is, female prisoners displayed affection openly and had regular 'deep' conversations. By contrast, in Ranby, expressions of warmth took on more latent and indirect forms (see Crewe, 2014), and bonding was largely achieved through activity. While intimate conversations were ongoing, they typically took place in private. These different patterns of affective bonding are now explored in turn.

To say that care was displayed 'openly' in Send had two meanings. First, it reflected the increased frequency and intensity of language used to express feelings, especially in comparison to the men's prison. Second, these displays were open in the sense of being highly visible across different areas of the prison—although this is not to say they happened everywhere, or all the time. A number of women prisoners engaged in a culture of 'gift-giving' or service provision that was indicative of their affectionate relationships. These practices were broad ranging and revealed a sense of social communion. For example, many prisoners spoke of sharing clothes and possessions: 'What's mine is yours sort of thing' (Amber). Others were able to 'spew their creativity' (Ula) by customising clothing, drawing, crafting, or 'making cards for people to cheer them up' (Olivia). Some utilised their prison jobs to serve their peers, offering discounted (or free) haircuts or treatment procedures in the beauty salons. Danielle worked for the St. Giles Trust and helped others find housing: 'I love finding someone somewhere to go…to give that feeling of belonging'.

Cooking and food consumption were routinised and significant activities in Send, bringing large groups of women together. Prisoners pooled together their canteen items on weekends to 'cook for each other like they would if you was at home' (Amber). Chantal further explained that she had chocolate stockpiled in her cell: 'The girls are like "let's go to Chantal cause she always has snacks". It's like being at home, my friends will always come round and have stuff. The references to 'home' in these accounts indicate that these culinary pastimes were attempts to 'domesticate' the living spaces, and, in doing so, to infuse care and comfort into the environment: 'I'm on my wing as the chef, so I'm constantly cooking. Where there's food there's laughter…if you're not hungry then you're happy' (Ula). Taken as a group, these activities seemed like collective attempts to manage emotional challenges and to soften the hard edges of imprisonment. Importantly, there was a kind of utilitarian division of labour among female prisoners. As Ula put it, 'Everybody uses their talent for the best of everybody else.'

Aside from these group affiliations, some women explained that they cultivated special relationships with particular prisoners that involved shared activities: 'We would watch movies together and would go to the library to play games even when we were meant to be working' (Gabriella). It was through these connections that displays of physical closeness occurred. It was common to see pairs of prisoners hugging, styling each other's hair, holding hands, walking arm in arm, or lounging on beds and chairs together. Many of these physical displays were affectionate but non-romantic—although some bonds were harder to distinguish or define: 'If she comes to watch a DVD she needs to be in the bed and I have to cuddle up beside her. I said "I'm gonna tell your boyfriend next time I see him that you're spooning me"' (Chantal). In these groups or friendship dyads, prisoners were openly exhibiting a desire for intimacy and showing care.

The yearning for a deep familial connection with others was compelling, and bonds that were hard to maintain outside prison were forged inside. This was manifested in the creation of surrogate families: 'People in here are gonna be like family to you. That's the only family you have in the moment until you get back into the real world' (Chantal). It was common to hear participants talk about other prisoners as 'sisters', 'aunties', 'grandmothers', or to self-identify with parental roles themselves

('They all call me mum' Wendy). For lifer prisoners, the longevity of these family units offered stability and enabled deep connections to flourish:

> We are a little family as a group. But it's a group of long termers and lifers. I've done about 14 years, so you know that person better than most other people do. You have seen their families grow apart, you've seen their children on family days, and now they're married and have grandchildren. So yes, it's your family. (Danielle)

Romantic dyads were also commonplace and fulfilled a need for emotional and physical intimacy. As Janice put it, 'a lot of women come in to prison and they just need that something, so they'll turn to a woman'. These relationships were often spoken of as temporary affiliations that replaced or supplemented strained relationships with partners outside: 'Gay for the stay, basically you're gay while you're here' (Amber). These relations opened channels for prisoners to share deep secrets and express love. Olivia explained that these ties 'bring you a lot of comfort, it's something else to focus on and it makes your time go a lot quicker'. That is, they were a method of soothing difficult feelings and provided an intense form of social distraction. Such relationships were not openly disclosed in Ranby and were, in all likelihood, far less frequent. Some interactions between male prisoners seemed to hint at pseudo-familial relations. That is, some male participants spoke of finding 'father figures' or treating their close friends like 'brothers'. In her study, Jewkes (2002, p. 153) explains that the role of 'paternalistic mentor is passed down through a chain of relationships' in prison. In Ranby, there were a number of instances where older parental prisoners were observed nurturing younger prisoners either on the wing, or through extended private discussions in their cells. Generally though, male prisoners were less likely to define their relationships in familial terms.

Moreover, the findings from the men's prison were strongly redolent of Crewe's (2014, p. 398) argument that 'men's emotional expressions are so often oblique, disguised, or communicated indirectly'. Prisoners in Ranby submerged care into their shared routines and activities:

82   B. Laws

Groups of lads walk around together, you eat together, you go to the gym together, you live together. That's the way it [affection] is shown. They become a close group of friends so to speak. They don't share feelings, but that's the way you know that he likes him and that he's got feeling towards him. They never say it. (Karl)

Through engaging in shared activities, prisoners were able to 'pick up a bond' (Kyle) with one another over time. A second contrasting feature was the adversarial structure of these bonding activities. That is, association periods were awash with competitive rituals, including: table tennis tournaments, pool and snooker matches, PlayStation games, play fighting (which sometimes escalated into real fighting) and gym workouts. Competition and displays of skill among prisoners provided a setting where displays of care could take place—but flows of emotion here were the 'background noise' and not the focus of these interactions.

Linguistic differences seemed important too. The use of the third person 'he' and 'they' was common in men's accounts (see Karl above, for example), whereas in Send, women were more likely to talk about feelings using first person pronouns ('I' and 'my'). This semantic difference reveals that male prisoners had a more detached relationship to their emotions. Indeed, men were more likely to communicate feelings to each other in non-verbal ways, for example through 'physical contact… high-fives, shaking hands, fist bumps' (Billy). The gym was a site *par excellence* for observing these interactions: prisoners were often seen squeezing each other's muscles—actions that seemed to blend encouragement, admiration and respect for one another's physical prowess. Karl further explained how special handshakes could communicate great depth of feeling and loyalty:

When I shake their hand or put a palm on their shoulder and say "you're good stuff you", that sends them a subconscious message…that he likes me and he is there for me, he's got my back and I can chat to him. That shows them enough. It doesn't have to be said, it is known. (Karl)

Similarly, Freddy reflected on the indirect, sub-verbal nature of these interactions

4 Relational Emotions in Prison   83

It's good to care and be nice, but you wouldn't necessarily show it. You can tell it's there. It's that subconscious thing isn't it, it's like unspoken words… It's just like a feeling, but a more in-depth feeling you just know. If I care, you just feel it. (Freddy)

For most male prisoners, then, affection was shown 'in an abstract way' (Bernie). The fact that some prisoners were able to actively comment on this process hinted at a level of awareness about how social and gender expectations governed the display of particular feeling states in men's prisons. For example, Howard described a situation where he restated the acceptable limits of male affection: 'He's [Howard's cell-mate] got this massage oil and he says "rub my back for me". I said "fuck off, we're in prison". But he's a top lad.' The emphasis on being 'in prison' here is a revealing indicator of the pull towards emotional restraint. Put simply, being too 'soft' was considered a signal of weakness and could generate ridicule or exploitation from other prisoners.

In spite of these risks, explicit displays of warmth sometimes emerged. Prisoners who hugged one another were communicating affection directly: 'when someone is a bit upset, someone will say "come here mate, give me a hug", and it makes a difference' (Billy). Similarly, during an outside workshop when a prisoner told his friend he was cold, the friend put the back of his hand on his face. Not all men exercised verbal restraint: 'With my close mates in here… I can have a good chat with them' (Jerry).[4] Other prisoners felt comfortable enough to say 'I love you, man' (Bernie) to their close friends. While such explicit displays were relatively isolated and atypical, they do serve as an important counterweight to descriptions of men's prisons as emotionally bereft environments.

Humour served as an important social lubricant in both prisons. Indeed, the litany of comedic interactions, pranks, and barbed retorts was a notable feature of day-to-day life both in Ranby and Send. These displays had an 'infectious' (Olivia) quality and served as a collective attempt to stave off negative feeling states: 'Humour is the number one thing that gets people through difficult times. It distracts you and can lead you down another avenue of emotions that result in you feeling

---

[4] A 'good chat' was understood here to mean a conversation that included openly exploring feelings.

better' (Billy). Andrew often used his exhibitionism to bring people together and lighten the mood: 'I will come onto the landing dancing [in a comical manner] and I will be laughing, and a couple of guys will join in…they call it the Andrew disease'. In Ranby, humour often had barbed edges as prisoners tended to 'rip the piss' (Alan) and compete to outwit one another, although these exchanges were usually good spirited. In Send, it was more common to hear accounts of communal mirth, especially in the context of Karaoke nights, parties, playing pranks, or roleplaying:

> A couple of weeks ago it was my friend's birthday, so we set-up the room like a casino hall. There was loads of card games and dominos, and it was nice cause everyone came down. Even the officers came down, and they were all confused. There was so much laughing…everyone was laughing and joking. We had music going in the background, we all bought stuff off of canteen. Everyone came down and had a drink. I acted like a waitress, taking the mick out of everyone: "Top your glass up love?", "red or white," "cherryade or lemonade". We do have to entertain ourselves the best we can in this place. (Blanche)

Through such acts, prisoners used humour to avoid succumbing to group inertia and promote positivity in their living areas. To this end, Tamara explained how group dynamics were highly sensitive to the contagion of moods:

> We are forever laughing and keeping ourselves up. But if one person is down it does kind of affect the group. When that person expresses how they feel, that other person that heard it will get down. It passes on. So we try and keep ourselves happy. Obviously it's not a happy place to be in. We've got to keep sane, otherwise we will just crack. (Tamara)

The various manifestations of care described above can be understood as an attempt to limit the spread and infiltration of toxic emotions from 'outside'. To some extent then, the careful policing of prisoner affiliations and various bonding rituals (cooking, shared gym routines) can be understood as attempts to make the environment predictable and positive.

However, such attempts were not always successful, as the stark realities of imprisonment penetrated these cocoons and hostile interactions with the wider prisoner community were hard to avoid: 'You're living somewhere where there's negative things going on all around, how's that going to make you feel?' (Yvonne). The remainder of this chapter moves in this direction by evaluating the 'negative' emotions that characterised wider interactions in both prisons.

Destructive Forces and Contagious Emotions

Displays of care in prison were hardly ubiquitous, especially outside of tight friendship groups. Those who tried to care for others described the pain of being taking advantage of: 'helping people out...only to be stabbed in the fucking back' (Wayne). That is, openness and kindness could easily be recast by exploitative prisoners as weakness. Prisoners explained that it was not just displays of affective warmth that were proscribed, but that displaying anger openly could also have dangerous consequences (including assaults, IEP reprisals and social exclusion). Put short, in the wider atmosphere of both prisons, the social display of emotions perpetuated destructive cycles that were difficult to contain. Indeed, emotions in this sphere resembled Douglas' (1966) notion of 'dirt'. Douglas argues that the presence of dirt constitutes 'disorder' (5), and anything dirty is considered 'as matter out of place' (36). In this context, the common slogans recanted by prisoners to 'do your own time' and 'keep your head down' were particularly pertinent to emotions. Expressions of feeling were 'out of place' in these broader interactions. The various allusions to prisoners having to traverse emotional 'tightropes' in the prisons literature (see Greer, 2002; Toch, 1992) seem particularly germane to these interactions.

The wider prison environment was full of uncertainty, both in terms of the people one encountered and the feelings that were triggered. A number of participants spoke in candid terms about feeling sudden shame.[5] This powerful emotion emerged in particular when they were reminded

---

[5] The oppressive physical environment sent a message to prisoners, and often eliciting shame. This notion is further developed in the following chapter.

about their offending behaviour. Sometimes these reminders were overt: 'Someone could come down after 15 years and bring up your past and the shame comes back again' (Ula). On other occasions, this process was more indirect: 'An officer is not going to come into this room and leave a bag there and leave you on your own…you're always under suspicion, you're always a suspect' (Haley). Shame was acutely experienced when prisoners felt they had suffered maltreatment. Zak, who could not control his pain, felt humiliated by nurses who downplayed his ailments:

> I was on my bed writhing in agony. I said "What's happening to me?" and she said "You're just having a panic attack, that's all it is." I said "Why am I in so much pain, panic attacks shouldn't cause this much pain." My arm was going boom boom boom [palpitating] and the sweat was pouring the fuck off me. She said "Do you know you're stopping us from having a night out tonight?"

Showing vulnerability in prison could be met with ridicule and irritation. The linkages between shame and anger are not always clear in the wider literature (Scheff & Retzinger, 1991), though Tangney et al. (1992, p. 673) note that 'shamed individuals may be motivated to anger because such anger is likely to produce some relief from the global, self-condemning, and debilitating experience of shame'. In line with this account, Mikey described an incident where he was prevented from using the bathroom in Ranby:

> I just came back from the library and I needed the toilet and I was desperate. I went to the officer and I said "Excuse me boss, can you let me-" He says "no you fucking can't, I'll do it when I'm ready"… So I kicked off and went mad. I told him I was going to knock him out and shit on him. (Mikey)

Neil shared a similar account: 'One morning I needed to shit all night and the officer wouldn't let me outside so I had to shit in a bag'. Being denied agency over the most basic bodily functions was a humiliating reminder that one could be perceived as sub-human by officers—and that such debasements were their lot. Liebling and Arnold's (2004) observation that 'the experience of being in punitive and disrespectful

4 Relational Emotions in Prison 87

environments is traumatic and damaging' is particularly apposite here. The language and general tone of officers' communication was perceived by some as excessive ('shouting when you don't have to shout' Rebecka), disrespectful ('they try and make us look stupid in front of people' Stacey), lacking sensitivity ('he's shouting "come get your methadone, you druggies"' Karl) and infantilising ('they make you feel small' Tamara). At times, these degradations were communicated physically. Being restrained by officers could be a particularly distressing experience: 'I ended up getting twisted up on the floor. Then I'm ashamed because why am I fucking kicking off? Why have I let you twist me up? And everyone's looking' (Craig). Throughout these accounts, the presence of onlookers appears to be a significant issue. Indeed, historically, shame has been connected to the idea of covering oneself—both literally and metaphorically—from being seen (Lewis, 1971). Prisoners were not just being personally reprimanded, they were being *publicly* humiliated. Being watched by a wider audience of prisoners magnified these incidents and intensified the difficult emotions that resulted. Scheff and Retzinger (1991, p. xix) claim that shame is the 'master emotion' that interferes with the management of all our other emotions. First, the authors argue, shame is the 'basic engine of repression' because we often become ashamed of our feelings once they are evoked, and therefore seek to stifle them. Second, shame is the 'runaway fuel of massive conflagrations of physical and emotional violence' (1991, p. xix). In sum, then, in these wider interactions between prisoners, emotions had a 'destructive' quality characterised by the presence shame, which served to increase social distance and friction between individuals.

Moreover, a number of other affective states appeared to have a 'contagious' (Hatfield et al., 1993) quality that spread over, or were absorbed by, other prisoners. The idea that social emotions disseminate in a manner 'akin to the transmission of social viruses' (Hatfield et al., 1993, p. 128) was intuitive to prisoners:

Ellie: You can all kind of feel like everybody gets the emotions, even if it's nothing to do with you. You can feel that, you can really feel it.

Interviewer: It kind of rubs off?

Ellie: It's in the air, and people do take it on.

This 'airborne' pressure to feel particular emotions had a different character in each establishment, though it emerged from a similar source: pent-up boredom, sadness and anger. In the women's prison, some felt fatigued by the seemingly endless litany of emotions: 'It drains me out…it's an on-going circle' (Katherine). Send was described as a prison with 'a lot of negative energy' (Blanche), and prisoners could easily get sucked into this emotional orbit. For example, women who were anxious had 'a domino effect' on those around them by 'making their life your life' (Ula, both quotations). Rather than containing their problems to those who knew them, these prisoners offloaded indiscriminately. Even if prisoners wished to withdraw, they were often 'brought into situations' and subjected to unsolicited sharing by prisoners 'who dump on you' (Lacey, both quotations). Under these conditions, supporting others was a non-consensual exercise, and emotional resources were being forcibly extracted: 'Being around them is emotionally draining. They're like siphons, they siphon the life and energy out of you because they're so sad, overwhelmingly sad' (Katherine). These accounts bring into focus a rarely discussed deprivation of imprisonment: the enforced exposure and proximity to others' moods, from which prisoners often had little means to escape.

Outbursts of collective anger appeared to have a similar degree of momentum or contagious quality ('It just all kicks off' Katherine). Some participants found it particularly hard to fend off these intrusions: 'If someone is in a bad mood, that is the sort of thing that I would absorb…if they were aggressive on the wing, it would raise all those emotions in me' (Olivia). Chantal explained 'We don't know where to put our anger, so we take it out on each other'. Put simply, other prisoners became the targets of anger and frustration precisely because there was a lack of viable alternatives for channelling difficult feelings. While physical outbursts were rare among the women, verbal aggression and anger were prevalent: 'I have seen people moved to tears…by people who take great pleasure in belittling and orally demoralising someone' (Olivia). In Send, a pervasive culture of gossiping ('bickering and nastiness'—Danielle) was described as toxic: 'It's like, why are we even discussing this, none of us were involved?' (Chantal). This behaviour functioned as a kind of collective venting, providing a cathartic outpouring of anger and frustration.

4 Relational Emotions in Prison 89

During conflicts in Send, personal information was a highly valuable tool: 'They'll use whatever you've given to them against you' (Haley). In light of this, prisoners explained that they had to be highly selective about who they trusted. There were other prisoners who went further, intentionally distorting information and spreading rumours to humiliate others ('I was being called a devil worshipper' Stacey). These individual confrontations often had wider social ramifications: 'Not just one person falls out with you, it will be a whole group of people' (Stacey). The social structure of the prison consisted of a web of different groups and factions that were most often ethnically ('Black girls', 'White girls') or geographically delineated ('Welsh girls', 'Travellers'). The fact that it seemed '*everybody* has a clique' (Ellie, emphasis added) hinted at a collective pressure to enter social relationships. This reflected deep insecurities about social isolation and bullying, which would make it far harder to cope with one's sentence. To some extent then, women were pushed together due to fears of exclusion rather than affection.

Unpredictability and fear were also central concerns in the men's prison, although the rationale for this concern had a different source: 'You don't know where the next shock is going to come from or where the next threat is' (Ian). In Ranby, then, confrontations more often had a physial edge, as arguments could quickly escalate into fights or violent attacks. 'It's all "he said, she said". The next thing you know, it gets twisted and your life is in danger' (Alan). There was a build-up of frustration and fear among prisoners that coloured social interactions with the underlying threat of violence. '[Violence] is the language being spoken in here. Imagine you're trying to speak French in a jail where everyone speaks English, it won't work' (Dean). To be 'fluent' in this language meant being able to avoid being an easy mark, and to stand one's ground and fight if necessary. Howard explained that it was the lack of institutional safety that forced him to respond violently:

I'm walking around, next thing some kid comes from behind and slices him [his friend]. And so today he came by and tapped me on my chest, and he says "tick tock, your time is next". You ain't walking away from that situation without you knowing what time it is… If you're not gonna create a safe environment for me, I'm gonna make sure he knows. You're forced to go along with people you wouldn't normally get along with. I'm not accepting it. Without blood, things are easily forgot. It's the only thing they understand. (Howard)

The spirals of fear, aggression and violence at work in men's prisons have been well documented (See Edgar et al., 2014). For current purposes, it is insightful to further explore the idea that, in Ranby, these volatile emotions had a contagious quality. That is, there was a kind of affective 'pull' that made it difficult for prisoners to avoid walking away from confrontations, and made them susceptible to 'catch the rhythms' (Hatfield et al., 1993, p. 1) of other prisoners' emotional states. Two large exercise yards that were surrounded by house blocks and other buildings created an exposed, highly visible space. This area functioned like a theatre in which prisoners observed and communicated with their peers. When confrontations arose in these public spaces, they were quickly seized upon by those in the vicinity:

Other people are getting involved, saying "What are you doing letting people treat you like that?" Then you're thinking if he speaks to me like that then other people will speak to me like that. If I don't do something now, I'm going to get tortured even more. (Dean)

The expectations of this wider audience placed strain or 'peer pressure' (Billy) on prisoners: 'I can't look soft in front of my boys, everyone will take the piss' (Oscar). This was perceived as a public test of one's boundaries, where failing to react assertively could open the floodgates for future challenges and exploitation (de Viggiani, 2012; Sim, 1994; Toch, 1998). Responding physically to provocation garnered admiration and sent a potent message to other prisoners: 'People will think fucking hell he's got a good punch' Karl). What stood out about these altercations though was the sheer hostility and scornfulness of prisoners on the periphery, who tried to provoke physical confrontations through goading and cajoling: 'They say "fucking hell, are you gonna let him get away with that?"' (Tommas). During these incidents, a circle of prisoners would form around potential combatants, shouting at them aggressively: 'Go on! Whack him' (Craig). These attempts to 'hype up' other prisoners into

4 Relational Emotions in Prison 91

confrontations were often hard to resist: 'If you're not strong minded, you're going to listen to them…you start thinking these [guys] are right, and you'll act on it' (Andrew). The hostile energy and aggression pent up among the prisoner population was being charged and channelled into their peers, creating a wave of momentum that swept them along.

These gladiatorial spectacles functioned as a way for prisoners to alleviate collective boredom and provided temporary entertainment. Some participants observed other prisoners daring or paying their peers to fight people. All of these incidents were ways to 'see some excitement, laugh at you, and see somebody get twisted-up' (Val). Similar forms of 'amusement' were sought when some prisoners spiked vulnerable addicts with synthetic cannabinoids:

> Someone's running around trying to buy drugs, and someone else says "You can have this for nothing [high dose of spice]", just because they know the effect it's going to have on them. It's like winding up a toy and then stand back and watch. They see it as entertainment' (Billy).

Finally, a recent suicide attempt on the landing was met with a mixture of encouragement and derision: 'There was prisoners shouting and screaming "You haven't got the balls", "do it!", "come on, come on"' (Dean). Taken as a whole, these accounts indicate that some emotions were infectious, sweeping across large groups of prisoners. These affective waves of energy were hard to ward off and resembled Randall Collins conceptualisations of 'ritual interaction' (1990) and 'forward panic' (2011). The former concept explains how individuals 'get pumped up with the emotional strength from participating in the group interaction' (1990, p. 32), while the latter term refers to the 'build-up of tension and fear' in violent incidents in which combatants are 'caught-up in each other's mood' (2011, p. 23). The spatial constraints of prison life compounded these dynamics, as it was not always possible for prisoners to retreat from unwanted social interactions, especially in cell sharing situations or tight living quarters. Prisoners were highly exposed to the vacillations of others' moods and contagious emotions, catalysing the potential for forward panics. Indeed, the critical role of spatiality, and the ways in which if could sometimes magnify hostility and aggression, features heavily in the next chapter.

Gender and Emotion

In the previous chapters, there was little to distinguish the gendered experience of emotions. Rather, it was suggested that the affective challenges of imprisonment appeared to be universal. However, here a number of differences have surfaced, forming three broad categories, relating to: emotional literacy; competitive and collaborative emotional expression; and finally, the internalisation and externalisation of destructive emotions. These themes are understood as differences *in general* rather than *absolute* contrasts.

First, the female prisoners were more emotionally 'fluent' than male prisoners. In Chap. 2, much was made of the long historical tendency to colour such observations in pejorative terms. These concerns resurface here. The finding that women display 'superior language use' is often translated into the idea that women 'specialize in bitchiness and verbal aggressiveness, while men's penchant for physical aggression is often seen as being up-front and direct' (Campbell, 1993, p. 73). Leaving aside the fact that 'men actually outdo women in terms of verbal as well as physical aggression' (Campbell, 1993, p. 73), the moral starting point of these debates is notably masculinist because separation and individuality is valued over attachment. Moral systems that recognise the 'continuing importance of attachment in the human life cycle' and that the world 'coheres through human connection' are typically disavowed in such accounts (Gilligan, 1992, pp. 23–29). Gilligan (1992) explains that the forgotten moral voice of women involves 'illuminating life as a web…stressing continuity and change in configuration, rather than replacement and separation, elucidating a different response to loss, and changing metaphor of growth' (48). In the context of emotions and imprisonment, these imbalances surfaced through 'gendered rehabilitative strategies which primarily take aim at *containing* women's emotions' (Kolind & Bjonness, 2019, p. 2 emphasis added) instead of emphasising the positive aspects of them. Further, Kruttschnitt and Gartner (2005, p. 144) found that female prisoners are often described by officers as 'more emotional, manipulative, and generally more troublesome than their male counterparts'. Prison staff can at times tend towards seeing emotion as a problem to be curtailed and swept away, like dirt, or matter that is out of place (Douglas, 1966).

In some instances, prisoners in this study reinforced stereotypes about gender that were matched by the empirical findings. For example, Ellie claimed that talking about emotions was part of 'being a girl', and Karl said 'men don't talk about feelings'. Female prisoners were observed to be more comfortable articulating their emotions than their male counterparts. The male prisoners—although not unfamiliar with the importance of empathy and relationships in prison themselves—were more likely to exercise verbal restraint and express their feelings through understated actions, such as nods of approval and small physical greetings, such as handshakes and fist bumps. It was more common in Send to drop in on 'deep' conversations in public places and to see women displaying a wide number of emotions together (for example: crying openly, talking enthusiastically, joyful dancing, and raucous laughter). This was further intensified by the various therapeutic programmes in Send that championed awareness and openness to emotional dialogues. But the detailed discussion of empathy introduced in the middle of the chapter rebalances the notion that emotional expression is inherently problematic, dangerous or always the subject of institutional containment. As Baron-Cohen (2012, p. 46) explains 'the pay-off of self-disclosure is intimacy' and 'the *upshot* of this' is that these relationships 'are more emotional'. This is the case because emotional intimacy 'forms and reinforces social bonds' and 'communication channels open so that any tensions that arise are then easier to diffuse' (Baron-Cohen, 2012, p. 55). In a similar vein, then, this chapter avoids the pitfalls of equating emotional expression with weakness and emotional restraint as a virtue. The argument emphasises the strengths of affective intimacy among female prisoners and the importance of emotional expression as form of social adhesion.

Second, while both sets of prisoners expressed emotions through shared activities, the nature of these activities had different distinguishing features. In Ranby, activities were far more competitive or adversarial— men played games against one another and gym partners spurred each other on through challenges and goal setting. These men were less likely to describe feeling dependent upon one another, though they clearly valued their group affiliations and relied upon them in times of need.

Though Crewe (2014) recognises that the case can sometimes be over-stated it is valid to conclude, in line with Baron-Cohen (2012, p. 55), that the men in this study refer 'less frequently to their relationships, tending to live them through joint activities rather than talking about them'. In Send, women engaged more often in communal pastimes, where group bonding was achieved through a combination of skills, generosity and mutual support with problems. Further, women were more dependent on these group networks, which were an essential feature of their daily lives and functioned like pseudo family units. This contrasts notably with Mandaraka-Sheppard's (1986, p. 135) finding that women were 'not inclined to form cohesive groups', exhibiting a general 'reluctance to stick together' because their relationships are characterised by hostility, mistrust and a 'quiet antagonism' (137). These results align more closely with Owen (1998) who found that interpersonal relationships are the anchors of prison life for women—although the presence of pseudo family units was less pervasive here than in Owen's study.

Third, female and male prisoners were also more likely to use different modes of emotional expression, especially in the case of anger and aggression. One contention of Chap. 2 was that prisons research has typically under documented the role of anger in women's establishments (Liebling, 2009). This trend aligns with findings outside of prison in that 'maleness and aggression have become linked to the point where it is easy to forget about women's aggression...[which] is private, unrecognized, and frequently misunderstood' (Campbell, 1993, p. 1). Campbell states that for women the threat often comes from within and that their anger represents an expressive 'cataclysmic release of accumulated tension' and a 'cry for help born out of desperation' (7). Campbell further explains (1993, p. 18) that women's anger follows a pattern of 'repression, frustration, then explosion'. This observation connects strongly with the artwork presented in the previous chapter, and the finding that bottled emotions appeared to return in 'explosive' forms.

When women's anger has been discussed in the prisons context, research has confirmed that while men are more likely to 'aggress against others or property [whereas] women direct their anger inward with either cognitive outcomes (such as depression) or behavioural outcomes (such as self-harm)' (Suter et al., 2002, p. 1096). Further, Mandaraka-Sheppard

(1986, p. 135) explains that the expressive qualities of women's 'outbursts of violent behaviour' in prison are individualistic, instant, and last for a short period of time. To some extent the current study reaffirmed these accounts, finding more internalisation of sadness and anger in the women's prison compared with instrumental externalisation among men in general. According to Easteal (2001, p. 99) the internalisation of pain and secrets is a rational response to austere prison settings that are 'anathema to the process of healing' and merely echo earlier childhood experiences of censure. Further to this point, the litany of social control mechanisms outside prison that govern women's feeling states are well documented (Howe, 1994). That is to say, the same 'psychic numbing' (Easteal, 2001) enforced on women as children is apparent in the 'psychic coercion' of imprisonment (Carlen, 1998, p. 83). Carlen (1998, p. 85) describes the 'humiliating pettiness of many of the rules and the rigidity with which they are enforced [in prison], and the erosion of control over the ordering of personal space and time' that women face.

One side-effect of this strict governance, particularly apposite for this discussion, is that women internally experience more secondary emotions when they express anger and aggression—such as guilt, anxiety and shame—because of a sense that they have breached society's expectations of feminine behaviour by failing to internally police themselves (Campbell, 1993). However, this study adds to these existing debates by exposing how emotional control and expressivity are cyclical and connected processes. Women were both *more emotionally expressive* and *more controlled*. That is, internal and external controls lead women to suppress the expression of certain feelings, but this was a generative as well as stifling process.

By contrast, the male prisoners externalised their anger, often in quite instrumental ways: the aforementioned gladiatorial, and sometimes predatory, displays of violence in association yards were representative of this. For men, anger and aggression is about defending against the loss of status, allowing them to repair wounded self-esteem, and gain social and material benefits (Campbell, 1993). Liebling (1992, p. 194) found that 'much of the self-destructive behaviour by the male groups…can be seen as instrumental, strategic or determined to achieve some outcome'. It seems a truism that in men's prisons, 'one can feel that the general mood may lead to something carefully organised and forethought' (Mandaraka-Sheppard, 1986, p. 137). The linguistic features of men's accounts in this study—which were less likely to use 'I' and 'me' terms—indicated a certain proclivity towards the 'outward projection' of their affective states. Though men's prisons encourage emotional fortitude and restraint in general, they actively license states of anger and 'kicking off' (Crewe, 2009, p. 437)—although these displays were carefully calibrated in Ranby. Instrumental displays of anger were not completely foreign in Send either, especially in the dining room where women initiated fights with the hope of being 'shipped out' to different establishments. In her study of anger and aggression, Campbell (1993, pp. 132–133) uncovers 'remarkably similar' stories from women in gangs, including accounts of 'threat and counterthreat, the bravado, and the pride in scaring the opponent into submission'. Campbell claims that when women follow these aggression scripts it is because they have been overwhelmed by 'fear and loneliness' in their families, schools and communities and must therefore use aggression to survive (133). They aggress, according to Campbell, because they have nothing to lose. This reflective analysis is not afforded to the men in her study, who are depicted as ruthless instrumentalists who 'eagerly exploit the full range of their aggression…materially as well as socially' (140). The findings in this current study do not deny that men's prisons have higher levels of instrumental violence overall, only that the biographical accounts introduced in Chap. 4 made it explicitly clear that isolation, fear, abandonment and trauma was present among *both* samples.

Care should be taken not to overemphasise gender differences either, as there was also much concordance between these prisoner groups. As Liebling (1992, p. 184) states:

> Any complete dichotomy between male and female experiences of imprisonment is misleading, despite the many differences existing between male and female penal establishment and their organisation. One of the important findings…has been the consistency of the pains of imprisonment, regardless of gender.

This was especially apparent in relation to the social sharing of emotions. In both prisons, it was customary to hear that other prisoners were the most common source for offloading emotions (as opposed to family members and officers). As wider psychological research has recognised, people 'prefer to interact with others who are experiencing similar emotions' (Townsend et al., 2013, p. 526) because it fills 'powerful needs for social recognition and validation, for listening and understanding, for unconditional acceptance and for social integration' (Rimé, 2007, p. 472). Prisoners, then, shared a powerful collective experience that put them in a position to be able to truly empathise with the feelings of those around them.

The extent to which these 'gendered' emotion differences in prison are indicative of wider trends in the population outside is a challenging question. In their study of mental health disorders in the community Eaton et al. (2012) found that women showed a higher mean level of internalising, while men showed a higher mean level of externalising. But specific aspects of the prison environment may crystallise and intensify these differences. An important strand of Mandaraka-Sheppard's explanation for why women prisoners were 'lacking the strength of an informal structure' (141) concerned the coercive nature of the establishment which reduced trust in their relations. Similarly, if the institutional consequences of outward aggression are more damaging than inward aggression prisoners may be more inclined to control their emotions (Suter et al., 2002). For current purposes, this argument raises difficult questions about the extent to which gender differences cause differences in emotionality, or whether the different cultural and operational priorities of the prison plays an important role in establishing or denying communal relations. Much has been written about the prevalence of 'toxic' and hegemonic masculinities in men's prisons (Toch, 1998; Kupers, 2005), and the opportunities for work and education in women's prisons often seem to endorse outmoded and passive feminine virtues (Bosworth, 1999). While these are important considerations, the extent to which gender moulded displays of emotionality in prison remains an unanswered question. To address this question, the spatial and institutional drivers of emotion are the primary concern of the following chapter.

In many ways, then, the findings in this current study confirm existing arguments in the literature. But by considering emotions from different perspectives, this study helps refine and augment these debates to reveal important tensions: female prisoners are both more fluent with their emotions *and* more controlled. Second, the extended discussion of empathy in this chapter goes some way to rebalancing the pejorative connotations that 'Females tend to show more indirect (or relational, covert) aggression...behind people's backs...like gossip exclusion and bitchy remarks' (Baron-Cohen, 2012, p. 37). Empathy had important integrative qualities that have been well documented in the chapter. More generally, an understanding of emotions in prison contributes to debates about the key dimensions of power, order and control. To conclude this chapter, some of these important arguments are addressed.

Emotions: Power, Order and Control

In their illuminating study Sparks et al. (1996) set out to understand how order is negotiated in different prisons, and how the use of power and authority facilitates or impedes the social organisation of these institutions. Though their account includes no explicit analysis of the role of emotions in this task, in a number of places feelings are indirectly introduced into the analysis. For example, the authors state that 'prisons quite commonly seethe and boil with human agency, passion, and conflict' (1996, p. 68), especially during riots where they are sites of 'sheer hedonistic thrill', even if most of the time they 'are boring' places, this 'boredom may be sought' (82). From the inverse direction, the current study can complement Sparks et al.'s account of order and control in prison by further developing the analysis of emotions.

Derek Layder (2004, p. 5) argues that there are 'deep-seated associations between power and the emotions' that are 'not simply contingent and haphazard', rather the 'two are to be found in each other's company in every instance...[as] constant companions'. Yet as stated above, research in women's prisons has often veered away from important topics such as legitimacy and power (Liebling, 2009). This is surprising given that Suter et al. (2002, p. 1095) found that 'women were significantly more likely [than men] to be angered by perceptions of unfairness and justice', and that their 'resentment toward unfairness' stemmed from traumatic life events that 'created a sense of inequity'. Further, the fact that women's prisons are often described as 'more emotional' and 'needy' places essentially serves to strips women of agency. As Kruttschnitt and Gartner (2005, p. 159) explain 'volition...is missing, as it always has been for female offenders'. In line with this, Carlen (1998, p. 91) describes the 'constant hijacking of any control' and the infantilisation process still inherent in many women's prisons. What is missing from this interpretation is the point that displays of emotionality are, to some degree, a direct response to militant policing and institutional regulation, and that these responses serve key functions. For example, explosions of anger and aggression reveal where the negotiations of power relations have frayed or broken down completely.

In their small groups and prisoner dyads, the exchange of emotions was indicative of the 'ongoing process of attachment that relates and sustains the human community' (Gilligan, 1992, p. 156). In this light, it becomes clearer that displays of care and empathy are also deeply related to establishing and managing power—or at least not separate from power entanglements. Gilligan explains that women can 'equate power with giving and care' (167), and understand 'nurturance as acts of strength' (168). Emotional expression in both prisons functioned like social glue, or 'connective tissue' (Davidson & Milligan, 2004, p. 524) that typically increased levels of intimacy, trust and brought a degree of harmony to these relations. The dynamics of emotions, then, have a lot to say about attempts to establish and maintain order and reveal some of the alternative ways in which it is achieved.

But this debate is not without interpretative complexity. The finding that there are high levels of emotional suppression punctuated by outbursts of anger, in both prisons, speaks to the institutional attempts to control particular behavioural expressions and the lack of trust prisoners have in officers. Restraining or internalising one's anger is a rational response where there are 'institutional consequences of outward aggression' that are 'more aversive than that of inward aggression' (Suter et al., 2002, p. 1096). Indeed, Mandaraka-Sheppard (1986, p. 199) articulates the 'subtle spiral effect' of such punishment or control on further misbehaviour and shows that the 'multiplication of offences and the 'multiplication of punishments' can engender bitterness. In a related manner, the high levels of anger and fear on display in Ranby in public spaces were indicative of direct threats to power and status. As Barbalet (2001, p. 26) explains: 'A power relationship which results in the dispossession of a participant also leads to their anger'.

Arguably then, the emotional dimensions of imprisonment provide an important micro-level lens through which to view the new penology (Feeley & Simon, 1992) and the 'culture of control' (Garland, 2001) close up. Imprisonment is, increasingly perhaps in the era of mass incarceration, an experience of depersonalisation that can have a clear 'impact on the emotional well-being of its charges' (Kruttschnitt & Gartner, 2005, p. 154). The idea that imprisonment is a dehumanising experience is hardly original, but understanding the precise mechanisms by which prisoners are made to feel 'somehow less than human' is important (Easteal, 2001, p. 99). At least part of this explanation involves understanding the constriction and limits placed on emotional expressivity in prison.

The institutional sanitation of feelings operated in the following directions: first, through a kind of *purging* that tried to clean up emotions from public prison spaces like dirt that is out of place (Douglas, 1966)— recall that prisoners who danced joyfully in the hallways received more mandatory drugs tests. Second, prisoners are placed under emotional strain and pressures to navigate the emotions of other prisoners. Indeed, a number of prisoners described a form of *enforced* empathy that they termed as a contagious and contaminating force. There are clear synergies here with Carlen's (1998, p. 83) claim that imprisonment can create an 'unspeakable, and always corrosive, fear of pollution'. Third, while therapy arguably facilitates an inverse process, encouraging expressivity, the next chapter reveals that this is a complex case and that 'special treatment can readily become special control' (Peay, 2010, p. 521). To bring these arguments together, in the context of control and order, it appears that emotion is both an important cause and effect. On the one hand, emotions are the result of particular coercive institutional rules and regulatory practices and the strain of adjustment. On the other, regulating and expressing emotions offers an active, agentic, way of reinterpreting prison space and establishing new forms of social connection, dignity, order and trust. However, this debate is further informed by the idea that prisons have an emotional geography, and that space is in an influential variable. The next chapter explores the contribution of space to the discussion of emotion in detail.

Conclusion

The theoretical perspectives introduced in this chapter ('social glue' and 'emotion contagion') provide ways to develop traditional dramaturgical frameworks of prison life that rely on the binary distinctions set out in Chap. 2: that is, between 'frontstage' and 'backstage' areas, or public and private spaces. Goffman (1961, p. 15) states that social actors are strongly influenced by a desire to shape 'the definition of the situation which the others come formulate' about them. Such frameworks emphasise the importance of impression management, and cast the individual as an agent who is compelled to hide authentic expressions of identity and emotion from the public sphere. Yet, while this perspective has value, it is also limiting. Indeed, Goffman recognises that the focus on the 'communicative role' of social interaction alone excludes the possibility of other functions such as catharsis or 'tension-release' (1961, p. 241).

By contrast, then, this chapter argues that emotions have deeply social roots and a range of applications that complicate the frontstage-backstage dichotomy. It may be more accurate to describe concentric circles of prison relations, including: romantic couples, friendship dyads, small groups, diffuse affiliations, interactions with strangers, and hostile groups. In each of these groupings feeling states take on different forms and meanings, and the pattern and flow of emotionality in these interactions cuts across binary conceptualisations of prison life. For example, in the innermost circles of relations (dyads and small groups), the mutual expression and experience of affective states was integral. In these groups, there were numerous displays of care shown through 'consideration, generosity, or support' that were 'triggered by visible reminders of another's humanness' (Liebling & Arnold, 2004, p. 219). Rather than banishing authentic emotions from their social worlds, then, these prisoner relations demanded them. These interactions were highly regenerative and provided an important source of emotional nourishment.

The second half of the chapter evaluated affective states that emerged from the social sphere. The metaphor of emotional contagion guided this analysis, shedding light on the ways in which social interactions had a kind of affective momentum. In this context, the imagery of disease was particularly germane, as participants often articulated fears of being 'contaminated' by imprisonment or described emotional states as being 'infectious' or 'in the air'. There are important connections here with scholarship on collective emotions (Collins, 1990, 2011), and especially the idea that emotions can spread like waves of energy. Collective emotions have been notably underexplored in prisons research. This is surprising given the unique aspects of the physical environment, including the highly constricted movement of bodies and forced (co)habitation in tight spaces, that concentrates and magnifies forms of emotional contagion. Among female prisoners, this analysis of shared emotions revealed a deprivation that is rarely discussed in the pains of imprisonment literature (Crewe, 2011; Sykes, 1958): namely, the enforced exposure to others' emotions and moods, from which prisoners often had little means to escape. Importantly, then, particular emotions are moulded by, and woven into the fabric of physical spaces in prison. This dynamic relationship, between emotions and space, is the subject of the next chapter. In the concluding chapter, more is said about the potential of these findings to develop, and add texture to, older frameworks of prison life rooted in limited formulations of impression management.

References

Barbalet, J. M. (2001). *Emotion, social theory, and social structure: A macrosociological approach*. Cambridge University Press.

Baron-Cohen, S. (2012). *The essential difference: The male and female brain*. Penguin London.

Ben-David, S., & Silfen, P. (1994). In quest of a lost father? Inmates' preferences of staff relation in a psychiatric prison ward. *International Journal of Offender Therapy and Comparative Criminology, 38*(2), 131–139.

Bosworth, M. (1999). *Engendering resistance: Agency and power in women's prisons*. Routledge.

Campbell, A. (1993). *Out of Control: Men, Women and Aggression*. Pandora.

Carlen, P. (1998). *Sledgehammer: Women's imprisonment at the millennium*. Springer.

Cochran, L., & Claspell, E. (1987). The meaning of grief: *A dramaturgical approach to understandng emotion*. Greenwood Press.

Collins, R. (1990). Stratification, emotional energy, and the transient emotions. In T. D. Kemper (Ed.), *SUNY series in the sociology of emotions. Research agendas in the sociology of emotions*. State University of New York Press.

Collins, R. (2011). Forward panic and violent atrocities. In S. Karstedt, I. Loader, & H. Strang (Eds.), *Emotions, crime and justice*. Bloomsbury Publishing.

Crewe, B. (2009). *The prisoner society: Power, adaptation and social life in an English prison*. Oxford University Press.

Crewe, B. (2011). Depth, weight, tightness: Revisiting the pains of imprisonment. *Punishment & Society, 13*(5), 509–529.

Crewe, B. (2014). Not looking hard enough: Masculinity, emotion, and prison research. *Qualitative Inquiry, 20*(4), 392–403. https://doi.org/10.1177/1077800413515829

Davidson, J., & Milligan, C. (2004). *Embodying emotion, sensing space: Introducing emotional geographies* (November 2014), 37–41. https://doi.org/10.1080/1464936042000317677

De Viggiani, N. (2012). Trying to be something you are not: Masculine performances within a prison setting. *Men and Masculinities, 15*(3), 271–291.

Douglas, M. (1966/2002). *Purity and danger*. Routledge.

Easteal, P. (2001). Women in Australian prisons: The cycle of abuse and dysfunctional environments. *The Prison Journal, 81*(1), 87–112

Eaton, N. R., Keyes, K. M., Krueger, R. F., Balsis, S., Skodol, A. E., Markon, K. E., & Hasin, D. S. (2012). An invariant dimensional liability model of gender differences in mental disorder prevalence: Evidence from a national sample. *Journal of Abnormal Psychology, 121*(1), 282.

Edgar, K., O'Donnell, I., & Martin, C. (2014). *Prison violence: Conflict, power and victimization*. Routledge.

Feeley, M. M., &; Simon, J. (1992). The new penology: Notes on the emerging strategy of corrections and its implications. *Criminology, 30*(4).

Fischer, A. H., & Manstead, A. S. (2008). Social functions of emotion. In M. Lewis, J. M. Haviland-Jones, & L. F. Barrett (Eds.), *Handbook of emotions* (Vol. 3, pp. 456–468). The Guilford Press.

Garland, D. (2001). *The culture of control: Crime and social order in contemporary society*. University of Chicago Press.

104 B. Laws

Gilligan, J. (1992). In a different voice: *Psychological theory and women's development*. Harvard University Press.

Goffman, E. (1961). *Asylums: Essays on the social situation of mental patients and other inmates*. AldineTransaction.

Greer, K. (2002). Walking an emotional tightrope: Managing emotions in a women's prison. *Symbolic Interaction, 25*(1), 117–139. https://doi.org/10.1525/si.2002.25.1.117

Harber, K. D., & Pennebaker, J. W. (1992). Overcoming traumatic memories. In S. A. Christianson (Ed.), *The handbook of emotion and memory: Research and theory*. Lawrence Erlbaum Associates.

Hareli, S., & Parkinson, B. (2008). What's social about social emotions? *Journal for the Theory of Social Behaviour, 38*(2), 131–156.

Hatfield, E., Cacioppo, J. T., & Rapson, R. L. (1993). Emotional contagion. *Current directions in psychological science, 2*(3), 96–100.

Howe, A. (1994). *Punish and critique: Towards a feminist analysis of penality*. Routledge.

Jewkes, Y. (2002). *Captive audience: Media, masculinity and power in prisons*. Willian Publishing.

Kolind, T., & Bjønness, J. (2019). 'The right way to be a woman': Negotiating femininity in a prison-based drug treatment programme. *Punishment & Society, 21*(1), 107–124.

Kovecses, Z. (2000). *Metaphor and emotion: Language, culture and body in human feeling*. University Press.

Kruttschnitt, C., & Gartner, R. (2005). *Marking time in the golden state: Women's imprisonment in California*. University Press.

Kupers, T. A. (2005). Toxic masculinity as a barrier to mental health treatment in prison. *Journal of Clinical Psychology, 61*(6), 713–724.

Layder, D. (2004). *Emotion in social life: The lost heart of society*. Sage.

Lewis, H. B. (1971). Shame and guilt in neurosis. *Psychoanalytic Review, 58*(3), 419.

Liebling, A. (1992). *Suicides in prison*. Routledge.

Liebling, A. (2009). Women in prison prefer legitimacy to sex. *British Society of Criminology Newsletter, 63*, 19–23.

Liebling, A., & Arnold, H. (2004). *Prisons and their moral performance: A study of values, quality, and prison life*.

Mandaraka-Sheppard, A. (1986). *Coping with the self in prison: inmates' self image and its relations with behaviour in prison*. The dynamics of aggres.

O'Donnell, I. (2014). *Prisoners, solitude, and time*. Oxford University Press.

Owen, B. A. (1998). *In the mix: Struggle and survival in a women's prison.* SUNY Press.

Peay, J. (2010). *Mental health and crime.* Routledge-Cavendish.

Planalp, S. (1999). *Communicating emotion: Social, moral, and cultural processes.* University Press.

Rimé, B. (2007). Interpersonal emotion regulation. In J. J. Gross (Ed.), *Handbook of emotion regulation.* Guilford Press.

Scheff, T. J., & Retzinger, S. M. (1991). *Emotions and violence: Shame and rage in destructive conflicts.* iUniverse.

Sim, J. (1994). Tougher than the rest? Men in prison. In T. Newburn & B. Stanko (Eds.), *Just boys doing the business.* Routledge.

Suter, J. M., Byrne, M. K., Byrne, S., Howells, K., & Day, A. (2002). Anger in prisoners: Women are different from men. *Personality and Individual differences, 32*(6), 1087–1100.

Sykes, G. M. (1958). *The society of captives. In The Society of Captives.* Princeton University Press.

Tait, S. (2011). A typology of prison officer approaches to care. *European Journal of Criminology, 8*(6), 440–454.

Tangney, J. P., Wagner, P., Fletcher, C., & Gramzow, R. (1992). Shamed into anger? The relation of shame and guilt to anger and self-reported aggression. *Journal of Personality and Social Psychology, 62*(4), 669.

Toch, H. (1992). *Living in prison: The ecology of survival.* The Free Press.

Toch, H. (1998). Hypermasculinity and prison violence. In L. H. Bowker (Ed.), *Masculinities and violence.* Sage Publications.

Townsend, S. S. M., Kim, H. S., & Mesquita, B. (2013). Are you feeling what I'm feeling? Emotional similarity buffers stress. *Social Psychological and Personality Science, 5*(5), 526–533. https://doi.org/10.1177/19485506 13511499

5

Space and Emotions

Theories of prison architecture have a long history (Bentham, 1791; Evans, 1982; Foucault, 1977; Jewkes, 2013;), and have drawn attention to the symbolic features of imprisonment, which are 'layered with meaning' (Jewkes, 2013: 27). For example, McConville (2000) argues that the prison façade figuratively resembles the force of the state and its power to quash crime. However, as noted earlier, this literature tends towards prioritising structure over agency and typically excludes prisoners' accounts from the research. This is to say, while prison architecture may appear oppressive to an outside observer, the extent to which prisoners actually feel oppressed by it is an empirical question. Indeed, Foucault's (1979) suggestion that imprisonment would lead inevitably to the creation of docility is challenged by recent empirical work that emphasises the emotional differentiation of prison spaces (Crewe et al., 2014). In contrast to these early accounts, then, this chapter shifts the focus to further understand the experience and appropriation of prison space, and the wide range of emotions that emerge in, and cut across, its various zones. Recent developments in the sub-field of 'carceral geography' are particularly apposite here (for a review, see Moran, 2015) and feature throughout. Indeed, the different affective zones described in this chapter closely

© The Author(s), under exclusive license to Springer Nature Switzerland AG 2022   **107**
B. Laws, *Caged Emotions*, Palgrave Studies in Prisons and Penology,
https://doi.org/10.1007/978-3-030-96083-4_5

resemble what Smoyer and Blankenship (2014: 564) term 'a patchwork of interior spaces'.

This account starts with the premise that physical environments affect people emotionally, but acknowledges that these effects are not uniform or predictable. That is, while architects may purposefully attempt to 'design in' particular affective responses, it is more accurate to say that at best, buildings shape certain 'possibilities of experience' (Massumi, 2002: 204). A non-deterministic account should consider how inhabitants experience different spaces, because there exists a 'copulating of live body and dead stone [that] is unique and unrehearsed' (Tschumi, 1996: 125). As Kraftl and Adey (2008: 226) put it, there is a sense of 'soaking and absorption, experienced by both bodies and buildings' that is 'beset with the unknown'. Because prisoners are not passive objects moulded uniformly by their environment, this account aims to blend objective description with subjective accounts of the experience of physical space. What emerges is a complex 'emotional map' of these establishments that resists simplistic generalisations—for example, the tendency to cast prisons as a kind of grey, homogenous monolith—or reductive binaries of emotion management (private versus public expression, frontstage and backstage metaphors) that have sometimes illuminated prior accounts of prison space (for a summary, see Crewe et al., 2014).

To chart a course through these emotion maps, this chapter divides prison spaces into three main sub-groups: living spaces; constrictive and volatile zones; and areas that can be termed 'free spaces' (Goffman, 1961). The first segment describes the range of emotions and feelings prisoners experienced in their cells, wings and on house blocks. These accounts uncover a sharp variance of attitudes towards the cell space. This discussion is conceptually guided by Turner (1974) and Jewkes' (2005a) development of the idea of *liminality* as 'a period…of ambiguity, a sort of social limbo' (Turner, 1974: 24, cited in Jewkes, 2005a: 374). Indeed, understanding cell experiences as a 'midpoint of transition' (Turner, 1974: 237) helps to explain why these spaces were containers for many forms of intense emotion. Cells were experienced as claustrophobic and unsettling for prisoners in the midst of transition, but were more akin to a sanctuary for those who had emerged from the other side of this process. A notable feature of this discussion is the way in which prisoners attempted to customise their living spaces. This active reshaping of the environment signalled an attempt to display and affirm newly formed identities and evoke feelings of comfort.

From this juncture, the discussion turns to spaces that prisoners found emotionally constrictive or highly volatile. These were areas characterised by high levels of fear, aggression, and physical violence. In the men's prison, the 'line route' was one such place, while in the women's prison the dining room served a similar function. These spaces shared a number of important features: the presence of multiple unknown prisoners; unpredictability; perceptions of poor supervision from offices; and the feeling of being crowded, watched and judged by one's peers.

In the third section, the discussion turns to so called 'free spaces' (sometimes termed niches), which 'refer to small scale settings within a community or movement that are removed from the direct control of dominant groups, [and] are voluntarily participated in' (Polletta, 1999: 1). These zones included libraries, classrooms, workshops, visits halls, chapels and gyms and all had different affective climates compared to other prison zones. One salient motif was that these zones did not 'feel' like part of the prison and offered temporary breaks from its more oppressive aspects. Again, Turner's (1974) perspective is instructive here. His conceptualisation of 'communitas' as an unstructured community which is 'undifferentiated, equalitarian' (274) and marked by a spirit of liberty helps to disentangle the various factors that distinguished these areas from the wider environment. The various features of these 'island[s] of respite' (Crewe et al., 2014: 68) that created this sense of distinction are explored in some detail. Especially significant here were the attributes of civilian staff and the different rules of emotional expression that permeated these spaces, where 'kindness, generosity and emotional disclosure were [all] permitted' (Crewe et al., 2014: 68).

Following this, the chapter introduces a brief section on 'therapeutic spaces' in prison. These intense spaces had distinct climates and were experienced as psychologically constrictive, personally transformative, or some combination of both. At the affective level, therapeutic zones were complex spaces for prisoners. Although the experience of psychological power in such spaces commonly evoked feelings of frustration and anger, these emotions often existed alongside joy and compassion as prisoners celebrated their own development trajectories or acknowledged the growth of others. The chapter concludes by analysing the possibilities or lack thereof of achieving privacy in prison. The attempt to locate privacy in prison facilitates a broader discussion of the 'spatial selection' strategies that prisoners used to either seek-out or avoid particular emotional states. In this final section, it is argued that the spatial constraints of the environment placed limits on these strategies and that enforced proximity with others at times acted as a catalyst for destructive emotions. Generally though, prisoners were able to shape many of their emotions, at least to some degree, through the careful selection of the spaces in which they operated. In this closing section the substantive analysis comes full circle, as these spatial strategies resonate with the individual emotional management strategies set out in Chap. 4.

Living Spaces

> It's a place for everything; all my emotions come out in that cell. (Olivia)

Cells, wings and house blocks were the places where prisoners spent most of their time, and when they spoke of prison life, it was typically these areas to which they referred. A more detailed physical description of these different living spaces was introduced in the methods section (Chap. 3), but it is worth reiterating that, in the men's prison, house blocks were typically larger and cell sharing arrangements far more frequent than in Send.[1] These differences had important implications for how the participants experienced their living areas. The following discussion begins with cell spaces, before panning out to the communal living areas.

Prison cells were complex and emotionally intense zones. For some prisoners, it was typical to experience a full 'range of emotions' (Dean) within cells—these feelings could oscillate rapidly or fuse into each other. For example, staring at pictures of family members could evoke bittersweet reactions where 'happiness is mixed with sadness' (Rebecka). Pictures offered positive reminders that prisoners were loved and cared

---

[1] In Send, cell sharing was limited to the small drug treatment wing.

for, while also evoking feelings of guilt, shame and loss. Ula explained that the cell evoked 'pure, more intensified emotions' because 'there is no one around you to stop or distract you from them'. Being cut off from many forms of external stimulation compelled prisoners to process and confront their internal states. This emotional intensity was embraced by some prisoners for its cathartic qualities but was highly challenging for others. There was a shared narrative that confinement—and the stark reality that one was being physically locked-in to a cell—was emotionally turbulent during the initial stages of imprisonment but that, over time, prisoners adapted to it, and in many cases, began to enjoy this time of relative privacy:

> I suppose you could say there's a bit of submission involved. You're having to just bite the bullet. You come to a certain time of the day where you know where you're going to be. As you can't leave from behind that door. So after seven o'clock at night, that's it. You know exactly where you're going to be. (Bernie)

> You have to learn to love your cell and your space. When I first came to prison I found it very difficult to be in a cell on my own. (Ellie)

Adapting to the cell space can be further understood as a kind of liminal process or transitional stage. For current purposes, liminality refers to 'states of being or states of mind…as we pass from a period of stability to one of ambiguity and undergo some kind of transformation' (Jewkes, 2005a: 376).[2] Prisoners who felt unsettled in the cells were often in the midst of this intermediate, 'ambiguous phase', experiencing complete upheavals of their identities accompanied by intense negative emotions. Prisoners who transitioned beyond this difficult stage embodied an idea 'frequently symbolised in ritual and myth' that the liminal space was like a 'grave that is also a womb' (Turner, 1974: 259). These prisoners felt a different range of emotions in their cells (characterised by serenity and affection) and decorated these spaces with a range of identity markers.

---

[2] This is a different sense of liminality than has been used in recent accounts. For example, in her article, Moran (2011) focuses on the liminal features of prison visiting room spaces as opposed to psychological processes of change explored here.

Claustrophobic Cell Spaces

Around a third of the participants held mixed or unfavourable attitudes to their cells, which they claimed evoked 'mostly negative emotions' (Lacey), including 'anger, sadness, boredom, frustration, depression, and anxiety' (Freddy). These accounts were emblematic of the idea that 'liminal spaces are characterised by disorder and chaos' (Jewkes, 2005a: 382). A key factor for these prisoners was a general fixation on their confinement. That is, they were locked in against their will and 'you just can't get out of it and you're stuck there, it can be really dreadful' (Ellie). The cell was framed here as a zone of deep internal strife and conflict that was hard to escape: 'You've got to fight through it' (Freddy). Some prisoners described a form of behavioural 'stereotypy' as they mechanically paced and circled their cells in a restless manner ('I walk up and down my room, that's the hardest part of my day' [Gabriella]; 'You get annoyed and angry, so you start bouncing around the pad' [Val]). These feeling were intensified by the restricted dimensions of the space: 'The rooms are so claustrophobic sometimes…I've got everything in there, but it just feels like I haven't got enough space' (Haley). Prisoners that progressed on to enhanced wings (in Ranby) or resettlement wings (in Send) explained the psychological liberation of receiving the key to their 'room': 'I've got the comfort of knowing I can escape from the stress. I can walk to the recess and have a shower and have a cuppa tea' (Karl).

As suggested above, time in cells created waves of intense emotional energy, but these prisoners felt overwhelmed by these forces, rather than able to navigate a course through them. Emotions were unwelcome intrusions that felt like barriers to wellness, raking up feelings of self-disapproval ('Why are you back here again? Why are you here?' Craig). Canvassing one's cell walls with pictures of family members and friends could, counterintuitively, stimulate feelings of shame: 'If I lay there looking at my photos for too long I feel sad because I've lost out on so many years of their life that I can't get back' (Molly). Similarly, Stacey explained that although she had pictures of 'children on the wall' she would 'try not to look at them'. As an attempt to mitigate against disturbing thoughts, Gabriella chose not to display her pictures at all: 'I need to separate myself from outside'. The onset of nightmares and acute states of anguish among these prisoners are consistent with Turner's (1974) argument that liminality involves an encounter with 'grotesque and monstrous forms' (239). Put short, for such prisoners, cells were psychological traps where they were pushed into a seemingly endless maze of uncomfortable feelings and rumination.

These participants did not feel attached to their cells nor did they find comfort in them. This was evidenced, in part, by the decision not to personalise these spaces:

Interviewer: *Do you decorate your cell?*
Gabriella: No.
Interviewer: *So it is just standard issue?*
Gabriella: Yes, I don't want anything to feel like home.

Indeed, the idea that cells constituted a kind of temporary home was, for these participants, a source of aggravation; 'In no way, shape or form can this place ever feel homely' (Bernie). Creating a domestic space, these participants felt, might threaten their outside identities or signal an admission of defeat:

> The walls in my cell are empty, it's not my home. It's just a passing through place for me. It can never be my home. The place I grew up in does not look like this awful place. It's just a room with a TV. (Wendy)

These prisoners did not want to feel like they had been co-opted into or institutionalised by the prison regime. On an emotional level, such responses were attempts to deal with deep existential fears, especially in relation to deterioration, stagnation and the loss of a sense of self in prison. These prisoners were unsettled further by a range of external sensory intrusions into their cells. It was impossible, they claimed, to escape the relentless screaming and shouting of loud prisoners. Bright security lighting pierced through curtains and under the doorways, meaning that 'you never have complete darkness' (Danielle). The possibility of achieving relaxation was sometimes thwarted in a more intrusive and direct manner. For example, experiencing a 'pad spin' (an unannounced cell search by officers for contraband) was an unsettling experience in itself, but it also left prisoners feeling apprehensive about the next time they might be inspected. Stacey had been through many such searches and spoke of her subsequent anxiety:

> They can't keep doing this to me. It was 11:45 at night and they burst into my room. I had to take my clothes off and get out of my room while they searched. I shouldn't have to keep doing that. Every time I hear their keys I feel like I can't relax. (Stacey)

Similarly, having to share a cell with another prisoner was described as a significant source of discomfort by male prisoners. The idiosyncratic behaviours and routines of others, concentrated in a small living space, could make it hard to relax: snoring, loud music, hygiene, and late night television viewing were some of the most frequent complaints. Having to use poorly screened toilets was seen as a particularly unwelcome degradation: 'You're in a double and your toilet is in the middle of the room, there's no curtain, you've got to take a shit while your pad mate is eating his tea. This is 2016' (Kyle). The primary emotion conveyed here by prisoners was disgust. This is reminiscent of Sibley and Van Hoven's (2009: 202) description of prisoners' powerful anxieties about 'contagion, contamination or pollution...[and that] imagining certain kinds of mixing, of bodily fluids... engenders disgust'. While some prisoners found ways to negotiate these anxieties over time and forged bonds with their cellmates that served to quell feelings of isolation, few preferred this arrangement to single cell living. It was further claimed that long-term prisoners suffered the most emotionally from sharing arrangements, especially if they were paired with prisoners on a short sentence. The regular upheavals of adjusting to new partners made it difficult to establish a fixed routine. But on a deeper level, long termers often expressed the sentiment that they had a different kind of prisoner experience—one more existentially intense and introspective than short-termers—and therefore it was unfair to combine them.

Taken together, the accounts introduced above present a general picture of prisoners in the midst of a 'profound experience of humiliation and humility' common to liminal experiences of transformation (Turner,

1974: 260). It is noteworthy that a large proportion of these prisoners either had little prior experience of being imprisoned in a cell, or were in the early stages of serving long tariffs. This is redolent of Crewe et al.'s (2017) assessment of long term prisoners: 'the early phase of the sentence was characterised by bewilderment, anger, denial, and a form of "temporal vertigo" resulting from consideration of the sheer amount of time in prison that lay ahead' (8). However, there were exceptions to this narrative. At least two prisoners in this research had had substantial prior experience of imprisonment and had served out the majority of their sentences. As a possible explanation for this variance, Jewkes (2005a) argues that in some cases individuals 'experience a permanent liminality in that they are not moving between established boundaries' (375) as in cases of terminal illness. While most prisoners in this study moved through this turbulent stage, it is significant that many of those who commit suicide in prison are overwhelmed by these initial entry shocks: 'prison suicides occur disproportionately at the earliest stages of custody' (Liebling, 2007: 426). The six self-inflicted deaths in Ranby that took place in two years prior to this research are a visceral reminder that the experiences of prisoners who commit suicide are excluded from research accounts on prison adaptation (Liebling & Maruna, 2013).

The Cell as Sanctuary

> I know that when my door is locked no one can get in and I can't get out; I feel safe in my own little bed. That's my safe haven. (Pia)

As Jewkes (2005a: 382) argues, 'liminal spaces are characterised by disorder and chaos…[but] if one can create a path through them, they can affect positive change'. After a period of emotional volatility, most prisoners were able to make peace with cellular confinement. Indeed, some began to highly value and look forward to time spent in their cell. A number of participants affirmed this, describing their cells in almost reverential terms: the space was 'like a sanctuary' (Billy) that instilled feelings of 'serenity' (Dean). A crucial step for these prisoners was the addition of personal touches through decoration and furnishings:

116   B. Laws

You're put in a cell with nothing. Nothing on the walls, there's no emotion and no life. Everywhere is dead. I thought I can't do 18 months like this. And then I started walking around and seeing other people's pads and seeing their pictures on the walls. If you see my cell now, I've got nice carpet down, cupboards how I want them, pictures all over the walls, I've got a DVD player and everything I want. It's like living in a temporary hotel room. So when my door is shut it's my chill out zone, I can relax. (Alan)

For Alan, a sparse cell was equated to an emotional void, whereas personal goods and visual aesthetics created a space where it was possible to *feel* tranquil. Importantly here, prisoners who exerted control over decoration and spatial layouts explicitly spoke to the effects this had on their feelings—put simply, they were shaping the physical environment to meet their emotional needs. For example, Blanche explained that displaying religious iconography was a way to design in optimism: 'I've got loads of pictures on my boards, the one in front of me is all my religious stuff, so when I wake up, the first thing I see is positivity'. The emphasis on the use of objects to evoke feelings symbolises a kind of 'prosthetic of the self' (Gonzalez, 1995), wherein material possessions represent an important extension of prisoners' personalities and the kind of emotions they wanted to feel. In a similar vein, colour was adapted to augment particular feelings:

I have my own bedding rather than the prison issue bedding. I made my room bright yellow. I put yellow curtains in, yellow in the bedding, yellow everything. The normal furniture they give you is dark blue curtains, green bedding. Everything was just sort of dull and grey and black. I think it makes the room very depressing…so I try and make it the brightest colour possible to try and make me feel not so dull. Even when it's night-time outside it still feels bright in there. I don't want to feel dark and depressed. (Amber)

By asserting a personal colour scheme, prisoners distinguished themselves from what they perceived as the uniform, drab, and alienating design choices of the prison environment. As Rebecka summarised, 'if I was to describe this prison as a colour I would say it's grey', and greyness was symbolic of lifelessness and deterioration. Indeed, the uniform pastel green tones that lined many of the corridors and the flaked paint in cell interiors were reminiscent of medical facilities and hardly communicated vitality. By customising their cell colours, prisoners created a contrast between the cold edges of the wider prison world and their 'warm and welcoming' living spaces (Chantal). Taken together these accounts reflect the ways in which prisoners appeared to 'make space from themselves' by building 'mental walls' and finding 'comfort in the construction of a purified space' (Sibley & Van Hoven, 2009: 201–202).

Cell decoration also signified the importance of ownership of space and its impact on identity. Jewkes (2002: 93) notes that individualising the cell is 'one of the few ways in which prisoners can publicly display their identities'. It was common to hear prisoners speak with pride as they asserted tenure over these spaces: 'The cell is *my* serenity, I have my *own* prison' (Amber, emphasis added); 'It is my space' (Nia); 'You make it your space' (Rebecka). Some prisoners went further, describing cells as a 'mini-home' (Jerry) or 'my little home' (Yvonne). Because the cell was personalised and comfortable, prisoners felt they could drop their defensive postures and behave more authentically: 'I can be myself when I'm in there' (Alan), or as Chantal put it: 'I feel free in my cell'. Looking at pictures of family members allowed prisoners to realign themselves with their identities as daughters, sons, sisters, brothers, parental figures and friends. These images also provided a reminder that one was loved and cared for by others. In line with these accounts, Sloan (2012) argues that by manipulating and taking ownership over space, prisoners 'move away from the prisoner identity that is inscribed upon [them]', and 'differentiate themselves from those who they perceive as negative' (408).

This reassertion of identity coincided with a renewed ability to experience authentic feelings. Cells provided a sealed 'container' for discharging emotions: 'It can be a sad place but I'm glad I'm in there; even though I feel sadness, I can still be relaxed and comfortable' (Billy). Even though the emotions that surfaced were often challenging, prisoners had a predictable amount of time to process them before re-entering more public areas. In this sense, time in one's cell provided an important emotional shelter for balancing moods and replenishing energy. Entering this space in the evening was also associated with the forward progression of time for some prisoners: 'It's the end of the day, another one ticked off, time is ticking away' (Jerry). It was ironic that during the most physically constrained, socially isolated periods of imprisonment, these participants did not suffer or experience temporal stasis, but rather felt a degree of psychological and emotional freedom to be most like themselves.

Some advantages of the cell space were distinguished by their absolute contrast with the wider prison environment. Because association areas and house blocks were often loud, unpredictable, and populous places, 'to finally be locked away' was often experienced as 'a relief' (Alan, both quotations). Indeed, some prisoners embraced the opportunity to segregate themselves from 'unpredictable situations' (Billy). Even if prisoners were not directly involved in confrontations, the threat of violent encounters was ongoing and could provoke anxiety. By distinction then, locked cells offered a modicum of quiet, order and solitude: 'it's silent and I love it, I love it when my door is locked' (Francesca). Because of these features, cells were often surmised as 'safe places' (Danielle) or semi-private cocoons 'away from people' (Katherine) where one did not have to 'be on edge' (Nia).

In sum, by customising their cell spaces with colour schemes, 'personal possessions and [other] signifiers of the self' (Sloan, 2012: 406), prisoners attempted to evoke particular feeling states and design in a level of comfort. Because cells were distinct from many oppressive features of prison life, they elicited a different set of feelings and a wider degree of emotional expression than other institutional spaces. These prisoners were able to process difficult emotions free from the gaze of their peers and were not subjected to the negative influence of others.

Taken together, these accounts suggest that the majority of prisoners developed strong positive attachments to their cells over time. But typically, prisoners first had to pass through a disorientating and chaotic period of liminality, where they experienced little ontological security and were trapped in cycles of negative emotions. As Jewkes (2005a) surmises, during the early stages of liminality 'the self may be temporarily suspended but may reassert itself at a later point as the initial feelings of fear and loss subside' (375). When prisoners transitioned through this process the reassertion of identity was apparent through the renewed sense of ownership that prisoners felt over their cells and increased levels of comfort with their emotions. What began as a space of disruption and isolation could become one of the few places where prisoners could exert control over the environment and their emotions.

Wings and House Blocks

> It's just the same old thing, just frustration. Just confined to this place; the same old people did the same thing. No one has overachieved today. You're not going to hear anything fantastic are you? As in when you go to work every day this colleague has done this and that, all this has happened at work. There's always something new and exciting when you're at home, but in prison it's not. You know that that person has just laid in the cell for 12 hours, because I've done the same thing; it's just a depressing place. (Freddy)

Almost unanimously, prisoners held negative feelings towards their shared living quarters, although a minority of participants living on smaller wings offered alternative perspectives. Life on the wings and house blocks was typically portrayed as vacillating between the mundane and the manic. The physical environment was most often described as uncomfortable, mainly due to a range of sensory incursions. For example, a common complaint was that the ongoing level of noise made it difficult to relax. These auditory disruptions came from a number of sources. The daily patterns of officers locking and unlocking doors and gates produced a jarring metallic percussion that reverberated around the wings and landings: 'I'll never get used to the slamming gates, metal on metal, chains and keys' (Freddy). For Tamara, these sounds were unwelcome reminders of her reality: 'when you hear the keys, it's like "shit I'm still in jail"'. Other prisoners could be equally disruptive: 'You can never switch off, you'll try to, then you've got someone smashing up or someone shouting all night "do you want burn [tobacco]?"' (Kyle). Similar accounts were related from the women's prison: 'You're in your cell and there's people screaming from their windows at night…you're trying to wind down, it's like "please stop it"' (Katherine). Lacey explained that the noise from the landings was often so intense that it was impossible to 'hear the telly, even if we turn it up to the max'. At the affective level, the force and prominence of sensory intrusions raised feelings of anxiety and anger among participants who were powerless to change these environmental features.

For Bernie, the problem was not so much the volume but rather the repetitiveness of hearing 'the same old sounds over and over again. There's never a new sound. There's just never a new sound'. This created a stark sense of monotony because prisoners were around: 'the same people, the same things, and hearing the same doors locking and keys rattling' (Rebecka). The lack of variation in the soundscape gave the wings a dispirited and jaded feel. Importantly however, Danielle explained that because noise was the status quo, silence was interpreted as an eerie and alarming disruption to the rhythm: 'When it's silent, you think 'what's going on?'. And you think, 'something is boiling, it's going to kick off''. Most prisoners felt caught in a bind, disliking the excessive noise on the one hand, but contributing to it on the other, because ultimately 'if you don't shout, you don't get heard' (Val).

The smells and scents of the living spaces provoked especially strong reactions among female prisoners. It was typical to hear expressions of disgust about 'women with hygiene problems' (Janice) who 'don't wash and their room smells' (Rebecka). It was claimed the prisoners with medical incontinence created a build-up of smells on the wings because their disposable pads were only emptied once a week. The visual stimuli in these living spaces further contributed to a sense of unease. Prisoners complained that the aesthetics of the wings and house blocks were visually oppressive: 'I loathe the building itself. You get sick of seeing it. It looks like a dungeon…you want to take every brick down, one by one' (Bernie). Bernie was describing the spurs on house block five in Ranby, which, because of the absence of natural light, had a subterranean feel. O'Donnell (2014: 96) explains that prisoners are 'involuntarily confined in ugly surroundings, unaffected by the passage of the seasons or the wonder of the natural world…The corridors and cells upon which the prisoner's gaze rests seldom inspire; drabness is integral to the design'. However, more important than the physical construction of these spaces was the sense that they were uncared for. Often these concerns centred on the presence of dirt and lack of maintenance:

5 Space and Emotions 121

It's like a shack, the building is awful, it's falling apart. It's probably the most grimy wing in any prison I've been on. It's all coming away from the walls, there's subsidence, there's a lot of damp. (Ellie)

Look at where we're at right now, what a load of shit it is. This is a shit hole, it's all crap. I mean look at that window, there's bird shit all over it. It's a horrible place. (Bernie)

If you were to come back home and your house was like this wing, it would make you depressed. If you walk into a clean house you're happy, you can just get on with it day-to-day... It's horrible on here, it's horrible. (Val)

The environment was producing feelings of disgust and shaping the mood of prisoners who did not appreciate the enforced proximity to dirt and physical decay. On a more symbolic level, however, these prisoners were hinting that the lack of care for the physical environment was a kind of commentary on their lack of status as a marginalised group—that they were unworthy of cleanliness. During a period of observation on a house block in Ranby, one prisoner was irate about the presence of flaked paint on the walls of the wing he had been moved on to. He explained that the decrepit walls made him feel worthless and subhuman. While Jewkes (2012) states that the physical design of a prison 'has a profound and moral influence on prisoners' levels of environmental cleanliness may have a similar impact.

The size, layout, and 'feel' of the house blocks and wings were also significant variables. The expansive rectangular house blocks (one, two and three) in Ranby were widely criticised as being too big for prisoners to live comfortably alongside one another. Indeed, the layout of these large accommodation blocks (which held around 240 prisoners each) resembled factories or warehouses. The open floor plan, presence of natural light and utilisation of modern materials in these areas was a complete contrast to the dark and constrictive feel of the older buildings. However, the trade-off to these design features was a kind of assault on the soul (Price, 2012)—in short, these house blocks could feel homogenous, lonely and anonymous.[3] For example, prisoners claimed that these spaces lacked any sense of social cohesion: 'On these massive big wings, there's no community' (Paul). By way of contrast, house blocks six and seven were significantly smaller units (holding around 60 prisoners) and had a very different atmosphere: they were noticeably quieter and the flow of foot traffic was less frenetic. Phil felt his house block was 'brilliant because it's small, there about 40 lads who all run the wing. People don't fight or do anything wrong because the ethos is really good. The wing is manageable.' These wings also had design features that prisoners argued had positive impacts on social interactions and indicated a kind of emotional tone that was 'softer':

> There's a dining hall, you're not going back to your pad eating food off your lap. You interact with other people at the table, you're socializing, having a crack with the lads. It's as simple a thing as eating at the table. (Kyle)

Space was more compartmentalised on these wings, with several rooms having dedicated functions (games rooms, dining rooms, screened-off phone booths, and corridors) instead of large, relatively undifferentiated areas. The small resettlement wings in Send had a similar kind of spatial versatility, and prisoners who were seen putting up decorations together in the break rooms clearly valued these areas. These environmental factors contributed to the domestic and relatively collaborative atmosphere on these wings, and shaped emotional possibilities for engagement and care.[4] This offers an alternative perspective to the deliberate 'designing-in' of disenchantment that so often characterises prison architecture in England and Wales (Jewkes, 2012): that is, prison space can be designed to encourage communion and social integration.

In sum, the various sensory intrusions (especially levels of noise and visual squalor) and the physical layouts (either too cramped or too large and homogenous) of the wings and house blocks were important

---

[3] There were other chaotic aspects to these spaces, unrelated to size, that are further elaborated below.
[4] However, it is important to note that spatial factors were only a part of the explanation. The characteristics of the prisoners living in these spaces (who were typically holding 'enhanced' IEP status) acted as a filtering mechanism, shaping the atmosphere on these wings: 'If there are lads that come on who don't behave themselves, they stand out straightaway' (Phil).

variables that left the majority of prisoners feeling uncomfortable or disaffected in these zones. As O'Donnell (2014: 112) highlights: 'the ordering of space influences the geometry of relations between people'. This section has attempted to describe the particular emotional outcomes of alternative forms of spatial organisation. At the affective level, then, these spaces most typically produced powerful feelings of anger, anxiety and disgust among prisoners who felt unable to exert control over the wider features of their environment or felt rejected by it. For other participants, these were affectively 'dead' zones that alienated prisoners through their blend of tedium and repetition. Haley's statement summarises a customary sentiment about these living spaces: 'To tell you the truth, the wing doesn't really mean anything to me'.

Hostile Spaces: Boiling Over

> It's like it's in the air. And people do take it on. You can feel in the dining hall, if there's stuff going on in the prison, the tension is in there, and everybody is kind of a little bit on edge, it's really strange. You can feel it brewing. (Ellie)

> It's intense on the wing, it can be really intense. There's riot bells going off every day, there's fights every day, there's screaming matches every day, there's people on the floor having fits every day, there's ambulances coming in all the time, there's suicides happening, there's self-harm happening, there's nurses on the wing. (Billy)

Beyond the stressors of the living quarters described above, there were zones in both prisons that had a more 'volatile' quality. In these areas, there was a social 'simmering' that tended or threatened to break out into open violence. These were the places where 'it's most likely to kick off' (Freddy) and prisoners 'fight all the time' (Gabriella). The most hostile areas shared a number of key attributes that contributed to the high levels of tension.[5] The following section briefly introduces the layout and social

---

[5] This use of the term 'hostile space' here is not to be confused with the defensive design trend called 'hostile architecture', which involves the 'design of buildings or public spaces in a way which dis-

fabric of three different areas in Send and Ranby, and then analyses them in unison.

The first area, the dining room in Send, was used by all of the women in the prison, apart from those in the therapeutic community (J-Wing), who had their own dedicated servery. It was a large box shaped building, with around 30 large circular tables for dining; prisoners used the dining room twice a day for lunch and evening meals. The second area of interest, house blocks one and two in Ranby, were sprawling modern upgrades of classic Victorian prison layouts, with two long wings that extended outwards in an 'L' shape from a central observation hub. These spaces housed around 260 prisoners each. House block one was being used primarily as an induction wing, with some residents living there for safety reasons. House block two was split between general population prisoners and those being treated for drug addiction. The third area considered here was the 'line route' in Ranby. This space was not characterised by the same obvious physical demarcations as the first two areas, but included various walkways and corridors that prisoners traversed between different areas of the prison—mainly from accommodation buildings to educational spaces, workshops, and gymnasiums. Because prisoner movement in Ranby had recently been delimited to a small number of windows in the regime day, line routes were highly populous events, and the main trails extremely congested during these times. The focus on the line route highlights the significance of exploring emotional expression and regulation in moments of transition to and from different prison spaces (Crewe et al., 2014).

These three prison zones elicited adverse emotional reactions in most participants, and they relayed different degrees of 'terror, fear, apprehension, sadness, rage, anger, annoyance, loathing, and all the other bad words' (Francesca). Upon entering these areas, prisoners immediately felt 'more on edge' (Oscar), describing a palpable 'tension in the air that you can feel', mainly because prisoners sensed that these were ripe 'climates for violence and disruption' (Simon, both quotations). The specific nomenclature used to describe these areas was revealing, often capturing

---

courages people from touching, climbing or sitting on them, with the intention of avoiding damage or use for a different purpose'.

5 Space and Emotions 125

the chaotic, desperate nature of these zones—for example, house blocks one and two were referenced as being 'like Beirut', 'the dark side', or the 'black holes' of the prison. However, such labels arguably masked as much as they revealed. It is important therefore to burrow beneath such visceral descriptions to understand the dynamics that engendered these strong reactions.

The first salient factor was that these spaces had unpredictable or unknown qualities. For example, on line route, prisoners did not know who they might be pushed into proximity with. This could be particularly stressful for those who owed debts or were involved in ongoing feuds: 'If you're in a beef with people, line route can be hell' (Tommas). Further, because this was one of the few opportunities for prisoners from different wings to interact and trade goods, there was pressure to make deals quickly, which added a level of affective intensity and desperation to these interactions. This sense of 'limited opportunity' for trade was also observed in the dining room in Send, being 'the only place people can meet up and do it' (Ellie). More specifically, it was perceived by prisoners in Ranby that trade in NPS had escalated violence on the line route. Because there were 'so many people desperate to get hold of it' (Oscar) dealers encouraged addicts to assault prisoners and settle their scores in exchange for NPS. More generally, prisoners who walked the line route knew they were particularly vulnerable at these times: 'You have to watch your back…somebody can just run and do you' (Andrew). The sprawling nature of the route made it difficult for prisoners to monitor all the different angles and directions from which they could be attacked. Similar perceptions of danger and unpredictability were operating in the women's dining room:

> The whole process in the dining hall is not controlled in any shape or form. There is actually no consistency with it, and then there are people that I'm unfamiliar with and they are looking. A lot of the time people sit down and people are coming and you swivel your head around. I feel really uncomfortable. (Katherine)

The feeling of disorder in the dining room was in part a by-product of fluctuating seating times. That is, in an attempt to ensure that particular

126   B. Laws

wings were not always the first or last to be served their meals, the regime alternated the seating order on a daily basis. However, Nia explained: 'It can be quite daunting...you don't know who you're going to run into, and you don't know if you're gonna have a problem'. These were chaotic places that lacked a clearly defined structure. Sparks et al. (1996: 75) explain that, while a rigid routine can be a source of 'deadening tedium', it can also be extremely 'reassuring and consoling', creating a reality that is 'sufficiently predictable and solid for us to be able to act capably within it'. In the absence of such mental security, the individual 'risks being swamped by anxiety' (75). In line with this argument, the Ranby house blocks lacked structure, and disorder flourished:

> Bruv, oh my goodness, I've been in grizzly jails, but there's still a level of decorum. I got to house block one and there's no decorum, there's just zombies, tramps and freaks...I'm big and I've got influence, but on that wing someone will rob your stuff straight away. I've seen someone get stabbed for a quarter of burn. (Liam)

An important element of unpredictability resided in the regular turnover of new intakes on the house block. Prisoners knew neither figuratively nor literally who or what was coming next. There were few set expectations that prisoners could establish to help navigate through these spaces, and they therefore had to be constantly on guard.

The unknown qualities outlined above were exacerbated by crowding, which amplified the chaotic, intense feel of these spaces. Gambetta's (2009) attempt to explain the reasons why prisoners enter physical conflicts is highly relevant here:

> The probability of entering into fights will be directly related to the number of prisoners any one prisoner will deal with while knowing nothing about their traits...where for instance, there is a high turnover of inmates or where prisoners are frequently reallocated to wing and cells thus frequently meet prisoners about whom they know nothing, the hierarchy will be more unstable and will have to be re-established at each new encounter. (83)

In a similar manner, the line route entailed a mass exodus of unknown entities and bodies circulating around the establishment—a significant proportion of the prisoner population were crossing paths simultaneously. These were places with extremely dense concentrations of prisoners ('There's just too many people'—Katherine; 'It's all the people in one space'—Olivia), which increased feelings of pressure and tension because there was less room to establish personal boundaries and less time to react. The large numbers also created difficulties for management: officers in the dining room were under pressure to make sure everyone got a chance to eat lunch in a timely manner, but a number of prisoners felt that their eating was being rushed by staff. Being hurried along contributed to feelings of tension and unease. Further, the dense concentration of prisoners formed a kind of human shield, concealing the outbreak of physical altercations: 'In the dining hall it takes a while for you to realise a fight is happening because it's so chaotic. You have so many wings down there at the same time…it's a real mix' (Molly). Andrew described a comparable situation on the line route:

> I was walking down there and out of nowhere four guys started fighting, it took officers about five minutes before they realised what was going on. As you've probably seen, when everyone is walking together it just looks like a big frenzy, you can't see much, it's crazy. (Andrew)

The concentration of prisoners in these spaces created deep insecurities of being constantly watched: 'There's too many eyes on you. It's that whole spotlight thing I don't like' (Katherine). Kyle explained that the atmosphere on the house block was marked by 'people staring at you'. This visual monitoring created anxiety ('It gets you a bit panicky. Even when you sit down you get a bit paranoid thinking who's watching me, who's watching me?'—Yvonne) and functioned as a trigger for altercations, as prisoners tried not to lose face in front of their peers.

The final important factor here was the perceived absence of officer supervision in these areas. Some prisoners felt there was either a deficit of institutional control ('there're no officers about'—Tommas; 'It is the one place where there's no cameras'—Molly) or that the institution simply turned a blind eye in these zones ('they accept it as a necessary evil'—Simon). What seemed more verifiable was that the physically expansive nature of these spaces created blind spots where it was harder for officers to always 'be in the right place to see what's going on' (Andrew). Poor visibility and the lack of natural sightlines engendered deep fears about personal safety:

> It's such a big wing yeah, most of the time the officers are in the office doing something else. I might be on the threes [the third floor of the wing] in the shower, so someone could just come in there and start attacking me. I found a huge knife in there. (Andrew)

All of the factors described above coalesced to create spaces that were buzzing 'hives of activity' (Billy) and at times felt 'lawless'. The imposing environmental stimuli and sensory intensity of these areas made them akin to highly-pressurised containers. That is to say, there was a striking affective force in these zones that was substantially different to the ambient areas around them, and even the smallest disruptive or destabilising events could result in an explosive discharge of anger. Prisoners either absorbed the pressure and emotional strain of these areas or found ways to minimise exposure or avoid them altogether: 'I don't go down to the dining room, I am terrified' (Wendy).

The following section explores the other end of the spectrum of prison space—the places where prisoners felt the most comfortable. These areas also shared and number features, but the form, location and intensity of these zones were a complete contrast to the volatile areas described above.

Free Spaces

In his respected book, *Asylums*, Goffman (1961: 205) describes:

> ...the emergence of bounded physical spaces in which ordinary levels of surveillance and restriction were markedly reduced, spaces where the inmate could openly engage in a range of tabooed activities with some degree of security. These places often also provided a marked reduction in usual patient population density, contributing to the peace and quiet char-

acteristic of them…The staff did not know of the existence of these places, or knew but either stayed away or tacitly relinquished their authority when entering them. Licence, in short, had a geography. I shall call these regions *free places*.

Across various academic literatures, such spaces are alternatively termed 'havens', 'niches', 'spatial preserves', and 'cultural laboratories' (See Polletta, 1999; Toch, 1992).There were a number of areas in Ranby and Send that functioned as 'free spaces', but in a broader, less closed-off, less illicit, sense than in Goffman's account. In these zones, institutional control was lighter, and there were more relaxed rules about the expression of specific emotions that might have been stifled in other parts of the prison. It was in these places that prisoners were likely to show their most authentic selves. This section is ordered thematically to further understand the common features of free spaces, and is theoretically informed by Turner's (1974) concept of 'communitas'. Communitas, Turner argues, is an unstructured community which is 'undifferentiated, equalitarian' (274) and marked by a spirit of liberty and freedom.

First, all of the free spaces were described explicitly as being distinct from the general prison atmosphere—as separate islands away from the main prison. For example, those with jobs explained: 'It's not prison, it's work' (Neil); 'It's more of a workplace environment' (Haley). The fact that it was 'cleaner on the workshops' (Val) seemed to mark an important contrast from living spaces that were often disordered and unclean. Alongside cleanliness, these areas often had softer design features and less visible emphasis on security. For example, in the hair salon in Send, barred windows were painted in lighter tones. Further, the liberal use of posters and artwork on the walls, the loud radio and bustling conversations of the clientele, made it easy to forget that it was a prison salon. In a related manner, the loud music in Ranby gym contributed to a vibrant atmosphere that was different to other prison zones and allowed prisoners to immerse themselves in exercise. This factor was reminiscent of Moran et al. (2013: 144) where 'the insulating noise [in one of the workshops] represent[ed] an escape of sorts from the challenges of communal living'.

Importantly, different 'temporal rules' appeared to be operating in these zones. In the gym, time seemed to accelerate, both in the grand

130   B. Laws

scheme of prisoners' sentences ('the gym course is the best thing that has happened to me, time has just flown' Jerry) and during daily workouts. An atmosphere of complete focus was intensified by the short windows of training time prisoners were allotted (45 minute sessions), and which they were keen to maximise. Prisoners who moved seamlessly between exercise machines and free weights, and who carefully negotiating their routines with their peers, appeared to be in the 'flow' states described by Csikszentmihalyi's (1991: 71), where: 'Concentration is so intense that there is no attention left to think about anything irrelevant, or to worry about problems. Self-consciousness disappears, and the sense of time becomes distorted'. Notably, Turner (1974: 238) explains that communitas is almost always 'portrayed by actors as a timeless condition, an eternal now, as a moment in and out of time'.

Meanwhile, non-uniformed staff members contributed to an important sense of community cohesion in these areas. They helped to 'keep the spirit up' (Yvonne) and made these areas feel nourishing. Participants expressed gratitude for the humanity of these staff members: 'The teachers don't treat you as if you're being punished…education is probably the only place in prison where you get as much respect as you might deserve' (Craig). In contrast to the wider environment, these were incentivising zones where prisoners were more likely to be encouraged than reprimanded: 'Mark and Jasmine [the course instructors] are all about giving you positives and the plus side of things—I have never seen anyone like that in jail' (Mikey). At the affective level, support staff assisted prisoners with difficult emotional states too: 'when I have a bad day they help me come down…Sometimes I get agitated and they let me take a walk. They're understanding' (Wayne). Prisoners felt that these staff members were non-judgemental, treating them like 'human totals' and 'integral beings who recognizantly share the same humanity' (Turner, 1974: 269).

Turner (1974) further argues that a defining aspect of communitas is a 'liberated spirit' which is 'universal and boundless'. In line with this sentiment, equality and inclusivity were key features of these free spaces. Indeed, the chaplaincy in Send was an exemplar of both equity ('everyone's got common ground, they're learning and going through faith together'—Rebecka) and inclusion: 'They never turn people away, they always make us feel welcome'(Chantal). This atmosphere of inclusivity in

5 Space and Emotions 131

these free spaces was infectious, and prisoners spoke about their complete surprise at befriending those with violent histories or sex offences: 'On paper you'd think this is going to be trouble, but then you meet him and he's laughing and joking all the time' (Jerry). The openness to receiving instruction and encouragement from others in these areas ('I've met a friend, he's always pushing me in the gym' [Phil]), and the clear displays of affection (for example, frequent physical touching and comparisons of muscles in the gym) were all signifiers of closeness and connectivity.

Furthermore, the nature of particular forms of work and activities constellated prisoners with shared interests: 'I'm with like-minded people, and I feel we are all equals' (Katherine). In these areas, then, prisoners felt able to glide into different identities (as a 'worker', 'artist', 'athlete' or 'student'), casting off the 'masks' of bravado that they typically wore on the wings. In further contrast to the wings and house blocks, Nia articulated feelings of safety and collaboration in the hair salon:

> I just happened to be on the course with a really good bunch of girls so I felt safe. I felt that I could like, if I needed help from any of the other student I could get it. They are all very encouraging to each other. They don't put each other down, it's like you're being nurtured and that was a nice experience. (Nia)

For all of the reasons set out above, then, free spaces instilled a sense of emotional tranquillity in prisoners. The soothing nature of the chaplaincy provided an opportunity to 'relax and gain knowledge in a calm space' (Haley). This climate enabled emotions to be channelled in a safe container. The gym was praised for its emotion transforming and 'stress relieving' (Phil S) qualities: 'I go to the gym when I'm angry or upset…It tires me out, which I love' (Rebecka). Intense exercise was a way of cultivating physical and psychological comfort, emotional stability and general feelings of peace. Moreover, while the most disliked places in prison were experienced as mentally constrictive, the gym had the reverse effect: 'It *gives me space* in my head' (Wayne, emphasis added). Free spaces were zones of emotional nourishment and prisoners felt replenished after spending time in them.

Finally, participants were emotionally open in these areas ('it's somewhere where I can just cry and I don't care who is there'—Ula). Prisoners developed 'a certain amount of trust' in these settings because they felt able to 'talk about anything that might be troubling' them (Craig, both quotations). Further, there was a freedom to 'ask anything' (Blanche), which stoked participants' curiosity, creativity and expression: 'people are writing their own stuff [songs and poems], and I'm thinking, how did you get all that out?' (Wayne). Prisoners were also able to express a broader repertoire of emotions. These were areas that evoked 'a lot of love, joy and peace' (Chantal), emotions that were rarely described in such unqualified ways in prison: 'It gives you joy and that kind of…what is the word? Serenity! It's uplifting and every time you walk in to the chapel, even when you're walking towards it, I can feel my body' (Rebecka). In a similar manner, Francesca explained: 'I feel joy because I like working there, I love my job. I feel interested. I feel optimism because I'm always looking to try and help people'. Some prisoners described intense blissful states: 'I've had some deep feelings in the chapel…but it has come out as tearful because I'm overwhelmed by whatever it is that's gone on…you just feel that presence within you' (Janice). These passionate testimonies serve to highlight a range of emotional experiences that are infrequently documented and contrast sharply with other areas of the prison. That is, if chaos and unpredictably were the norm, these areas provided a stabilising and replenishing oasis for prisoners.

Visits Halls

The visits halls in both prisons were also exceptional spaces of emotionality in that, because of their function, they generated intense happiness and excitement but also great sadness, anxiety and guilt. The focus here, then, is exploring the intensity and fluctuation of emotions on display during visits. These vacillations are touched on by Crewe et al. (2014):

> The emotional landscape of the visits room was palpably different from most other areas of the prison. Here, men held their children and touched their partners with tenderness, longingly embraced family members and

friends, and openly displayed joy and affection, as though their emotional identities had been resuscitated en route from the wings. Some were visibly upset as their visitors left, or sat in silent contemplation, their stolidity contrasting with the animated tone of a few minutes earlier. (67)

Indeed, a number of prisoners felt joy during visits ('The only time I feel in here is on visits. It feels like the prisoners are coming back to life'— Rebecka), followed by 'a big comedown' (Olivia) when visitors left. In these joyful moments prisoners were able to temporarily immerse themselves in nostalgia for the outside world: 'You feel good about yourself and you remember your days out there' (Wayne). These accounts are strongly redolent of Moran (2014) who argues that these spaces are also 'liminal' in the sense of fusing the inside with the outside world. That is, 'prisoners come face-to-face with living embodiments of their previous life outside the prison' and can 'suspend the immediate reality of incarceration', enjoying a 'taste of home' (347). Tamara was so immersed in the experience of 'suspension' that she accidently tried to leave with her family: 'my head was still on the outside' (Tamara). The realisation that 'you've got to go back to your world in prison' (Tamara) was a crash landing for many participants. Seeing one's children leave was particularly excruciating for parents: 'It's horrible, it's horrible, it kills me inside, all you want to do is go home with them' (Oscar). For many prisoners, then, the dynamic of visitation involved experiencing an initial 'high' followed by a depressive 'come-down'.

However, some participants had quite different experiences of visits. Those in romantic relationships felt deep insecurities about whether their partners would still love them, for example. In a few extreme cases, prisoners suffered from panic attacks before or during their visits, where excitement and anticipation fused with more intense feelings:

All of sudden I just felt ill, I felt sick and everything. All the pressure of seeing them and realising that I'm in here for my stupid actions. And for me the guilt of realising what I put my family through because my crime was big in the newspapers and media. Things happened to my family after I got sentenced, so I think I've got a lot of guilt and I feel bad about it, so that contributed to the anxiety. (Karl)

For Zak, attempting to present a strong façade in the face of ongoing health problems was overwhelming:

> I couldn't move properly and I managed to sit down and my back started to spasm. I said "Love, I can't sit on a visit like this". I burst into tears because she travelled all the way from Manchester. I said "please don't think it's you but I can't let you see me like this. I'm an emotional wreck right now, I can't do it".

The visits hall was an emotionally raw zone that could intensify feelings in every direction. But it was also a zone of contradiction: for example, emotional closeness operated alongside the enforcement of distance. This is to say, some elements of the interaction were experienced as artificial by prisoners, evoking bittersweet reactions. Loved ones were physically present, suggesting the possibility of intimacy, but as Francesca explained, 'It's not like a normal environment, like you'd sit at home and watch telly. On visits it's like two hours, you're here and there and you struggle to think of things to talk about'. In line with this, Karl explained the pressure to show positivity:

> You've got to sit there for two hours on a visit, and you feel like you've got to have a good time. You don't want your family travelling two or three hours for you to sit there moaning about things, so you got to force yourself to have a good time. (Karl)

These interactions were abstracted, lacking the organic feel that defined them outside prison. This tension between closeness and distance was exacerbated by the limits placed on gestures of affection: 'You can't be as tactile as you want to be or show your true emotions' (Olivia). Prisoners were not denied physical contact entirely—hugging and kissing was tolerated when visitors arrived and left—but beyond this there were strict limits: 'You don't have any time to be intimate' (Janice). During the visit itself, the physical environment reinforced the social distance between prisoners and visitors, as if intimacy had been purposely designed out of the arrangements:

The tables annoy me; if you have one person visiting you, you have chairs on the other side of the table. If you both sit back in your chair, you can't even reach one another…there's a big distance between you, you're trying to shout to that person to hear them talk. All I want to do sometimes just hug my mum or hold my mum's hand or lay my head on her lap, and yet I can't even touch the tip of her finger. (Molly)

Because of these tensions, some prisoners felt 'fucking relieved' (Katherine) to leave the visits hall. Taking all these accounts together, the visits hall concentrated some very powerful emotions in prisoners. The presence of romantic partners, children and parents and the extreme vacillations of feeling states differentiated this space from all others zones of the prison.

The various free spaces introduced here had qualities that contrasted sharply with other, less favoured areas of the prison. For example, whereas shared living spaces were often frenetic, dirty, loud, destructive, poorly supervised, and hostile, these spaces had the inverse qualities. That is, they were often cleaner, quieter, more ordered, nurturing, creative, and safer spaces for prisoners. In terms of emotional outcomes, there are strong resonances here with Crewe et al. (2014), in that these zones made it:

> …possible for prisoners to forge a space that was comparatively free from the oppressive oversight of their peers on one side and the institution on the other. Within limits, and only temporarily, spaces emerged for a more authentic presentation of emotion and selfhood. (70)

Furthermore, in these free spaces, peers and staff members offered collaboration and insight as opposed to resistance: these were judgment free zones. Staff members often rewarded and incentivised positive behaviours rather than penalising prisoners for their mistakes. There was a form of emotional 'attunement' between peers and non-uniformed staff, which provided an outlet for difficult emotions. Moreover, unlike other prison zones, there was a spontaneous and organic quality to the relations and manifestations of care that emerged. Many of the features of these free spaces align with Turner's (1974) concept of communitas: especially the

136   B. Laws

different temporal rules, inclusivity, openness, and liberated spirit that operated within these spaces.

Therapeutic Spaces

In contrast to all areas hitherto discussed, therapeutic treatment spaces were distinct in that they actively attempted to reconfigure prisoners' emotional responses and disrupt their thinking patterns. In Ranby, exposure to therapeutic treatment was limited to attendance in psychological programmes or placement on the small Kainos wing.[6] In Send, therapeutic spaces were more pervasive, encompassing the therapeutic community (J-Wing), Psychologically Informed Planned Environment (PIPE) on A wing, and the alcohol and substances programme (RAPt) on D-wing. Given the broad range of services on offer and the relatively small number of total prisoners in Send, the proportion of women undergoing some form of therapy was high (around 35 per cent). The large proportion of long-termers in Send also meant that a contingent of prisoners had already experienced one (or more) of these spaces.

Prisoners in both establishments seemed to be polarised by their therapeutic experiences. A number of participants spoke enthusiastically about their transformational effects, such as developing awareness about how behaviours could 'hurt people' and the empathic importance of 'understanding their side of the story' (Wayne). Prisoners cultivated a degree of emotional self-awareness in therapy and learned about the processes underlying their destructive feelings: 'I've had an angry life man, and anger eats away at the soul' (Liam); 'With this SCP [self-chance programme] course, it's all about sussing out my own anger cues' (Dean). Importantly, the therapeutic communities provided participants with an ongoing opportunity to work on their problems collaboratively, in real time. That is, they were not learning abstract skills divorced from everyday life in prison. In this respect, the PIPE unit was particularly valued by

---

[6] Kainos is a charity that works with adult male offenders. It uses cognitive behavioural therapy methods (CBT) within a group therapeutic community setting on a prison wing. It is a round-the-clock programme that requires total immersion in the programme, typically over a period of six months. There were around twenty male prisoners on this wing during the research period.

Ellie, who saw it as a highly practical way to use 'the skills you learned on TC and prove them'. Living and learning alongside peers going through therapy provided direct windows for insight and self-reflection. For example, the therapeutic expectations of openness and inclusivity challenged individuals who did not feel comfortable around prisoners with particular offence histories:

> I'm pushed into a small environment with paedophiles and wrong uns, it was difficult listening to some real explicit shit, I wanted to write them off. At the end of 27 months I was playing table tennis with sex offenders. That was only due to me exploring so much shit. (Liam)

Liam's account is reminiscent, in a more restricted way, of the forms of communitas articulated above: especially the idea that communitas is 'spontaneous…[and] not shaped by norms' (Turner, 1974, 274). That is to say, outside of the therapeutic environment, prison norms would typically stigmatise the formation of affiliative bonds with sex offenders. The therapeutic communities, in particular, encouraged horizontal affiliations, which often led to learning opportunities and shared emotional introspection. For example, Paula explained that during group therapy, another prisoner downplayed the impact of a crime (shooting someone) that Paula had also been victim of. 'I said to her "I've been shot and it's not so easy, it really fucking hurt." I've never been able to identify with the physical and emotional pain that it caused me until that day in therapy.' Hearing other women's testimonies provided a further avenue for cultivating self-awareness and insight. Other prisoners were like mirrors for each other's pain, growth and collective healing. Deep relationships and 'really strong bonds' were forged in these settings, because to some extent 'the people you do therapy with are your therapists too' (Ellie, both quotations). In short, the formalised culture of emotion sharing and learning in these therapeutic spaces made these areas feel distinctive from other prison zones. Over time, some prisoners absorbed the language, tools and perspectives of the psychological environment in which they were being immersed:

Paula:	The TC helped me to manage my emotions better and helped me to understand myself better, to understand my emotions and where they came from. It taught me to break it down and understand patterns of behaviour in myself and others.
Interviewer:	*How?*
Paula:	By reality confrontation, by challenging people and being challenged. By learning to work through those challenges of being defensive, and it helps you to work through denial and then you start to see it on other people, and in the end you do feel like a therapist. Because you are saying to someone "you're in denial" and "you're lying, I want to challenge you and I want to confront you because you did this", you're saying to her "but this is what you did". So you're learning all the different skills of deflecting and of being challenged, and taking criticism, and being able to reflect and look at yourself, and being able to think: hang on a minute. Being able to see things in other people, it's a mad process; at the time you think it's a load of shit, but it's actually really powerful.

However, in direct contrast, a number of prisoners felt alienated by therapeutic treatment and experienced these spaces as psychologically suffocating. Indeed, some prisoners felt that when they questioned the wisdom of the programmes, they would be crushed beneath an avalanche of clinical labels. The expectation of level-headed, open sharing by prisoners was at times in conflict with the seemingly intense level of psychological scrutiny over participants' testimonies. This left some prisoners feeling like there was no way to turn, and that they were lost in a kind of psychological maze: 'Sometimes you can't win on there…if you don't share enough you're deflecting, if you hold the same opinion as your mate, you're colluding' (Pia); 'Psychologists read into everything you say' (Billy). These accounts are strongly redolent of Kruttschnitt and Gartner (2005) who expound the inherent constrictions of expectations for prisoner sharing:

5 Space and Emotions   139

Prisoners were told to open up, disclose problems, and embrace the potential of treatment and getting well. Yet, as these women acknowledged, failing to partake in the rhetoric of disclosure would earn them the ire of staff while fully accepting could undermine their chances of release. (159)

Prisoners had to walk an emotional tightrope wherein both expression and disclosure were subject to psychological scrutiny. Most importantly for current purposes, any outburst of emotion, especially anger or frustration, was admonished as being *reactionary* and *defensive*. Anger was not interpreted by therapists as cathartic or expressive, but rather as an aberration that needed to be identified and corrected. Paul felt that the feedback received always gravitated towards stigmatising prisoners, emphasising 'everything absolutely negative' and providing 'nothing positive' or incentivising.

Sometimes prisoners appeared to be pressured to embrace particular interpretations of their lives and psychological states, rather than internalising these messages freely. In a related way, Katherine explained that 'succeeding' in these spaces meant having to sacrifice one's true identity and beliefs: 'There's a lot of talk but there's no meaning behind it, it's just mechanical, it's just bullshit'. Katherine felt alienated by prisoners who co-opted the language of psychologists and clinicians because, she claimed, it seemed like robotic and disingenuous 'psychobabble':

Use a bit of colourful language, swear if you have to, just don't be mechanical. As soon as you do that, you put me on guard and I feel very defensive very quickly, because I feel like you're trying to manipulate me, you sound like a therapist. I find it uncomfortable very quickly. Because you're quoting off people. They're not people. They go on there and become brainwashed and like zombies. (Katherine)

Prison therapy raised fears among some prisoners that they were being broken apart and re-programmed. At the affective level, this raised discomfort about having to contain authentic feeling states to align with therapeutic culture and values. Such feelings were exacerbated by the closed-off nature of therapeutic community in Send: J-Wing residents did not associate with other parts of the prison, adding to the feeling of

140   B. Laws

constriction and control: 'It's really intense, because you don't come off the wing' (Francesca).

What united these divergent perpectives was the deep immersion and psychological entanglement that was experienced in these zones. Even the advocates of these environments acknowledged their invasive and bureaucratic qualities: 'It's helped, but if there was somewhere where you could just unload things, that would be better, rather than box ticking that is used against you in a negative way' (Billy). The therapeutic lens and constant incitements to openness made it difficult for prisoners to conceal their emotions: 'Everything we feel is exposed' (Katherine). Interestingly, the older men's library on house block five functioned like an informal version of official therapeutic culture. In this space, prisoners engaged in cathartic conversations outside the typical realms of formal prison therapy and without the presence of staff or trained clinicians. Most importantly, in this area, prisoners did not have to worry about institutional consequences and could retain some degree of emotional privacy.

Privacy and Selection of Space

> You know when you can have private time; when the last check is done at 8:30, then no one is going to check on you until the morning. So you've got that private time, but you never really do feel alone. There's that little pinprick in the door, you can see people look through it, you can see people's feet going under the door, and the light turns on in the landing…So although you can be on your own, you are never truly alone. (Danielle)

Throughout the accounts above, privacy has emerged, both implicitly and explicitly, as an important explanatory variable. However, as Moran (2015: 31) explains, 'defining what 'privacy' might mean is a challenge in itself' as it is a 'complex arrangement…specific to particular contexts'. Rather than resolve these tensions entirely, Schwartz (1972) provides conceptual guidance for assessing privacy in prison by drawing a contrast between 'forced exposure' and 'forced spectatorship'. For current purposes, this distinction is useful, revealing the different ways in which

5 Space and Emotions   141

privacy was limited, and raising implications with regard to emotional expressivity and the use of prison space.

A significant contingent of prisoners felt that specific design features and institutional decisions largely eroded the possibility of achieving complete privacy. As an example of forced exposure, even when participants were locked in their cells, officers and other prisoners could 'just walk up and open the flap' (Olivia) to observe their behaviour.[7] This could be experienced as particularly intrusive and embarrassing for prisoners who were observed naked in their cells: 'They [officers] see your bum' (Francesca). Zoe stated that 'it's horrible because I'm in my room and this is my private space, but then they're telling me that I'm meant to be dressed'. O'Donnell (2014: 80) notes that peep-holes and viewing flaps deny prisoners the opportunity for real solitude through 'the intrusive burden of an unwelcome gaze'. Prisoners are cut off from meaningful social contact on one hand, and subjected to unsolicited and disembodied observation on the other.

In a different manner, prisoners were forcibly exposed to the habits and idiosyncrasies of others. Indeed, institutional control over cell sharing arrangements created considerable challenges to privacy for male prisoners: 'It's impossible to have privacy when you're living with somebody 24-7, eating, shitting, and pissing. He's shitting where your head is' (Tommas). Although some prisoners draped blankets and curtains around the sides of their beds to create a visual screen, and negotiated times for music, TV, silence and bathroom usage with their cellmates, single cells were still idealised as providing the 'next level of privacy' (Simon). Given that most prisoners agreed that it was better to ventilate sadness alone in their room 'rather than cry in front of people' (Francesca), cell-sharers were denied this outlet in their living space.

Participating in the social world of the prison created acute difficulties for finding time alone, as acquaintances were prone to 'come and just barge into your room' (Ellie) when they needed help or wanted to talk. Two prisoners claimed that they could only achieve privacy by segregating themselves from the prisoner population completely:

---

[7] Most cell doors had a small metal flap, the shape of a vertical letter-box, which could be opened or closed to see inside the cell and observe prisoner behaviour.

142   B. Laws

You can have privacy. I don't think it's healthy but you can…I've seen something where men don't leave their cells. I've even been through it. I had my cell pitch black. It's black where I needed to turn the light on just to get a cup from the sink. And I just wanted to stay in there, and I didn't wanna leave. (Freddy)

I don't want to know people's business and I don't need to know it. I don't want to be involved in it. So it's quite a lonely existence for me as well. (Ian)

The price of privacy, then, was a degree of social isolation that could have damaging effects over time. Ellie claimed that there was a trade-off between association time and privacy that fluctuated across different living areas: 'E and F [resettlement wings] are good, you've got time out of your cell but you lose some of your privacy. On main block you get locked in early but you know you're going to get time alone'.

By contrast, a number of prisoners reflected that, while privacy was never absolute, it was still possible to a degree 'when you're in your cell' (Mikey). These prisoners felt that privacy was something that had to be forged or sought-out, rather than something guaranteed by the establishment. They set firm boundaries with their peers: 'You have to make sure they don't walk straight in, and say "No, not today"' (Zoe), or explicitly ask for 'some time alone' (Janice). Some prisoners simply refused to answer their doors or pretended to be asleep ('I will have my room in total darkness ready for when they knock' Ula), knowing that eventually their peers would get the message. Others benefitted from having screened-off sanitary cubicles that allowed them to hide: 'You can go in the toilet and people can't see you' (Oscar). Privacy was also found outside of cell spaces: Danielle explained that she was able to cry in the showers because the sounds of the water and the heat would make it difficult for anyone to hear or notice changes in her affect. Transitions between the wings and other buildings opened up space for some prisoners to break away from their social groups and find brief moments of solitude:

I like getting away from people. If I was outside and had something wrong, if I felt annoyed with everything I would just go somewhere and chill out for the night. I like looking at the moon, so when the moon is out I'll be out and find a nice spot to chill out I like doing that. (Tamara)

Spatial Selection and Emotion

I like to use the spaces all over, I don't like to sit in a room all the time. (Yvonne)

This discussion of privacy has revealed one way in which prisoners attempted to use space to serve and soothe emotional needs away from the eyes of others. However, finding private time for offloading emotions was only one aspect of a broader strategy. Indeed, as well as *seeking out* particular emotions, it was common for prisoners to manipulate space *to avoid* particular feeling states. Evading spaces where unrest was likely ('I avoid the association room and dining room as much as I can' Gabriella) or sequestering oneself away ('I retreat to my room' Haley) during peak times of activity decreased the 'chances of getting into trouble' (Mikey). These decisions were motivated by conflict avoidance and the cycles of fear and aggression that were more probable in specific areas. Some prisoners tried to evade any area that increased feelings of uncertainty: for example, Bernie explained that he 'avoided places where there's people I don't know'. Boredom also drove prisoners away from certain spaces: 'I avoid J-Wing because it's a very dull landing. It's like the Addams family house' (Rebecka). In a related manner, regulating space was not only used to escape the onset of emotions, but was also a method of diluting the intensity of feelings at a point subsequent to conflict: 'If someone upsets me, it's better to remove myself from that situation completely' (Amber). This stopped feelings from escalating to a point where prisoners had to defend themselves or risked losing face.

In a different way, prisoners sometimes distanced themselves out of compassion for the feelings of others: 'If I don't take myself away, I'll just take it out on other people' (Rebecka). These prisoners did not want their peers to feel obligated or weighed down by their feelings. By contrast, Dean explained that the physical environment could also be manipulated to intensify personal aggression and instil fear in others, rather than minimise it. Two prisoners had soiled Dean's mattress and bedsheets with food as a prank:

> So I shut the door and went in their pad. I said "take that bedding and wash it now, if you don't there will be consequences". I said "it's not about being a bit of fun, it stops now". I told them what to do, "I want it all washed by 4 pm". That got it done because I used violence and aggression. Closing the door and walking in the pad, that was the threat straight away. Think about the psychological thoughts you're having. If I leave the door open, you've got an escape route. Once I close this door, you're in the room by yourself with me. Just by opening or closing the door…but that's prison, that's how it is. (Dean)

Denying other prisoners an exit and confining them to a small space added edge to the situation and evoked fear. More typically, it was the prison regime that denied prisoners freedom of movement and ignited unwelcome emotions and there were many situations where prisoners had only limited control over space. This chapter has already referenced the spatially challenging nature of cell-sharing arrangements, but more importantly, here, are the ways in which participants attempted to minimise these difficulties by controlling space. As suggested above, material screens were used around beds to divide the cell into different areas, but prisoners also negotiated times when they could leave the cell to create a limited form of privacy and avoid conflicts entirely. Further, prisoners did not passively accept cell-sharing arrangements: they repeatedly petitioned officers for newly available cells or asked to share with friends instead. In this sense, spatial selection was not just an immediate situational strategy (for example, walking away from a conflict) but also involved substantial planning to carve out more harmonious space in the longer term.

The chaotic living quarters on house blocks caused a range of emotional discomforts that were difficult to circumvent. Particular frustrations arose when unplanned 'freezes' to prisoner movement meant that activities and association times were curtailed or cancelled. Some prisoners were commonly left waiting for long periods of time just to get back onto their wings and house blocks. Indeed, the use of 'movement slips' in Send, that had to be administratively approved by officers, was a stark reminder that the institution was attempting to formalise and control prisoners' use of space. It was not surprising, then, that some prisoners felt completely devoid of any spatial control:

> There's a lot going on. It's quite circular, it's all around you. There's no room you can go in and chill to get out. You can't do that in prison, you can't escape; it's constant, it's aggressive. It's 24-7. It's manic. (Freddy)

Living on wings that were awash with new psychoactive substances constituted a form of spatial entrapment for some prisoners: 'You just can't take yourself away from it, it's always there, you have to deal with it' (Val). A number of prisoners shared experiences of being passively intoxicated by second hand NPS smoke or saw other prisoners having distressing panic attacks while taking it. Being forced into proximity with people and substances one did not like was arguably the principal driver of anger, fear, and tension in prison. It was when prisoners felt cornered that volatile emotions and confrontations seemed most likely to arise. But these concerns notwithstanding, most prisoners strove—and achieved—some degree of control over space. By seeking out particular areas, and particular people within them, and sidestepping other places, they could increase the potential for feeling desirable emotions while diminishing the likelihood of facing emotionally unsettling situations (Gross, 2008; Laws & Crewe, 2016).

Conclusion

The data presented at the close of this final substantive chapter of Part I connects back to earlier findings. That is, the substantive chapters began with a discussion of individual emotional management strategies, and through an analysis of space, the focus has returned to the ways in which prisoners attempt to exert control over space to regulate their feelings. These accounts indicate that while prisoners did not have complete control over spatiality, they could exercise some degree of bounded agency. Prisoners managed to forge out space for themselves by exploiting gaps in the system or finding ways to co-opt it. Indeed, the careful attempts by prisoners to establish routines (as discussed in Chap. 4) can be understood as a way to work within the parameters of the regime to seek out preferred spaces and avoid areas that they disliked. Importantly, too, in the 'hostile zones' it was the precise absence of order that was striking and fear inducing. Routines have a 'double-edged' nature which can be both stifling—raising fears of institutionalisation—but also ontologically reassuring, making environments feel more predictable and less chaotic (Sparks et al., 1996).

This chapter has clear connections with aspects of the carceral geography literature which emphasises the 'spatially mediated nature of the articulation of emotion'; traces the various 'ways in which individual spaces of the prison elicit and facilitate different emotional expression' (Moran, 2015: 29, both quotations); and draws attention to the emotional geography of institutional spaces (Crewe et al., 2014; Smoyer & Blankenship, 2014). Indeed, this chapter argues that prisons have complex 'emotion' maps (Crawley, 2004), and that the affective feel of particular spaces was dynamic, changing as prisoners moved to and from particular areas. Further, the analysis of the 'line route' in Ranby revealed the significance of exploring *transitional* spaces and areas with less clearly demarcated boarders. Shadowing prisoners as they completed their journeys across these different routes provided an intuitive way of understanding these more diffuse spaces.

This chapter broadened Goffman's (1961) original conceptualisation of 'free places', and developed a more recent contribution (Crewe et al., 2014), by introducing the notion of 'communitas' (Turner, 1974). These areas provided prisoners with a respite from chaos, and facilitated a wider repertoire of emotional experiences. Exploring the different features of communitas—which is characterised by spontaneity and a spirit of liberation—helped to decipher the factors that made these places feel distinctive. Importantly, these zones typically had 'softer' architectural features and contained staff members who embodied an ethos of inclusivity and acceptance. This created an atmosphere of emotional 'attunement' where feelings could be expressed openly without fear, judgment or reprisal. In a different manner, the appropriation of liminality (Jewkes, 2005b; Turner, 1974) was introduced here to further understand cell spaces. The description of cellular living as an almost 'developmental' process underscores a wider finding in prisons research and concentration camp literature that, at least for some prisoners, painful experiences can give way to 'the possibility of resurrection', and that 'bleakness and abandonment' is sometimes followed by 'joy and reunion' (O'Donnell, 2014: 97). The experience of imprisonment was fluid, not fixed; it was possible for prisoners to shift from finding the cell oppressive to finding it liberating. The second part of this book attempts to explore and contrast these findings in the context of solitary confinement, a context which require a quite different analytical lens.

References

Bentham, J. (1791). *Panopticon or the inspection house.* T. Payne Mews Gate.

Crawley, E. M. (2004). Emotion and performance: Prison officers and the presentation of self in prisons. *Punishment & Society, 6*(4), 411–427. https://doi.org/10.1177/1462474504046121

Crewe, B., Hulley, S., & Wright, S. (2017). The gendered pains of life imprisonment. *British Journal of Criminology, 57*(6), 1359–1378.

Crewe, B., Warr, J., Bennett, P., & Smith, A. (2014). The emotional geography of prison life. *Theoretical Criminology, 18*(1), 56–74.

Csikszentmihalyi, M. (1991). *Flow: The psychology of optimal experience.* Harper Perennial.

Evans, R. (1982). *The fabrication of virtue: English prison architecture, 1750–1840.* University Press.

Foucault, M. (1977). *Discipline and punish.* Random House of Canada.

Foucault, M. (1979). *Discipline and punish.* Random House of Canada.

Gambetta, D. (2009). *Codes of the underworld: How criminals communicate.* Princeton University Press.

Goffman, E. (1961). *Asylums: Essays on the social situation of mental patients and other inmates.* Penguin.

Gonzalez, J. (1995). Autotopographies. In G. Braham & M. Driscoll (Eds.), *Prosthetic territories: Politics and Hypertechnologies.* Westview Press.

Gross, J. J. (2008). Emotion regulation. In M. Lewis, J. M. Haviland-Jones, & L. F. Barrett (Eds.), *Handbook of emotions.* Guilford Press.

Jewkes, Y. (2002). *Captive audience: Media, masculinity and power in prisons.* Willian Publishing.

Jewkes, Y. (2005a). Loss, liminality and the life sentence: Managing identity through a disrupted lifecourse. In A. Liebling & S. Maruna (Eds.), *The effects of imprisonment*. Routledge.

Jewkes, Y. (2005b). Men behind bars 'doing' masculinity as an adaptation to imprisonment. *Men and Masculinities, 8*(1), 44–63.

Jewkes, Y. (2012). Aesthetics and anaesthetics: The architecture of incarceration. In L. K. Cheliotis (Ed.), *The arts of imprisonment: Control, resistance and empowerment*. Routledge.

Jewkes, Y. (2013). The aesthetics and anaesthetics of prison architecture. In J. Simon, N. Temple, & R. Tobe (Eds.), *Architecture and justice: Judicial meanings in the public realm*. Ashgate Publishing.

Kraftl, P., & Adey, P. (2008). Architecture/affect/inhabitation: Geographies of being-in buildings. *Annals of the Association of American Geographers, 98*(1), 213–231.

Kruttschnitt, C., & Gartner, R. (2005). *Marking time in the golden state: Women's imprisonment in California*. University Press.

Laws, B., & Crewe, B. (2016). Emotion regulation among male prisoners. *Theoretical Criminology, 20*(4), 529–547. https://doi.org/10.1177/1362480615622532

Liebling, A. (2007). Prison suicide and its prevention. In Y. Jewkes, B. Crewe, & J. Bennett (Eds.), *Handbook on prisons*. Routledge.

Liebling, A., & Maruna, S. (Eds.). (2013). *The effects of imprisonment*. Routledge.

Massumi, B. (2002). *Parables for the virtual: Movement, affect, sensation*. Duke University Press.

McConville, S. (2000). The architectural realization of penal ideas. In L. Fairweather & S. McConville (Eds.), *Prison architecture: Policy, design, and experience*. Routledge.

Moran, D. (2011). Between outside and inside? Prison visiting rooms as liminal carceral spaces. *GeoJournal, 78*(2), 339–351. https://doi.org/10.1007/s10708-011-9442-6

Moran, D. (2014). Leaving behind the 'total institution'? Teeth, transcarceral spaces and (re)inscription of the formerly incarcerated body. *Gender, Place & Culture, 21*(1), 35–51.

Moran, D. (2015). *Carceral geography: Spaces and practices of incarceration*. Ashgate.

Moran, D., Pallot, J., & Piacentini, L. (2013). Privacy in penal space: Women's imprisonment in Russia. *Geoforum, 47*, 138–146.

O'Donnell, I. (2014). *Prisoners, solitude, and time*. Oxford University Press.

Polletta, F. (1999). 'Free spaces' in collective action. *Theory and Society, 28*(1), 1–38.

Price, T. (2012). *The mythic modern: Architectural expeditions into the spirit.* ORO Editions.

Schwartz, B. (1972). Deprivation of privacy as a functional prerequisite: the case of the prison. *J. Crim. L. Criminology & Police Sci., 63*, 229.

Sibley, D., & van Hoven, B. (2009). The contamination of personal space: Boundary construction in a prison environment. *Area, 41*(2), 198–206. https://doi.org/10.1111/j.1475-4762.2008.00855.x

Sloan, J. (2012). 'You can see your face in my floor': Examining the function of cleanliness in an adult male prison. *The Howard Journal of Criminal Justice, 51*(4), 400–410.

Smoyer, A. B., & Blankenship, K. M. (2014). Dealing food: Female drug users' narratives about food in a prison place and implications for their health. *International Journal of Drug Policy, 25*(3), 562–568. https://doi.org/10.1016/j.drugpo.2013.10.013

Sparks, R., Bottoms, A., & Hay, W. (1996). *Prisons and the Problem of Order.* Clarendon Press.

Toch, H. (1992). *Living in prison: The ecology of survival.* The Free Press.

Tschumi, B. (1996). *Architecture and disjunction.* MIT press.

Turner, V. W. (1974). *Dramas, fields and metaphors.* Cornell University Press.

Part II

Solitude and Segregation

Introduction to Part II

> There is a great diversity in the nature of the environments that are lumped together under the label "solitary confinement"
> Suedfeld et al. (1982, p. 312)

During my time researching in HMP Ranby I met a prisoner who was self-isolating on one of the main living wings. Given what I had read about the enduring, damaging, effects of isolation I was surprised to learn that prisoners might *choose* to do this. This prisoner was being threatened by a group of rivals in the prison and felt unsafe. to take part in work activities during the day or even associate with other prisoners on his housing unit. He was desperate to avoid being attacked and lived with the fear of that prospect hanging over him. He acknowledged that extended periods of isolation were not good for his health and that it may have caused damage. He did, however, find time in his solitude to cultivate his passion for reading and photography. It was this interaction that sparked my interest in solitary confinement in a quite particular way. It raised the following questions: Why do some prisoners, in some contexts, actively seek out segregation? What might this tell us about the pressures of the broader prison environment? What kinds of emotions lead to, and are experienced in, solitary confinement?

152   Solitude and Segregation

The following analysis, then, is based on 16 in-depth qualitative interviews with segregated men serving their sentences in HMP Whitemoor, a high-security Category-A prison. Access to the prison was sought through a formal application through the National Research Council. The prison was selected because it is attempting to think of creative ways to help transition long term 'seg dwellers' from the segregation unit back into the general population of the prison. A 'Bridge unit' had recently been conceived and implemented in the prison. The unit attempts to provide tailored, individualised, support for prisoners who were recently segregated and help reintegrate them. However, this transition unit was struggling at the time of the study. The segregation unit was consistently over-capacity and the surplus prisoners were placed on the Bridge unit. This created difficulties in running separate regimes as intended. Prisoners on the segregation regime typically received two of the following three choices in their morning: a phone call, shower, or time on the yard. The remainder of the day (around 23 hours) was spent in cells unless there was a segregation review, or another appointment (medical or legal) planned ahead of time. There was some communication between prisoners on the unit, via 'conversations' shouted through the doors or pipes. Sometimes conversations took place through windows to other units in the prison. Segregated prisoners were often surprisingly well informed about events happening around the prison.

As will be discussed in some detail in Chap. 6 this approach to solitary confinement, and the study that emerged from it, is shaped by the research outlined in Part 1. The aim is to connect the relationship between the emotional experience of imprisonment in general and how the desire for isolation and separation *sometimes* emerges out of it. As Chap. 6 argues, not all prisoners 'seek out' solitary confinement, but a surprising number of them do. While it is important not to misrepresent the important work of human rights scholars and their calls to end solitary confinement practices, that work is sometimes divorced of an appreciation of the broader imprisonment practices that lead prisoners to segregation units. It is accurate to say that much less attention has been paid to prisoners' own motivations for segregation than the brutalizing effects of isolation. To address this imbalance Chap. 6 foregrounds the importance of motivation. The argument involves a detailed description of the complex, and sometimes contradictory, motives that may lead prisoners into seeking isolation. It further attempts to explore the relationship between segregation and the wider prison environment. For many prisoners, segregation has a 'negative benefit' or amounts to a form of 'lesser evil'. Such phrasing hints at the difficult decisions that prisoners navigate and offers an alternative perspective on solitary confinement debates.

In Chap. 7, the discussion turns from motivation towards the impacts of segregation on prisoners bodies in particular. A salient feature of segregation units is disembodiment. The body can be viewed as a particularly important site of analysis in solitary confinement and offers an important window into the world of prisoner emotions. Given the sedentary nature of the body, inherent material deprivations, and absence of social connection in these spaces, focusing on embodiment helps to increase understanding about how prisoners experience this form of isolation. This chapter forwards a framework that views the body as both object and subject: both acted *on* and acted *through*. The analysis is separated into three parts: first, it considers *damaged bodies* that bear the scars and distortions of imprisonment on the one hand, but that strike back on the other. Second, it describes various methods of *bodily maintenance* such as exercise, diet, cleanliness, and dirty protest in the context of a highly restricted regime. Third, attention is drawn towards the so called *spiritual body* which considers embodiment as a vehicle for transcendence and escape. The discussion brings these perspectives on the body and emotions together, exploring the dissolution of boundaries of the self (See Laws, 2020), and the inherent dangers of disembodied relations between prisoners and officers.

Finally, Chap. 8 attempts to bring both studies into some relief, by articulating the major findings of both research projects. However, this is not a deep analytical exercise, which might not be possible or relevant, given that both studies reflect very different contexts and security categorisations.

References

Laws, B. (2020). Reimaging 'the Self' in criminology: Transcendence, unconscious states and the limits of narrative criminology. *Theoretical criminology*, https://doi.org/1362480620919102.

Suedfeld, P., Ramirez, C., Deaton, J., & Baker-Brown, G. (1982). Reactions and attributes of prisoners in solitary confinement. *Criminal Justice and Behavior, 9*(3), 303–340.

6

Motivation for Segregation

Among its potential benefits, solitude provides relief from the pressures involved in interacting with other people. This is a 'negative' benefit, that is, a retreat from an unpleasant situation. If the retreat is motivated by social anxiety or depression, as it sometimes is, there is an obvious danger of exacerbating a pre-existing maladaptive condition.
Long and Averill (2003, p. 35)
I don't want to stay down here [in Segregation], I'd rather be on the wing, but it's the only way I can get myself out of a worse situation. If I go there, I'll end up coming down here. Either me or them will end up doing something serious. I'm trying to avoid it. This is the outcome of what happened last time. So even though it's not good, it's the best thing.
(Ernest, Prisoner*)*

Do prisons need segregation units? Recent calls from senior prison managers, human rights activists and number of academics continue to scrutinise this question. But answering it requires formulating two slightly different questions: first, what is the relationship between segregation units and the

---

A version of this chapter was first published with *The British Journal of Criminology*

© The Author(s), under exclusive license to Springer Nature Switzerland AG 2022 **155**
B. Laws, *Caged Emotions*, Palgrave Studies in Prisons and Penology,
https://doi.org/10.1007/978-3-030-96083-4_6

wider prison environment? A central contention of this chapter is that this relationship is deeply embedded, especially in the jurisdiction of England and Wales. While segregation units are often isolated from main prison quarters—in that they tend to exist in secluded parts of the grounds—they are not islands separate from it. Indeed, it is hard to understand the puzzle of segregation units without mapping the broader framework of incarceration and the individual prisoner journey within it. Existing research on solitary confinement tends to bypass the interplay between specific segregation practices and wider experiences of imprisonment.

The second question is whether the solitary confinement literature can augment the discussions of *effects* in helpful ways? For very understandable reasons, decades of literature have focused squarely on the effects of deep isolation. There are few debates in prison studies that are as contentious. At times, the discussion feels like impasse. The second aim of this chapter, then, is to shift the focus from effects to prisoner motivation. Much less has been written about the extent to which prisoners might seek out solitary confinement, though Shalev and Edgar (2015) offer a valuable starting point. A detailed account of prisoners' motives can shed light on segregation practices and the complicated decision-making processes involved—ultimately adding a different perspective to debates about effects. In their psychological account of solitude introduced above, Long and Averill write of the 'negative benefits' of solitude seeking. This kind of thinking, which could read like contradiction, offers the right frame to understand prisoners in this study who speak of segregation as a 'lesser evil' or as an opportunity for 'getting out of a worse situation'. Christian Smith and Eric Fromm both offer important perspectives to shape and guide a more nuanced analysis of prisoner motivation to guide this argument.

By looking at segregation in the context of 'broader' prisoner experiences on the one hand and by focusing on their motivations on the other, this chapter attempts to partly respond to Richard Vince's (2018) instructive statement:

If we are to truly reduce the over reliance on segregation we need to get upstream of the problem. The typical use of segregation by staff and often prisoners is either in response to an act of violence or indeed avoidance of such an act.' (26)

In both aspects of the analysis this chapter attempts to look 'upstream'. Before forwarding this argument, however, it is necessary to briefly survey the solitary confinement literature and introduce the methodological orientation of this study.

A Contentious Debate About Effects

This review of the solitary confinement literature is not exhaustive, but rather, aims to draw attention to the underlying fractures that frame this chapter. An important caveat here is that not all solitary confinement is the same. Suedfeld et al. (1982) question the inclusion of studies of POW literature and laboratory studies of sensory deprivation in relation to discussions of prison solitary confinement. Furthermore, very few scholars defend the use of American Supermax style punishment. O'Donnell (2014, p. 149) calls such prolonged ultra-segregation 'crucifixion without the prospect of resurrection' because it involves 'harm unmitigated by benevolence' and includes a brutal admixture of 'pessimism and unconcern'. But aside from these more extreme formations of isolation, the context for this study revolves around contested debates about the physiological and psychological effects of solitary confinement in more traditional prison designs.

One group of researchers have quite consistently described solitary confinement as a form or torture, that is both psychologically crippling and damaging, only serving to promote self-harm among prisoners (Jackson, 1983). Advocates of this view have been fixed in their position that solitary produces a repertoire of pathological effects and prolonged emotional damage, functional disability, and psychosis (see Grassian, 1983; Scharff-Smith, 2006; Kupers, 2008; Haney, 2012). But in stark contrast, a second group of researchers claim that segregation produces much less intense effects and only for some prisoners in institutions where basic standards of humane care have not been met (Suedfeld et al. 1982; Gendreau & Bonta, 1984; Wormith, 1984; Clements et al., 2007; O'Keefe et al., 2010; Gendreau & Theriault, 2011; Valera & Kates-Benman, 2016).

The tone of this debate includes absolute statements on both sides that can feel un-scholastic. On one level, there are strong existential claims about human nature. Pendergrass and Hoke (2018, p. 8) state that 'Isolation everywhere does terrible things to the human machine'. Casella, Ridgeway and Shourd go further:

In solitary confinement, a grey, limitless ocean stretches out in front of and behind you—an emptiness and loneliness so all-encompassing it threatens to erase you. Whether you're in that world a month, a year, or a decade, you experience the slow march of death. Day by day you lose your connection to everything outside the prison walls, everything you once knew and everything you once were. (2016, p. viii)

Casella et al. argue that human nature as irreducibly social:

Being human is relational, plain and simple. We exist in relationship to one another, to ideas, and to the world. It's the most essential thing about us as a species: how we realize our potential as individuals and create meaningful lives. Without that, we shrink. Day by day, we slowly die. (2016, p. xii)

These positions are unrelenting and leave sparse room for alternative perspectives. Indeed, scholarship that attempts to deviate from this script is sometimes scrutinised in ways which waiver from the aspirations of academic neutrality. For example, in his extended review of the Colorado study (see O'Keefe et al. 2010)[1] Craig Haney (2018, p. 369) argues that the study is 'riddled with serious methodological problems' and 'fundamentally flawed', that the results are 'impossible to decipher', that their acknowledgments of limitations are 'opaque and oblique'. Haney's argument that the Colorado study has 'become a last bastion of resistance against a widespread and growing consensus' (369) is in tension with his acknowledgement that other academics have endorsed the Colorado findings. Haney claims that the influence and reach of the Colorado study 'has been amplified by an equally flawed meta-analysis' by Morgan et al. (2016). He continues, arguing that 'the influence of a

---

[1] The Colorado study suggests that time spent in Segregation results in negligible psychological and physiological effects when used for short durations.

fundamentally flawed study can grow if it and the data it produced are included in literature reviews that overlook glaring weaknesses' (2018, p. 369).

Attacks on methodological procedures are sometimes espoused with equal veracity in the opposite direction. In their critique of Sharff-Smith (2006)—who's review discusses the various detrimental effects of confinement—Gendreau and Labrecque (2018, p. 348) take issue with the author's vote-counting method, first noting 'substantial inaccuracies in summarizing the magnitude of effect size'. Second, the authors take issue with the notion that administrative segregation is *solely* responsible for the psychological malaise of inmates, claiming that Sharff-Smith's reasoning is 'textbook radical behaviouralism' (348).

A key consideration for current purposes is that the emphasis given to experimental studies of segregation, and time spend debating them, is particularly unusual given the inherent constraints. O'Donnell (2014, p. 122) reflects that there is no ethical way to demonstrate the effects of segregation with 'sufficient scientific rigour to satisfy everyone', and therefore 'research findings will always be contestable'. Haney (2018, p. 378) similarly concludes that 'conventional research designs are nearly impossible to implement and necessary trade-offs are especially costly to the quality of the data collected'. In addition, systematic reviews of the solitary confinement literature make subjective distinctions between the 'correct' inclusion and exclusion criteria that feel inconsistent. For example, by choosing to exclude studies without control groups on one hand while including those relying solely on survey instruments or official records on the other. Further, while the emphasis on control groups is a thoughtful, in jurisdictions where prisoners move haphazardly through different prisons establishments, and occupy numerous units within each prison (e.g. mains wings, therapeutic treatment centres, healthcare, segregation etc.), such measures are hard to execute. Finally, experimental approaches risk excluding extremely valuable research that adopts alternate epistemological approaches. For example, O'Donnell's meticulous accretion approach which 'layer[s] excerpt upon excerpt' (2014, p. 67) from a rich pool of solitary confinement and isolation testimonies would be excluded from such reviews. The debate about the effects of solitary confinement stirs deep academic emotion and Suedfeld et al.'s (1982,

p. 303) comment that 'the amount of light shed by the disputants is tiny in comparison to the degree of heat' still gives pause for reflection. The argument below does not seek to bypass this discussion about effects but rather create the ground for re-approach. This approach is guided by a consideration of prisoner motivation.

Motivation Reconsidered

Given that segregation is often perceived to be an involuntarily sanction, focusing on prisoner motivation could appear nonsensical. However, a number of scholars note that some prisoners 'select' segregation. Gendreau and Labrecque (2018) estimate that between 20–30 per cent of Canadian prisoners are placed in administrative segregation 'for reasons of personal preference' and predict that the reactions of 'volunteers' will be different from those placed against their will (352). Suedfeld et al. (1982) explain that segregation may serve as a 'desirable time-out from the pressures and impositions of the general prison routine' (308), with some prisoners reporting that they 'welcomed, and had sought, a period in SC in order to "get their heads together"' (330). A number of Pendergrass and Hoke's (2018, p. 8) prisoner testimonies explain that solitary is 'tolerable, even desirable, because it was a respite from the violence and chaos of being housed in the…general population'.

The most relevant piece of recent research in the jurisdiction of England and Wales is Shalev and Edgar's (2015) 'Deep Custody' report. This detailed study sought to 'examine how segregation units and CSCs are used; describe the skills and views of staff who work there; and to explore prisoners' perceptions of fair processes and their treatment' (2015, p. v). There is some tension in the conclusion of the report where the authors argue on the one hand that: 'We explored both segregation units and CSCs as a *continuum of exclusion*, because both are forms of *involuntary separation* from the main population' (131, emphasis added). On the other hand, the authors report: 'Among the 50 segregated prisoners we interviewed, 19 had deliberately engineered a move to the segregation unit' (131). Shalev and Edgar go further than others in describing prisoners who 'orchestrated their segregation' (20). The most common reason

6 Motivation for Segregation 161

for seeking segregation included trying to engineer a transfer (or a 'ship out') to another prison. Alongside this motivation:

> Other reasons for wanting to be taken off the wing included having a debt which they couldn't repay; not wanting to share a cell; being exploited by other prisoners; or to get away from drugs on the wing. Increased access to governors, health professionals and others. (20)

However, while there are numerous references to motives for segregation across these accounts, they are not expounded in detail nor brought together into an analytical framework. Described in such terms, prisoners' reasoning can appear linear, functional and instrumental. It appears possible to reconsider motivation for segregation without compressing the breadth and intricacies of human motivation for action. To chart a course through this discussion of motivation Christian Smith (2015) is instructive, he explains that:

> ...an adequate theory of motivated action must recognize that human motivations, even basic motivations, are multiple. Human action is usually deployed to try to satisfy numerous, different, often competing motivations. Motivations are also complex. They do not usually organize into simple or neat sets, but are instead fraught with complications, intricacies, and difficulties. (75)

To say that motivations are complex and intricate, Smith continues, is to see that the 'action implications' of different motives can 'complement or conflict' with one another depending both on the 'time horizons' and 'particular conditions' in which people find themselves (75). A harder question perhaps is the extent to which motivation can include a degree of unconscious activity. Smith includes the contribution of the unconscious, but not in the sense of 'free-floating, random, or materially determined forces' but rather as the 'experiences, perceptions, and reactions rooted in lived reality' that means 'people's actions can be motivated even when the motives are unconscious' (79, *all quotations*). In his discussion of the different manifestations of violence Eric Fromm (1964, p. 15) argues that violence is 'based on the distinction between their respective

162   B. Laws

unconscious motivations'. While it is beyond the scope of this chapter to excavate a firm position on the role of prisoners' unconscious contributions, based on previous work (see Laws, 2019; Laws & Crewe, 2016) particular importance is given instead the underlying intuitions, feelings and emotions that prisoners may find hard to verbalise and articulate fully. Feelings and emotions therefore can be taken seriously in discussions of motivation as important elements in the composition of their decision making. Taken together, then, a deeper account of prisoner motives is presented here to contribute to debates about effects of solitary confinement and shed light on wider practices and processes of imprisonment.

The Broader Patchwork of Imprisonment

In their discussion of solitary confinement, Suedfeld et al. (1982) do not allow comparative aspects of their argument to fade into the background. For example, in the context of a discussion of anxiety levels in segregation they argue that:

> Stressful conditions of this sort could easily be (and in some prisons are) imposed in the normal dwelling quarters of the population. Conversely, SC [solitary confinement] units that are arranged more pleasantly along these dimensions would clearly be less aversive and might be in fact be no more so than the normal living arrangements. (311–312)

Without affirming or denying the accuracy of this argument, it is possible to accept that comparative dimensions are essential. Indeed, many of the participants in this current study did not discuss segregation in isolation, even when questions encouraged them to do so. This appeared in two ways. First, most participants had spent time in multiple other prisons. Arnie brought a book of poems and song lyrics to the interview. One of the most striking 'poems' was a list of around 30 different HM Prisons and YOI Institutions he had lived in: 'That's history right there, it's my story…I think about what happened in each place' (Arnie). Similarly, Charlie explained that he had been in institutions for almost 40

6 Motivation for Segregation 163

years: 'I come into the care system when I was 10, secure care at 12, borstals 13,14. I've been in prison all my life. 29 out of the last 35 [years] in prison'. In answering a question about time spent in segregation, Fred explains that his journey is non-linear, spending years alternating between the high-security estate and therapeutic units: 'I started off in Gloucester on remand, from there I went to Long Lartin for 5 years, then Gartree, then Grendon, I've been there twice. Dovegate, therapeutic Unit. Where else...Bullingdon, Cardiff. Swaleside.' Nate struggled to accurately recall the specific time periods but knew he had been 'in and out of seg' throughout his entire six-year sentence. In one sense, then, it was hard to intuit the impact of Whitemoor segregation because participants' experiences of imprisonment were geographically dispersed, and they were inclined to give comparative answers to non-comparative questions:

I: What's this seg lik e?
Kadeem: This is one of the best, more settled segs, because they have to facilitate lifers.

In a quite different sense, segregation blurred into the multiplicity of psychological and emotional challenges prisoners faced. In order to contextualise his experience of segregation *now* (in Whitemoor) Lenny explained that he previously spent 'six months down the block' in HMP Frankland, and then on the segregation Unit in HMP Full Sutton because he had 'trouble with forced conversion'. As Whitemoor has a reputation for housing a high proportion of Muslim prisoners Lenny reflected: 'I was upset about coming here'. Clearly, his ongoing entanglements followed him around the high security estate and become inseparable in his thoughts. Two participants in the study were serving sentences for Joint Enterprise. Ernest explained his initial feelings of despair and anger about his sentence: 'I just came from the YOI system where I was fighting a lot' (Ernest). Barak did not want to talk about segregation *per se* but wanted to share his frustration about being a B-Cat prisoner stuck in an A-Cat establishment.

Taken together, Gendreau and Labrecque (2018) appear correct to question the extent to which segregation 'is the primary driving force that creates the psychological malaise of inmates' (348) given that the contribution of wider life events is hard to differentiate. If segregation experiences mesh and merge with other experiences, it begs the question whether a narrow analysis on the effects of segregation is appropriate? This is not merely an issue of geographical complexity (e.g. the quantity of institutions experienced by prisoners) but speaks also to the psychological and emotional enmeshment of participants in the study whose concerns fell both *within, and simultaneously, beyond* the horizons of segregation.

Complex Motives

Situating segregation in the broader context of imprisonment experiences helps to understand why some prisoners may be motivated to seek out segregation. In this chapter, motivations are considered complex in three different senses of the word. First, they can be hidden, overlooked or misunderstood by others (e.g. from official records of why prisoners have been segregated compared to the reality) and also from our own awareness—the reference to unconscious motivations above addressed this point. Second, motivations are not fixed but change over time. Third, motivations are often layered, multiple and competing. According to Smith (2015), then, the movement from motivation to action is never zero to one, rather it involves 'developing stages of wishes, current concerns, intentions, decisions, and implementation' (81). The following sections of analysis explore the various motivations to seek out segregation, with these concerns held in mind.

Avoiding the Toxic Social World

> I don't want to be around characters who bring out the dark side, you either end up going to hell, or end up confused… I'd rather be here.
> (Hector)

In their description of gated communities and 'fortress' housing in the United Kingdom, Atkinson and Flint (2004) introduce a conceptual language that is highly relevant. The authors explain that when elite residents leave their homes they travel along secure geographical 'corridors' that attempt to 'shield or to immunise against casual or dangerous encounters' (888). The 'shielding of spatial patterns of movement' is achieved by using large SUVs and luxury vehicles designed to 'promote feelings of safety'. They term this activity 'bubbling', which is contrasted with 'gating' and 'walling', these latter terms describe the more sedentary activity of living within their 'fortress' houses. The dynamic use of space and mobility enables elite residents to largely circumvent and disconnect from the perceived risks of the local area. For current purposes, the movement of prisoners to segregation units can be similarly understood as an exercise in 'bubbling', 'walling' and 'gating'.

At one level, participants said that isolating themselves was about avoiding fear inducing situations altogether. Arnie was attacked by a gang of men within minutes of arriving on the wing from another prison.

I: Would you rather be on a wing with people?
Arnie: Not now mate, I can't trust no-one now.

A repeated concern of many prisoners was the fear of Muslim gangs and pressure to convert to a warped version of Islam that some termed a 'crazy ideology' (Gill). Hector, a Muslim prisoner, explained that there is a complex web of wing politics which can be difficult to avoid: 'On there you can't separate yourself…different parties were playing each other. Paranoia took over and I'm stuck in the middle.' While Lenny felt, in an ideal world, he would be in a prison closer to home, the segregation unit was one of the 'best places' to be at the current time. Lenny contrasted segregation with mains wings that were full of psychological uncertainty: 'If I go on the wing it would be an ongoing cycle with this issue [pressure to convert]. It might be one day or ten days, but once you don't want to be in their gang they don't like it'. Ernest said that on the wing the question 'Could I bump into them?' was always on his mind, and that 'It's just a matter of time'. Segregation was a way of temporarily escaping the cycle of fear and victimisation. It also constituted a desperate attempt to avoid a situation where they might feel compelled to retaliate or strike first.

They are trying to put me in a situation where I'm going to have to attack these people. I'm not gonna wait. I've seen what they do over the years. What am I meant to do? Am I just meant to let them beat me? Am I just meant to let them beat me? I know how it works. I am their number one person to get now. (Gill)

The repetition in Gill's account and the tense affective tone which he delivered it communicated the powerlessness and fear of violence on the wings. Charlie concurred with this reasoning: 'At least in here no one gets hurt'. Animosity between prisoners was exacerbated by institutional decisions that participants found hard to comprehend. For example, Fred had been involved in repeated violence with Muslim prisoners and sex offenders and felt that the institution understood 'I'm not allowed around them and they are not allowed around me'. However, there were instances where he was unwillingly brought into contact and Fred attacked a prisoner during a therapy group. Such retaliatory or pre-emptive violence, participants explained, would only serve to jeopardise their sentence or their family ties outside of prison:

I don't want to get into more trouble. I'll take myself out of that. Try and get to somewhere where I can show good behaviour… I'm certain I made the right choice. There's stuff like that going on in here… my family is gonna be worried. My mum is gonna be worried…I don't wanna worry about that. My mum and family worries every day. I want to get somewhere I can chill out and get stuff done. Not worry about guys coming down with suicide vests trying to stab me. Seg is the best option for me. Try to ride it out. Try to change. Hopefully get to a D-Cat. Try to progress. (Ernest)

Charlie explained that his understanding of protection changed over time:

That brick wall is supposed to protect me from society. Now it's become the other way round. That's my safety zone. That cell protects me. When the door shuts I'm protected…I can relax a bit. I know staff have got keys, but at least I can relax a little bit.

The idea of being placed on mains wings with other prisoners was described as 'claustrophobia in reverse' for Charlie because there's 'too many possibilities'. The temporal shift in Charlie's attitude towards segregation is important, reflecting the relative malleability of motivation. In line with Long and Averill (2003, p. 23), one important dimension of solitude is the 'disengagement from the immediate demands of other people' and a more general description of privacy is the attempt to 'control the degree to which other people and institutions intrude upon one's life' (23).

An alternative reading of participants' accounts above is a pernicious form of institutionalisation and adaptation to otherwise abnormal conditions. This maladaptation may undercut prisoners long-term capacities to relate socially. However, the intense atmosphere in the prison at the time of the research strongly resembles the fears of radicalisation and violence relayed in Liebling and Straub's (2012) previous study of Whitemoor. In that study the authors described a time period characterised by the 'presence of an omnipresent but "diffuse threat"' and an atmosphere of 'generalised suspicion and mistrust'(17):

> This fear was abstract (but a number of incidents, at Whitemoor and elsewhere, gave it edge). This meant constant staff vigilance as to any information that could be useful in preventing expected attacks, resulting in stress and tension, and obvious relief when 'key players' were moved elsewhere (Liebling & Straub, 2012, p. 17).

In this kind of context, the risk of long-term maladaptation and institutionalisation cannot be discounted but rather is subsumed to more immanent safety concerns. In this sense, 'seeking' isolation, or to revisit Atkinson and Flint's conceptual language, 'gating' and 'walling' oneself away appears a practical response in the face of both imagined and real risks, though not a complete negation of risk *per se*.

Developing Insight and Discipline

> The block breaks down the sentence a lot. Without seg it can be boring on the wing. Here you step back from it and assess.
> (Kadeem)

A second motive for moving to segregation was the pursuit of personal insight and discipline. Kadeem described isolation as a kind of psychological reset after which 'you come out fresh' and said: 'if I could come back to the seg every two months I would do it'. The particular appeal for Kadeem was being 'away from distractions' like TV and oversleeping on the wing that numbed and impeded development. In line with this, Long and Averill (2003, p. 23) explain that solitude wards off 'the potential perils of overstimulation'. Ernest stated that he is 'putting things to use' in Segregation, and described a more focused engagement with time. A number of prisoners engaged in disciplined, but immersive daily routines, including: reading, writing, washing, praying, exercising, painting and meditative reflection. This resonates with O'Donnell's (2014) explanation of 'raptness' as one of the various ways in which isolated prisoners learn to 'tame' time. Raptness is described as absorption in an activity that results in 'truncating duration and investing time with meaning' (2014, p. 226).

Having a regular and predictable rhythm to their routines was grounding for participants, suspending some of the risks of living on the mains wings. Hector explained: 'I've worked on myself without having to watch over my shoulder, having to watch my behaviour around other people'. It was not only the absence of particular individuals that helped instil a relative sense of safety and discipline, as Lenny stated: 'There's no temptations down the block…there's no drugs'. Having relatively quiet, extended time without interruptions, could be soothing and stabilising: 'It calms the soul…it stops me from being led by dark forces over God' (Hector). Sparks et al. (1996, p. 75) explain that while a rigid routine can be a source of 'deadening tedium', it can also be extremely 'reassuring and consoling', creating a reality that is 'sufficiently predictable and solid for us to be able to act capably within it'.

6 Motivation for Segregation 169

Living temporarily in segregation, then, ironically *opened* space for reflection. This included an opportunity to take stock of the current situation and set priorities: 'There's time to think about the important things…I'm planning for Mother's day' (Lenny). But it also included developing insights about particular emotions: 'Sometimes I'll be in my cell and I think why do I get angry so quick?' (Barack). And reflections on the institution, people and processes: 'I've had loads of time to reflect and see how prison works. See how people work'(Ernest). Hector explained that reading fiction 'helps to bring sense to the world'. For some, solitude presents and facilitates spiritual insights: 'when I'm silent it opens my thought processes and a channel to God' (Charlie). In this language, *brief* visits to segregation could resemble monastic retreats. However, gleaning insights was not always comfortable:

> It hurts me sometimes though… I see the badness and see the evil. I see the situation I'm in. And I see the sad…I feel sorry. This is our own Sodom and Gomorrah…sometimes it's hard to find hope in these places…because there's so much loss of hope, pride and respect…there's no truth. Everyone lies in here. We've lied to ourselves, to our families…we've got violence in common. (Charlie)

Reflecting on personal feelings and emotions is not a straightforward process, but such insight is further complicated by the kind of chaotic and tense 'social' areas of the prison described earlier in the chapter. Aside from the fact that solitude physically removes the individual from others, it also alleviates the psychological weight of identity markers.

> The people we see and the places we frequent reinforce our identities… by extracting us from our customary social and physical contexts (or at least altering our experience of them), solitude facilitates self-examination, reconceptualization of the self, and coming to terms with change. (Long & Averill, 2003, p. 26).

Self-work requires a certain kind of different psychological space to flourish. While segregation units are far from idealised 'retreat' settings, participants may be able to forge new insights and cultivate aspects of

170   B. Laws

their character because of the change of context. Whereas the first motivation was negatively framed, in that it involved moving away from something toxic, this involved moving towards something generative.

Frustration and Movement

> I won't live under no regime. I'm not living under your regime.
> (Gill)

A common motivation for seeking out segregation was to express frustration with the establishment and to forge change.

> I've been pushed into this situation. I've been in this jail for 4 years… I've explained to the officers I've done my courses…There's people who get caught with phones and get shipped out…do you want us to act out to get a ship out? (Barack)

Barack conveys the desperation and stasis of being a Cat-B prisoner in a Cat-A establishment: 'this jail is not made for prisoners like me'. But he argued that the formal channels to express this frustration were unreliable and inefficient. Fred similarly felt that the lack of procedural fairness was a major irritant:

> They speak to you and then shut the door…for me…I have to threaten or do something…I'd do everything the right way, and do apps, but when they keep mugging you off that's when I switch. They say "what you do that for", I say "well I was trying to do it in the right manner". (Fred)

Some prisoners explained that displaying threatening behaviours towards staff, issuing ultimatums ('If I don't get my RC1 [sentence progression] I have to act'—Barak), or creating chaos by jumping on the netting were viable routes to segregation and, secondly, increased the likelihood of getting a 'ship out' to another prison. There are strong connections here with Shalev and Edgar's account of prisoners who orchestrated their segregation (2015):

The segregation cell became a negotiated space. By occupying a cell, the prisoner put pressure on managers to meet their objectives. Despite the hardships and potentially negative health effects of segregation and the negative implications of having segregation on their record, some prisoners believed that occupying a segregation cell would be an effective tool for gaining a transfer or some other concession. (22)

By acting out, then, some prisoners stated that they actually received enhanced attention and arguably progression—though a better word might be *movement*—in their penal journey. Movement is more apposite as 'horizonal' transfers to similar prison establishments (in the same security category) did not, at least on the surface, constitute sentence progression. But there could be less obvious benefits from transferring around the high security estate, including: increased proximity to home, to friends and family, and being reunited with preferred prisoner groups. One prisoner suggested that institutional indifference and the general sluggishness of prison bureaucracy, could be inverted to their advantage. In theory, spending time in multiple segregation units and prisons should disadvantage prisoners, but in practice officers and staff did not always have time to update and read prisoners' records. If prisoners 'span the wheel' often enough by frequenting multiple establishments they could end up in a more favourable circumstance.

Using segregation to vent frustration was not a straightforward process and sometimes it amplified rather than alleviated pressure. Two participants explained their willingness to cooperate with staff and return to the main wings only to be denied: 'I've asked to relocate and they won't let me' (Jamie); 'I'm willing to locate and now I'm being punished for nothing' (Kadeem). Jamie felt he was placed in an almost Kafkaesque circumstance of being held in segregation right up until his release date, which was only eight weeks away: 'They are keeping me here and then straight on to the street'. In a different sense, Lenny explained how a recent attempt to take his own life was the culmination of 'a million issues' converging together:

I found out that Frankland posted my [property] to Manchester...so I'm telling them "I'm upset and I don't want to be here"...the officer says "I'll put your phone numbers on your pin[2] tomorrow and look into your Prop"...So I'm freezing in my cell, with ripped blankets and old dirty sheets, the window doesn't shut, there's hairs everywhere, can't have my own food...I want a hot drink...I bit my tongue...I was upset at every-thing...and then it was the tip of the iceberg. The phone numbers were not even on my Pin. I said "you've just broke my back boss, thin mattress, no vapes, no phone calls, I'm finished boss". I ligatured. It's over big big things...there's loads of things going on.

The wide-ranging nature of Lenny's frustration reaffirms the impor-tance of the argument set-out above about situating prisoner's testimo-nies in a broader context. Lenny's troubles are deeply rooted, clearly exacerbated by his current segregation and treatment but not wholly *caused* by it. That frustrated prisoners are motivated to seek out segrega-tion does not mean that strategy is always effective, for some it serves only to exacerbate and accumulate their pain. To revisit the nature of motiva-tion, the other main strand of this chapter's argument, Charlie explained that his use of isolation and silence changed over time: 'My silence started as a way to ignore them. A way to frustrate them'. But over the course of many years Charlie explains that silence 'became creative...now when I'm silent it opens my thought processes.' Motivations for isolation and segregation are transient and non-linear.

Taken together, the kind of aggression and violence that prisoners used to orchestrate their segregation is strongly reminiscent of Fromm's (1964) account of compensatory violence, where: 'Such aggressive behaviour constitutes an attempt, although often a futile one, to attain the frus-trated aim through the use of violence' (18). Importantly, Fromm contin-ues, there is a sense of generativity in this kind of violence, because 'it is clearly an aggression in the service of life, and not one for the sake of destruction' (18).

---

[2] Prisoners are granted access to a limited number of phone-numbers by using a personal pin code. These numbers have to be formally approved and processed by staff in advance of their phone calls.

Barometers and Prisons without Segregation Units

At the front and centre of their closing set of policy recommendations Shalev and Edgar (2015) argue that: 'The number of prisoners who engineer a move to segregation should be seen by managers as an important barometer of conditions on normal location and they should target efforts to improve treatment for all prisoners accordingly' (137). Further, in a later publication, Shalev (2018) elaborates:

> That a sizeable number of prisoners are seeking out segregation, with its austere conditions and impoverished regime, seems to me to be a clear marker of a system under pressure. It is not an argument for segregation as a force for good, nor does it suggest that segregation is harmless. To recognise that segregation is a place of refuge for some, must surely be an indictment of conditions in the general prison population. (11)

In light of these circumstances, a number of prisoners may orchestrate segregation as 'a lesser of two evils' (Shalev, 2018, p. 13). This article strongly aligns with many of these sentiments and has attempted to further understanding in this area by expanding accounts of various motivations for segregation. In general, the relationship between segregation and the wider prison quarters—or wider experiences of criminal justice for that matter—tends to be overlooked in favour of a detailed, and sometimes myopic, discussion of the effects of solitary confinement. In one sense, then, this chapter attempts to follow O'Donnell's (2014) lead in adding nuance to debates about effects. For a meaningful discussion of effects, the broader context of prisoners' lives is essential. Participants' accounts of segregation did not exist in a vacuum, their life stories are rich and complicated as was their decision-making process. Many of the interview discussions were as much about the overall conditions and events that *led to segregation* as they were about *current* conditions and effects. The fear and uncertainty surrounding radicalisation that accompanied the three high-profile violent events described in the methods section was crucial. The long-standing tensions relating to Muslim gangs and concomitant pressures to convert, well known to the prison, had seemingly peaked. Every interview included at least some discussion of these events. With this background in mind, this chapter has argued that prisoners' motivations are layered, complicated and temporal. Prisoners rarely espoused linear motives for orchestrating segregation nor were they triumphant about finding ways to leverage the institution in this manner. Their actions often felt like acts of desperation rather than opportunism.

There are some important limits on these findings. First, around a third of prisoners in the sample did not want to be in segregation. For them, segregation could not be said to be a lesser evil and the analytical approach developed above does not fully describe their experience. Further, it is hard to know what views would be articulated by the two men who declined to be interviewed. Clearly, the proportion of prisoners seeking out segregation will undoubtedly fluctuate from sample to sample. Yet, even in situations where this number is low, this approach can make an indispensable contribution to understanding segregation use and conditions within a particular establishment.

Second, there are lingering questions about institutionalisation. One way to frame this problem is in terms of a toxic combination of acute and chronic stress. While prisoners who orchestrated segregation may temporarily escape the reality of acutely stressful events they are perhaps subject to more insidious ongoing damage in segregation that is harder to articulate and measure. According to Gabor Maté (2003, p. 35):

> Acute stress is the immediate, short-term body response to threat. Chronic stress is the activation of the stress mechanisms over long periods of time when a person is exposed to stressors that cannot be escaped either because she does not recognize them or because she has no control over them.

As the analysis above attempted to emphasise, the prisoners who said they benefitted from some aspects of segregation typically described short rather than prolonged time periods. Long term 'seg dwellers', to use the prison argot, appeared to be psychologically troubled. One prisoner produced artwork that showed distorted faces appearing out of his cell walls, and eyes peering through his key-hole. That some prisoners choose segregation is an indictment of the social world of the prison rather than a celebration of their isolation experiences. Choosing the lesser evil, then,

6 Motivation for Segregation   175

does not negate the fact that damage can still be inflicted. But this point is sometimes inverted in the solitary confinement literature with potentially damaging consequences. That is, prisoner pain is ubiquitously attributed to segregation alone, and recast the cause and compounder of damage to the soul, body and psyche. While this kind of analysis is viable in interpreting experiences of long-term prisoners in supermax prisons it makes far less sense in the context of jurisdictions where the internal prison architecture is less severe, and where prisoners routinely move through numerous different living spaces.

As a closing companion argument, our research team recently wrote about hope in the context of a particularly high-performing prison (Liebling, Laws and Lieber et al., 2019). For current purposes, it is particularly intriguing that that prison did not have a segregation unit. A number of important factors were identified in that chapter that align strongly with the main argument set out here. That prison had 'a deep community ethos, built on strong relationships and a sincere belief in personal transformation' (108) and sentence progression. We discovered a senior management team that was 'deeply invested in the personal development of prisoners' (110) and who 'knew a considerable amount about individual prisoners' backgrounds and circumstances' (111). There was a strong sense of procedural justice and prisoners themselves 'had a "voice" in the prison, sitting on committees and attending meetings' (111) and overall they said they felt 'trusted, cared for, and recognised as persons of value' (112). The broader investment by management 'upstream', to recall Richard Vince's language, allowed the prison to flourish without relying on segregation as a management tool. The main point here, then, is that we learn much about the need—or lack of need—for segregation units by understanding the broader prison conditions that drive prisoners towards isolation. This understanding can help to situate calls from scholars and human rights activists to end segregation practices by placing them in the context of wider experiences of imprisonment.

References

Atkinson, R., & Flint, J. (2004). Fortress UK? Gated communities, the spatial revolt of the elites and time–space trajectories of segregation. *Housing Studies, 19*(6), 875–892.

Casella, J., Ridgeway, J., & Shourd, S. (2016). *Hell is a very small place: Voices from solitary confinement.* New York Press.

Clements, C. B., Althouse, R., Ax, R. K., Magaletta, P. R., Fagan, T. J., & Wormith, J. S. (2007). Systemic issues and correctional outcomes: Expanding the scope of correctional psychology. *Criminal Justice and Behavior, 34*(7), 919–932.

Fromm, E. (1964). *The Heart of Man. American Mental Health Foundation.*

Gendreau, P., & Bonta, J. (1984). Solitary confinement is not cruel and unusual punishment: People sometimes are. *Canadian Journal of Criminology, 26*(4), 467–478.

Gendreau, P., & Labrecque, R. M. (2018). The effects of administrative segregation. In *The Oxford handbook of prisons and imprisonment* (p. 340). Oxford University Press.

Gendreau, P., & Theriault, Y. (2011). *Bibliotherapy for cynics revisited: Commentary on a one year longitudinal study of the psychological effects of administrative segregation.* Corrections and Mental Health: An Update of the National Institute of Corrections.

Grassian, S. (1983). Psychopathological effects of solitary confinement. *American Journal of Psychiatry, 140*(11), 1450–1454.

Haney, C. (2012). Prison effects in the era of mass incarceration. *The Prison Journal,* 0032885512448604.

Haney, C. (2018). The psychological effects of solitary confinement: A systematic critique. *Crime and Justice, 47*(1), 365–416.

Jackson, M. (1983). *Prisoners of isolation: Solitary confinement in Canada.* University of Toronto Press.

Kupers, T. (2008). Prison and the decimation of pro-social life skills. In A. Ojeda (Ed.), *Psychological torture: Phenomenology, psychiatry, neurobiology and ethics: Vol. 5.* Trauma and disaster and psychology (G. Reyes, Series Ed.). Praeger.

Laws, B., & Crewe, B. (2016). Emotion regulation among male prisoners. *Theoretical Criminology, 20*(4), 529–547. https://doi.org/10.1177/13624806 15622532

Laws, B. (2019). The return of the suppressed: Exploring how emotional suppression reappears as violence and pain among male and female prisoners. *Punishment & Society, 21*(5), 560–577.

Liebling, A., & Straub, C. (2012). Identity challenges and the risks of radicalisation in high security custody. *Prison Service Journal, 203*, 15–22.

Liebling, A., Laws, B., Lieber, E., Auty, K., Schmidt, B. E., Crewe, B., ... & Morey, M. (2019). Are hope and possibility achievable in prison?. *The Howard Journal of Crime and Justice, 58*(1), 104–126.

Long, C. R., & Averill, J. R. (2003). Solitude: An exploration of benefits of being alone. *Journal for the Theory of Social Behaviour, 33*(1), 21–44.

Maté, G. (2003). *When the body says no: Exploring the stress disease connection.* Wiley & Sons.

Morgan, R. D., Gendreau, P., Smith, P., Gray, A. L., Labrecque, R. M., MacLean, N., Van Horn, S. A., Bolanos, A. D., Batastini, A. B., & Mills, J. F. (2016). Quantitative syntheses of the effects of administrative segregation on inmates' well-being. *Psychology, Public Policy, and Law, 22*(4), 439.

O'Donnell, I. (2014). *Prisoners, solitude, and time.* Oxford University Press.

O'Keefe, M. L., Klebe, K. J., Stucker, A., Sturm, K. and Leggett, W. (2010). *One Year Longitudinal Study of the Psychological Effects of Administrative Segregation.* Colorado Department of Corrections, Office of Planning and Analysis.

Pendergrass, T., & Hoke, M., eds. (2018). *Six by Ten: Stories from Solitary.* Haymarket Books.

Shalev, S., & Edgar, K. (2015). Deep custody: Segregation units and close supervision centres in England and Wales. *London: Conquest Litho, 93*, 14.

Shalev, S. (2018). Can any good come out of isolation? Probably not. *Prison Service Journal, 236*, 11–16.

Smith, P. S. (2006). The effects of solitary confinement on prison inmates: A brief history and review of the literature. *Crime and Justice, 34*(1), 441–528.

Smith, C. (2015). *To flourish or destruct: A personalist theory of human goods, motivations, failure, and evil.* University of Chicago Press.

Sparks, R., Bottoms, A., & Hay, W. (1996). *Prisons and the Problem of Order.* Clarendon Press.

Suedfeld, P., Ramirez, C., Deaton, J., & Baker-Brown, G. (1982). Reactions and attributes of prisoners in solitary confinement. *Criminal Justice and Behavior, 9*(3), 303–340.

Valera, P., & Kates-Benman, C. L. (2016). Exploring the use of special housing units by men released from New York correctional facilities: A small mixed-methods study. *American Journal of Men's Health, 10*(6), 466–473.

Vince, R. (2018). Segregation—Creating a new norm. *Prison Service Journal, 236*, 17–26.

Wormith, J. S. (1984). The controversy over the effects of long-term incarceration. *Canadian Journal of Criminology, 26*, 423.

7

The Body and Solitary Confinement

There is something about the exclusion of other living beings from the space we inhabit and the absence of even the possibility of touching or being touched by another that threatens to unhinge us.
—*Guenther* (Solitary confinement: Social death and its afterlives. *University of Minnesota Press, 2013: 145)*

One salient feature of segregation units is disembodiment. Prisoners in solitary confinement spend vast quantities of their day 'deprived from the bodily presence of others' (Guenther, 2013: vii); interaction with officers is infrequent and often occurs behind a door or screen; there is a notable absence of warm human touch and prosocial interaction. Indeed, when bodies do come into contact this is often hard-edged, taking the shape of violence or frisking prisoners for contraband—an action that binds touch with suspicion. The body in solitary confinement is prone to become more sedentary. What happens to *a body* under these conditions, and what can understanding the body tell us about prisoner emotions? This final substantive chapter sets out a framework of analysis that attempts to address these questions.

© The Author(s), under exclusive license to Springer Nature Switzerland AG 2022   **179**
B. Laws, *Caged Emotions*, Palgrave Studies in Prisons and Penology,
https://doi.org/10.1007/978-3-030-96083-4_7

The significance of the body is clearly recognised by scholars of imprisonment. Foucault's (1979) development of Bentham's panopticon is apposite. Foucault suggested that the construction of the panopticon prison design—which enabled prisoners to be inspected 'during every instance of time' (Bentham, 1791: 3)—would produce 'docile bodies' (1979). As Bosworth and Kaufman (2012: 195) surmise: 'For Foucault, the state's power to punish gets expressed on and through the physical body, whether it is tarred and feathered, incarcerated, or electronically tagged. The sociology of punishment is in this sense about bodies'. In his book *Asylums*, Erving Goffman (1961) describes various rituals of entry during the detailed admissions process of closed institutions, which include:

> taking a life history, photographing, weighing, fingerprinting, assigning numbers, searching, listing personal possessions for storage, undressing, bathing, disinfecting, haircutting, issuing institutional clothing, instructing as to rules, and assigning to quarters. Admission procedures might better be called "trimming" or "programming" because in thus being squared away the new arrival allows himself to be shaped and coded into an object that can be fed into the administrative machinery of the establishment, to be worked on smoothly by routine operations. (16)

Clearly, many of these protocols constituted attempts to measure and mould the body in explicit ways. More recently, the communicative nature of imprisoned bodies has been recognised (see Chamberlen, 2018; Moran, 2014). Crewe et al. (2014) describe marks on the body in prison as a kind of bridge between the person and the social: 'Acts of self-harm occurred in private, but left scars that were publicly visible' (66). Feldman (1991: 156) argues that 'under hierarchical observation [the prisoner] is manipulated by his body's visibility; the body is thereby transformed into a text to be read by authoritative observers'. The idea that the prisoner body can be 'read' also applies to release and the bodily inscriptions prisoners 'take' with them such as rotten teeth. As Moran (2014: 38) puts it: 'inscriptions of incarceration thus become corporeal markers of imprisonment, blurring the boundary between 'outside' and 'inside' the prison and extending carceral control through stigmatisation'. Taken together, these accounts explain how institutional practices mark the body. But, as a number of the authors cited above recognise, the body is not merely a passive receptacle to be inscribed.

Bodies are acted on, but they also *enact*. Bodies are at once receivers and transmitters of information (Lock, 1993), recipients of cultural imprints and 'self-developable means' for shaping the world (Asad, 1997: 47). In the context of prisons research, Chamberlen has gone furthest in balancing these mutually important perspectives, considering: 'The body as an event, active and reactive to its social environment' (2018: 143). Liebling (2014) recognises that this holds true for prison researchers too, who can strive to use their bodies actively for 'detecting cues, recognizing danger, sensing tension, or sharing frustration' (483)—though she acknowledged that this is complex territory. But less has been said about the prisoner body as a site of analysis in the context of solitary confinement. There are two notable exceptions. First is Brian Keenan's (1992) personal testimony of his four years as a hostage in Beirut in torturous conditions. What is distinctive about Keenan's account is the extended description of his bodily sensations and reactions to solitary confinement and torture. These insights influence the analytical framework developed below. Second, Guenther's (2013) monograph explicitly addresses the various ways in which solitary confinement can be said to 'unhinge' prisoners from their normal bodily relations with themselves and others. More attention will be paid here to the *range* of bodily adaptations that prisoners establish even in the face of such challenging conditions. That is, because in Guenther's account the body is cast as 'a root and a vehicle for [the] open-ended exploration of the world' exploration is essentially obliterated entirely by solitary confinement. This article sets out to develop these existing orientations by considering various other forms of body work and (mal)adaptation in the face of challenging conditions *beyond* obliteration.

More specifically, this involves a detailed discussion of three different themes. First, the chapter considers *damaged bodies* that bear the scars and traumas of imprisonment one the one hand, but that learn to violently strike back on the other. Second, it describes various methods of *bodily maintenance* such as exercise, diet, cleanliness, and dirty protest in the context of a highly restricted regime. Third, attention is paid towards what I have termed the *Spiritual body*, which considers the body as a vehicle for transcendence and escape. After setting out this framework, I attempt to establish connections between the body and prisoner emotions. Given that 'emotions use the body as their theatre' (Damasio, 1999: 51), the argument attempts to draw wider connections with emotions in prison (see Crewe et al., 2014; Laws & Crewe, 2016; Laws, 2019) set out in Part 1 of the book. Second, the implications of disembodiment are considered because the challenges posed to forming staff-prisoner relationships in this context is pronounced.

Damaged Bodies

Chamberlen's argument that prisoners experience captivity both '*on*' and '*through*' their body' (2018: 141–142 emphasis in original) is particularly apposite when thinking about the potential damage of solitary confinement. Keenan (1992) described feeling 'crucifying despair' during his prolonged periods of isolation. This stark phrase draws a specific connection between psychological turmoil and bodily pain. A number of the men in the study related that they had received numerous 'lumps and bumps' (Lenny) from altercations with officers and prisoners over the years. These injuries were often severe and traumatic. Gill said that officers had 'dropped me, split open my lip and knocked out my tooth and brought me to the block'. Arnie shared that the event that led him to segregation was when prisoners attacked him from behind and 'sliced my face, and there was blood all over'. Many prisoners showed examples of burns, cuts and breaks on their bodies during the interviews. Charlie's account included a litany of such graphic attacks on his body:

> I've been in the system, stabbed 9 times, I've been tortured, I've been burned, I've got scars all over me. Stab wounds all over… All over my arms… I've got plates and screws in my body…they've snapped my tibia and fibia…all my knuckles and all my fingers…they've snapped the fucking lot.

7 The Body and Solitary Confinement   183

Goffman (1961) describes how prisoners face anxieties of *defacement* and *disfigurement*. The former 'comes from being stripped of one's identity kit' and the latter 'comes from direct and permanent mutilations of the body' (21). Some prisoners in this study did not need to articulate their pain in words. Upon opening the cell viewing flap, one man presented with deep purple 'sleeves' of self-harm scars running down both of his arms. These visual markers of damage were unmissable; pain was being worn on the body. However, Asad's (1997: 42) observation that the body is both a 'medium of voluntary and involuntary communication' is relevant here. The wounded body raises all kinds of reactions and interpretations from staff ranging from empathy and care to hostility, suspicion and mistrust.

Prisoners' relationships to their scars and cuts was sometimes complex. As established in previous research (see for example Chamberlen, 2018; Laws & Crewe, 2016), some explained that self-harm was a 'source of relief' and a way of forging a 'deeper connection' with a lost part of oneself (Charlie, both quotations). Arnie noted that cutting was a way of 'dealing with pain'. Arnie articulated his active relationship with his scars and self-harm:

Arnie: I fucking self-harm myself…these are tattoos. These are tattoos to me. I haven't got any actual tattoos on my body but I've got hundreds of scars.
B: *Your body tells a story in that way?*
Arnie: Fucking hell mate 100 per cent…like I say mate…scars on top of my head mate…they all tell a story mate, and they all have a meaning, the all have a meaning.

Arnie wrote song lyrics in which a number of lines referenced damage and his 'HMP stitches'. At one level, these sentiments could be seen as attempts at integration and meaning making. In line with Chamberlen (2018, 179), scars on prisoners' bodies could 'act as enduring reminders of their painful experiences and as reflections of their sense of self'. The evocation of the idea that scars tell stories aligns with another point Chamberlen notes: scars have a kind of temporality that marks the passing of time. However, for the men in this study the experience of damage was not an historical artefact that could be tidied away. Their bodies continued to unsettle them in the present. According to Bessel Van der Kolk (2014), the principal feature of trauma is feeling unsafe in one's own body, which often reacts as if past danger is still ongoing. This can be evidenced through states of hypervigilance, numbness, extreme irritability, dread, uncomfortable emotions and sensations such as heartbreak and gut wrench. In van der Kolk's words: 'The past is alive in form of gnawing interior discomfort'. Damage is something that most prisoners lived with *through* their bodies in the present moment. Gill, who was still in pain from a violent altercation, spent the majority of a two-hour interview repeating and restating one traumatic incident. He explained that officers had hurt him while we was trying to break up a fight between two prisoners. As Leder (2016: 30) comments, pain can 'poison the "now" with suffering'. Furthermore, living in an environment that could not guarantee physical safety exacerbated fears about future assaults.

Another prisoner was observed in a state of complete overwhelm, crying and shaking behind his door with saliva in his beard from his remonstrations. He had been trying to explain to officers, the seemingly small issue that he had been underpaid for work he had completed in his cell. His desperation was visible and visceral. Herman (1992: 36) explains that 'irritability and explosively aggressive behaviour' represent a shattered fight/flight response and are the hallmarks of severely traumatised men. Such episodes can leave prisoners feeling embarrassed or even betrayed by their bodies. In pain 'the body surfaces as strangely other' (Leder, 2016: 16). Brian Keenan's (1992: 67) account of his captivity in Beruit is relevant here:

> For many days now I have tried to scream, but nothing will come out of me. No sound, no noise, nothing. Yet I try to force this scream…My own words becoming bricks and stones that bruise me. I have been lifted up and emptied out.

Experiencing damage and pain creates internal disconnection. It also increased the probability that prisoners would feel external frustration and strike back. Feldman (1991), writing about political prisoners in solitary confinement in Northern Ireland, explains how they learned to

7 The Body and Solitary Confinement   185

'deploy their bodies like weapons' (79). In this vein, Charlie outlined a hardening process that he had absorbed through his treatment:

> When they tell me I have to come out of my cell and I say no…well eventually they will use violence to get me out and remove me from the cell. If I say to somebody "move to there from there" and they say "no"…and if I then use force to put them there I am an animal I am a monster. If I need something, I've learned to take it by force. It's not democracy what [staff] use, it's dictatorship. They are violent by what they do.

Most participants in the study could articulate multiple instances of physical altercations with officers and other prisoners throughout their sentences, often connecting these experiences to feelings of hurt: both physical and psychological. Winlow and Hall (2009: 291) claim that for persistently violent men 'backing away from physical conflict can generate intense feelings of humiliation and regret', and that by striking first they avoid the 'risk that the new event will become a time-portal through which the humiliating historical tragedy will repeat itself' (2009: 297–298). On one morning, an officer was observed limping and out of breath after restraining a prisoner who had attacked staff. For current purposes, the main point is the need to recognise various forms of *bodily dissent* (Lock, 1993), which is to argue that the body serves as 'an active forum for the expression of dissent and loss' (Lock, 1993: 141). Bodily dissent and physical violence in prison are not unique to segregation units. Numerous studies have examined the prevalence of violence in wider prison environment (see Edgar et al., 2003 for a review). However, the peculiarities of solitary confinement arguably foster conditions where the body becomes the primary site of conflict. As outlined in Feldman's (1991) study, a unique pressure of solitary confinement is the highly disembodied relations between prisoners and officers, and the subsequent risk that this can create a downward spiral of attack and counter-attack. Further, Haney (2008) explains that the language used to describe segregated men such as 'the worst of the worst' and ultra-hardened prisoners risks creating a toxic atmosphere where inhabitants are seen as 'fundamentally "other"'. This dehumanises, degrades, and demonises segregated prisoners as essentially different, even from other prisoners. It provides an immediate, intuitive, and unassailable rationale for the added punishment, extraordinary control, and severe deprivation that prevail in supermax' (Haney, 2008: 963). The segregated prisoners' body is shrouded in an kind of mythology where it is seen as somehow 'impervious to the pains of imprisonment' and 'constitutionally more capable of standing up to the harshness of life' (Haney, 2008: 963). In a number of ways, then, segregated prisoners wear their punishment on their bodies and (re) enact damage through their bodies.

Maintaining the Body

In response to the challenging living conditions they faced, a number of prisoners articulated ways in which they tried to develop and maintain their bodies. Chamberlen (2018) elucidates various strategies of body care:

> Coping within such punitive and debilitating settings requires an active awareness of and exercise of care towards one's body. Protecting the body in this sense acts not only as a resistance to the system of confinement, but also as a pragmatic means of survival. (160)

One of the primary ways in which body care was realised in segregation was through exercise and diet. Because of the spatial limitations of segregation it was particularly important to embrace some form of human movement: 'you don't want to be in bed all day' (Ernest) or be 'sitting down all the time' (Hector). Ernest unscored the importance of 'keeping your bones active and your blood flowing'. In comparison with other areas of the prison, segregation workout routines were relatively modest: 'I do bits and bobs…a little walk and jog gets the blood moving' (Ernest); 'It does help to do a few push ups. To elevate the pulse' (Hector); 'I just want to keep loose and stay healthy' (Arnie).

There appeared to be a distinction between the function of segregation exercise and typical accounts of prison gyms away from segregation. For example, De Viggiani (2012: 278) describes the prison gym as a site of 'competitive oneupmanship' where prisoners are largely preoccupied with 'the use of weights to build muscle bulk'. As Crewe et al. (2014) put it, the gym is a place where 'strength could be built and demonstrated'. Prisoners in segregation were more likely to emphasise the stress relieving properties of exercise. 'I'm not trying to get big. I do cardio and I do it for my mind state, it releases stress' (Barak). These differences could be partly attributed to the limits on access to equipment and free weights that facilitate muscle hypotrophy. However, it seemed significant that in segregation prisoners spent far less time exercising in the visual line of, or in close proximity to, other prisoners. Omar explained feeling fatigue from the rigors of building up one's body: 'I'm resting from the gym…mentally I'm prepared for rest. It was all about muscle mass, it came naturally on the wing.'

The comments about exercise in segregation placed emphasis on emotional control and cardiovascular routines. Prisoners were often observed jogging around the small concrete yards, liberating their bodies rather than physically building themselves up. Some prisoners felt that the segregation diet was precisely calculated to induce a kind of vegetative stage: 'They try and pad you up with carbs—8 slices of bread a meal' (Jamie). Arnie shared this concern: 'Got more of a choice out there [on the wing]…in here, they all try to fatten you up'. These fears give a different accent to Crewe's (2011a) point that imprisonment is experienced as a kind of 'weight'. The burden of an overweight body raises fears that imprisonment is changing one's identity irreversibly and that personal virility is being syphoned. Maintaining the body in segregation, then, involved trying to take some agency over diet in the context of a highly restrictive set of food choices: 'On here you can't cook properly' (Fred). While in principle some segregated prisoners still had access to their canteen—some had it removed as a punishment—this relied on having accessible personal funds, as opposed to a prison job to finance extra food. There were no shared cooking facilities to create alternative dishes on the unit. On a number of occasions prisoners were observed rejecting the food options brought to their doors, sending part or whole meals away. Chamberlen (2018) argues that the emotional distress of a prison sentence can result in the loss of appetite; another clear way in which imprisonment can be said to directly damage the body. But, viewed in a different way, the conscious choice to refuse food was *agentic*. It communicated dissatisfaction to officers and provided a reliable channel to do so given that officers had to prepare and present food multiple times a day. As Keenan (1992) argues, rejecting food returns to the prisoner 'the full sanction of his own life and of his own will' (55). Much has been said about the ideological significance of hunger strikes employed by those interned in Northern Ireland, 'where the body of the dying hunger striker exerted a determining political presence that exceeded the structures of confinement' (Feldman, 1991: 198). Outside of the political dimensions of food refusal however, there were direct personal benefits. Ibrahim explained the various ways in which he felt 'fasting was good for the body'. Fasting could open space for personal reflection and insight about addictions and relationships—not only to food but also about emotions and faith. As Charlie reflects:

> You appreciate food more. You appreciate your body more. You feel your body needing something…feel it inside you. I don't crave… I feel that pull when I talk to God… You learn self-restraint.

Fasting cultivated a kind of bodily discipline that could be an indispensable aid in coping with the rigors of segregation. The final way in which prisoners tried to maintain the body was through defending against various forms of contamination: both physical and psychological; perceived and actual. Carlen (1998: 83) notes that imprisonment can create an 'unspeakable, and always corrosive, fear of pollution'. In Keenan's (1992) account physical and psychological pollutants are woven together in a way that is mutually reinforcing:

> I am reduced to sleeping in the smell of my own filth. Excrement, sweat, the perspiration of a body and a mind passing through waves of desperation. All of everything is in this room. I am breaking out of myself, urges, ideas, emotions in turmoil are wrenched up and out from me; as with a sickness when nothing can be held down. (67)

As Goffman (1961: 55) identifies: 'the most obvious type of contaminative exposure is the directly physical kind—the besmearing and defiling of the body or of other objects closely identified with the self'. Indeed, a number of prisoners in this study complained about the intrusion of

7 The Body and Solitary Confinement   189

dirt or filth: either they had recently been moved into unclean cells or explained the challenges of staying clean in small living spaces with limited cleaning materials. The regular turnover and movement of prisoners onto segregation units created challenges to personal hygiene that did not exist on prison wings. First, on the wing prisoners may be able to live in and maintain the same cell for extended periods of time. Second, the prevalence of dirty protest is less frequent on the wing. Barak emphasised the importance of washing in his daily routine:

Barak: Trust me…I'm in the shower for at least half an hour.
B: *You like the hot water?*
Barak: I just love showers…it's like in a sauna…it proper smokes.

Though it is not explicit in Barak's account that 'washing [constitutes] a form of coping and survival' (Chamberlen, 2018: 160), there did seem to be an important *cleansing* function at work as implied by the relaxing and purifying function of a sauna. After receiving a brutal beating from officers, Keenan (1992) explains: 'As I stood in the shower, languishing in the steam, I washed him away. I washed myself clean of his brutality and of his putrid sickness.' In a different sense, the regular washing and ablution practices that are deeply woven into Islam, and more metaphorically integrated into Christianity ('washing away sins' etc), fused cleanliness and spirituality together for prisoners in segregation. More will be said about the role of 'embodied faith' in the following section.

Some forms of intrusion were more sensorial and emotional rather than immediate physical pollutants that directly attack the body. For example, hearing the distress, altercations, or noise of other prisoners could be particularly unsettling. On some occasions prisoners targeted each other in ways that also affected bystanders. During one of the interviews, a prisoner in a cell 10 meters from the interview room was loudly insulting another man (calling him a 'screw boy'). This sound reverberated around the unit for at least fifteen minutes. The repetition of the words and intensity of the noise was jarring, an interpretation which was validated by other prisoners on the unit who were shouting 'shut up, shut up'. Again, Keenan's (1992) account is instructive:

It was as if their own distress was a kind of contamination running rampant around the prison. It beat around the walls of my own cell...Their despair, their fear came crashing in on me and I wanted no part of it...These were hellish days for all of us because in that silence each of us shared and partook in each other's suffering. We breathed in great lungfuls of it, and had to regurgitate the foulness of it and find some way to protect ourselves from it: in so doing, hopefully protecting those who had become engulfed in it. (170–171)

The references here to 'breathing in', and 'regurgitation' give some sense of the embodied nature of emotional distress. Indeed, the effects of trying to cope in the face of others' discomfort was extremely challenging. A few prisoners hermeneutically sealed themselves in their living spaces, using loud music as a kind of auditory cocoon, partly cancelling out the background sounds of the wing. But the sensory intrusion of dirty protest in segregation evoked particularly strong feelings and were harder to defend against.

Again, the important political dimensions of dirty protest are not the primary focus of this analysis. Rather, the emphasis here is with the visceral immediacy and embodied power of dirty protest. Throughout the duration of the study there was always at least one prisoner on the unit engaging in dirty protest: at one point there were three. The psychic dimensions of this behaviour are complex. According to Brown (2019: 47): 'Odour very concretely signals a difficulty in containing intimate aspects of the self, which...are felt to be unmanageable and 'namelessly' alien.' Brown goes on to discuss the ways in which smell can be viewed as a signal and repetition of trauma, neglect and intrusion at the hands of others often rooted in early childhood experiences. That segregation units are sites which appear to concentrate the incidence of dirty protest says much about both prior and ongoing traumatic experiences of prisoners held in them. In this respect, Guenther's (2013) thesis that extreme isolation unhinges prisoners from their bodies appears accurate, and dirty protest reflects a kind of (re)capitulation of the body.

However, without seeking to contradict this position there were other important aspects of dirty protest. Numerous officers and prisoners spoke of the ways in which the smell of urine and faeces 'hit you' as soon as you

7 The Body and Solitary Confinement 191

walked on the segregation unit. The implication that one could be metaphorically 'struck' by a smell, at sizeable distances from the offending body, recalls Feldman's (1991) point that prisoners can learn creative ways to weaponise the body. Feldman (1991: 190) explains in his study that IRA prisoners enacted a systematic *ecological revenge* on officers: 'There was no way to limit the flow of excreta, urine, or the accompanying stench into the prison short of the death of the prisoner'. Smell has powerful effects that skip over the rational mind: 'While we can avert our gaze from what we would rather not see, we are helpless and passive recipients of odours' (Brown, 2019: 39). Brown argues that to some extent 'odour speaks of the avoidance of further impingement or intrusion, functioning to keep others at a distance' (2019; 43). In a similar vein, Sidoli (1996) draws on the adaptive behaviours of skunks to describe how one boy used smell to both protect and aggressively attack. To some extent, then, prisoners who inverted the expectations of hygiene policed the boundaries of their bodies, creating distance and reducing the possibility of further harm. In this sense, dirty protest can be viewed as a roundabout way of maintaining the integrity of the body and forging a degree protective shelter and privacy in their cells. Indeed, Feldman (1991: 175) argues that by smearing faeces and urine prisoners transform their skin into a 'repellent surface of resistance' and that cells no longer existed as 'a unidimensional and totally transparent optical stage' for staff members. It was notable that the plastic transportable sanitary booths used to try and contain the fluids and odour of dirty protests in this study served, unintentionally, as an extra layer of visual shielding from the institutional gaze.

Taken together, even in the face of various unwelcome intrusions and attacks prisoners do not merely capitulate. In various ways, they attempt to maintain and cleanse, and 'develop the body's capacity and skills' (Leder, 2016: 77). As hinted, sometimes this development led them towards various forms of spiritual practices.

The Spiritual Body

In the first two sections above, the body is largely framed as the recipient/respondent to the rigors of solitary confinement and it develops outward-facing, active, responses to various threats and challenges (i.e. striking back). By contrast, an alternative embodied response is an inward turn to contemplation, meditation or spirituality.

Prior accounts in the literature have emphasised the importance of religious conversion in prison as helping prisoners to transform their life narratives and bring about identity reformulation. For example, Maruna et al. (2006) explain that:

> the conversion narrative "works" as a shame management and coping strategy in the following ways. The narrative creates a new social identity to replace the label of prisoner or criminal, imbues the experience of imprisonment with purpose and meaning, empowers the largely powerless prisoner by turning him into an agent of God, provides the prisoner with a language and framework for forgiveness, and allows a sense of control over an unknown future. (161)

Kerley and Copes (2009: 240) similarly argue that 'religious epiphanies tend to create a shift in how inmates reconcile their past and current selves. It provides a new lens for viewing their lives and allows them to reinterpret their current situation into something more positive and manageable'. However, the identity management functions of religious practice sometimes eclipse the important embodied aspects of faith. According to Carl Jung (1939: 28) the 'highest truth grows from the deepest roots of the body'; or to use Meister Eckart's words 'God is found in the heart' (1994: 10). Many prisoners in this study described such a kind of 'inward facing' relationship with the body that was highly significant, emotional, and deeply connected to their personal faith. Guenther argues that turning inwards is made more likely by the loss of possibility of 'outward' experiences:

> Even when prisoners are forced back on their own bodies and blocked from external experience of spatial depth, they may be able to retain and recover

a sense of internal depth—an "inscape" or "breathing space"—within their own bodies. (2013: 190)

A number of prisoners described secular or religious practices that clearly had embodied elements. Regular meditation practice brought a level of peace: 'Meditation yeah, meditation is like just...*calming* for me...*calming*...I often do meditation once, sometimes twice a day' (Arnie, emphasis added). Reading the Koran was a warm and connecting experience for Hector: 'my heart is open when I study. I look at it and I think...feel my heart... I feel the power of God and Allah. I've known for a long time, I feel good. In my heart.' In a similar vein, practicing Christianity was a sensory experience for Charlie: 'In different ways I hear what's needed. In different ways *I feel it*, I feel the love'. Peter explained that: 'meditating on the word of god let's it get *into your heart*' and a way from escaping the 'battlefield of the mind' (emphasis added).

Interestingly, while meditation appeared to lead to feelings of peacefulness, prisoners practicing Islam noted how it evoked a wide repertoire of emotions and affective states in them. Omar pointed out the importance of having an 'emotional connection with your faith' and explained: 'It's like a melody of feelings stir within you. It could be a happy verse. It could bring out emotions like happiness and sadness'. In a similar manner, Kadeem spoke of the dual nature of his faith and the role of fear: 'Prayer brings tranquillity and peace...hope as well. It's hope isn't it...It's fear at the same time because it stops you from doing something negative.'

The embodied nature of faith becomes apparent through particular turns of phrase used above that could be understood solely at the level of metaphor (i.e. references to 'the heart'). For example, describing his spiritual relationship with his music Arnie explained that 'it's forged in my heart...When it comes from the heart you can't go wrong. You can't go wrong when it comes from the heart.' The contention here, however, is that such phrasing indicates prisoners are attempting to convey direct embodied processes, beyond metaphor, primarily involving an affective shift in their feeling states and physiology (See Laws, 2020).

Faith-based practices instilled a range of emotional effects in prisoners' bodies, but in other ways they involved working *on the body* directly. Ibrahim spoke of the importance of practicing 'ablution before prayer' and explained how 'washing before prayer...at least 3 times a day' was a significant and ritual part of cleanliness. As Omar stated: 'purity is part of the faith'. It is possible to view ablution as an embodied purification process that led to psychological and emotional refreshment. It is this body 'work' and embodied aspect of faith, then, that forms a foundation or gateway for broader identity change outlined in previous research. As Asad (1997: 48) puts it: 'embodied practices form a precondition for varieties of religious experience'. In alignment with this view, Hector summarised: 'the body triggers [the teachings of the Koran] in the mind'. These accounts resonate with prior accounts in the literature that describe transcendence in prison.

Crewe et al. (2020) summarise that faith is important 'not just in helping prisoners to survive the present, but in some ways to transcend it, through states of meditation, philosophies of acceptance, and the possibility of seeing goodness and godliness in the otherwise profane'. There are further resonances here with the literature on the efficacy of yoga programmes in prison (see Auty et al., 2017 for a review; Karup, 2016). Though Yoga is often appropriated as a secular form of exercise Karup (2016) describes a process of transition in her study: 'Many of those who took up yoga for physical reasons—who were initially uninterested in personal development or spirituality—reported that yoga and meditation led them to become more introspective or even spiritual' (31). Taking all these accounts together, it is possible to understand a bi-directional process where faith in prison involves embodied practice, and embodied practices can pave the way to various forms of faith and meaning making. Focusing on the body can help to develop Crewe et al.'s point that faith helps some prisoners transcend the present moment. That is, looking at the embodied aspects of faith helps to understand the underlying mechanisms of transcendence processes beyond the level of narrative 'identity work'. Tuning in to one's bodily sensations and emotions could create important shifts in psychological mood and hint at the numinous. This is a more local, imminent, variety of faith similar to that described by Keenan (1992):

7 The Body and Solitary Confinement   195

In its own way our isolation had expanded the heart, not to reach out to a detached God but to find and become part of whatever 'God' might be…We had each gone through an experience that gave us the foundations of an insight into what a humanized God might be. (99)

Understanding Bodies in Conflict

Solitary confinement involves bodies in conflict. The results of this conflict can be viewed as various *contractions* and *extensions* of the body outlined above. The site of conflict is both external (clashing against officers and prisoners) and internal (navigating one's body states and emotions in confined space). At worst, the intensity and duration of living with conflict could lead to a destructive dissolution of boundaries. Some of the artwork that Charlie presented in the interview hinted at a kind of obliteration: 'The wall is screaming in that one. The face is coming out of the wall…it's like you're melting into the wall. You become part of the wall…part of the building…melting…'. The idea that prisoners could become absorbed into the very fabric of the building is indicative of an extreme form of institutionalisation. Guenther (2013: 35–36) argues that such effects occur precisely because solitary confinement 'exploits the most fundamental capacities of [prisoners'] embodied existence'. By this she means the erasure of 'constitutive relationality' with others and the 'power of co-constituting a meaningful world'—both of which become turned-in on the self in destructive ways. Put in different terms, in Guenther's thinking the body is indispensably relational, and without the continual possibility of interaction the foundations of reality are irrevocably disturbed.

Prisoners may panic and try to fight against this erasure of boundaries. Keenan (1992: 67) describes a disturbing episode in his cell where he was 'thrust suddenly into agonizing torrents of tears…I [would] crush myself against the wall to assure myself that I have a body'. Again Guenther's (2013) interpretation is stimulating here:

To bash one's hands or body against the walls of a cell is both to refuse and to confirm the enclosure of one's available space. Perhaps it is a way of emphatically marking the difference between body and cell in a situation where they have begun to merge, where the cell has become a kind of exoskeleton for the body. (183)

In prior accounts, humiliating prison practices have actively attacked and infiltrated the most personal boundaries of prisoners' bodies. In extreme, Feldman (1991) describes the practice of rectal cavity searches as 'Colon-ization'. Such debasing 'ceremonies of defilement' turn the body into 'a periphery' or 'margin of the state' rather than an independent human agent (174, all quotations). The absence of relationality and possibility for warm human touch—that is integral to solitary confinement—heightens the risk that prisoners become seen as 'fundamentally "other"' by staff and 'essentially different, even from other prisoners' (Haney, 2008: 963). Liebling (2015) highlights the importance of understanding dehumanisation through processes of "othering" and the risks of transforming prisoners into 'experienced objects' rather than 'experiencing subjects'. Again, it can be emphasised how this process works *on, and at the level of,* the body and that prisoners reel against this process of othering though not always successfully. Franz Fanon (1961), writing about slavery, describes the process by which human bodies become transformed and reconfigured into 'black flesh'. The differentiation involves a produced difference between the advanced mind of the westerner and primitive flesh of the slave. In the context of understanding torture, Scarry (1985) argues that because the torturer does not see or identify with the prisoner's pain: 'The prisoner experiences an annihilating negation so hugely felt throughout his own body' (36). Keenan's (1992) testimony is littered with references to feeling like 'a bag of flesh and scrape, a heap of offal tossed unwanted' (67); 'unclean and untouchable' (131); 'rancid meat to be kicked and beaten'(195); and 'a corpse' (22). The degradation and disturbing loss of normal bodily boundaries is magnified with extended periods of isolation and in its more extreme formulations.

The extreme damage that many prisoners in this study communicated indicates that solitary confinement—and the emotional dimensions of this experience—is often written on, and into, to the body. Prisoners may carry visible bodily inscriptions for the rest of their lives which may be a source of identifiable stigma (Moran, 2014). And as Van der Kolk (2014) states, writing in the less-visible context of trauma: 'the body keeps the score'. Past traumas affect prisoners in the present through the prevalence of uncomfortable emotions, unwanted sensations, hypervigilance, anxieties and lethargy. However, the wounded body is also 'the bridge back' to healing (Van der Kolk, 2014: 261). Increased body awareness and 're-habitation' of the body is an essential part of the healing process (Levine, 2010). It was striking that in spite of the rigors of solitary confinement a number of prisoners sought out isolation (see Laws, 2021). This clearly signals the challenges of communal living and certain opportunities, or at least 'lesser evils', presented by brief periods of isolation as articulated in the previous chapter. A number of participants in this study found a variety of ways to develop and discipline their bodies. These descriptions both confirm and disturb prior accounts of segregation. They confirm it in the sense that prisoners' testimonies echo the physical and psychological damage of segregation experiences—though such damage often began long before segregation in the wider prison or in life experiences before it. It is worth reiterating that disembodiment is fused into the solitary confinement experience. This alone can exacerbate physical and psychological deterioration.

However, this article also disturbs prior accounts of segregation by evidencing a degree of agency over their bodies to develop, adapt, and sometimes transcend some of the pains of deep custody—though this in no way reflects an endorsement of solitary confinement. That is to say, the destructive dissolution of boundaries outlined above could also have a positive accent, where the cell became a space of inner exploration, emotional expression, and a form of contemplation reminiscent of Lozoff's description of 'prison monks' (1985). There are strong resonances here with O'Donnell's (2014) nuanced account of isolation and solitary confinement experiences that emphasises how 'accounts of its positive aspects are glossed over' (61). The body is both a site of damage *and* a potential source of healing. There is scope to think creatively about how prison interventions could harness such 'body knowledge' in more creative ways. In a recent article (Laws & Lieber, 2020) the authors argue that the decline of boxing programmes in prison reflects 'a kind of institutional denial of the body as a site of knowledge and learning' in place of risk-based thinking. The challenges of having a body in prison generally, and in solitary confinement in particular, is complex and deserves more attention. This responds, in another way, to Liebling's (1999: 287) call to pay sufficient attention to 'affective understanding' in prisons research. Bodies feel, sense and react to the experience of imprisonment in important ways. This chapter contributes to the growing criminological literature on emotions and the sensorial dimensions of imprisonment. It might also supplement prior accounts of narrative identity change in prison that sometimes forget the role of the body in processes of change.

References

Asad, T. (1997). Remarks on the anthropology of the body. In S. Coakley (Ed.), *Religion and the body*. Cambridge University Press.

Auty, K. M., Cope, A., & Liebling, A. (2017). A systematic review and meta-analysis of yoga and mindfulness meditation in prison: Effects on psychological well-being and behavioural functioning. *International Journal of Offender Therapy and Comparative Criminology, 61*(6), 689–710.

Bentham, J. (1791). *Panopticon or the inspection house*. T. Payne Mews Gate.

Bosworth, M., & Kaufman, E. (2012). Gender and punishment. In J. Simon & R. Sparks (Eds.), *The Sage handbook of punishment and society*. Sage.

Brown, G. (Ed.). (2019). *Psychoanalytic thinking on the unhoused mind*. Routledge.

Carlen, P. (1998). *Sledgehammer: Women's imprisonment at the millennium*. Springer.

Chamberlen, A. (2018). *Embodying punishment: Emotions, identities, and lived experiences in women's prisons*. Oxford University Press.

Crewe, B., Warr, J., Bennett, P., & Smith, A. (2014). The emotional geography of prison life. *Theoretical Criminology, 18*(1), 56–74.

Crewe, B., Hulley, S., & Wright, S. (2020). *Life imprisonment from young adulthood*. Palgrave Macmillan UK.

Damasio, A. R. (1999). *The feeling of what happens: Body and emotion in the making of consciousness*. Houghton Mifflin Harcourt.

De Viggiani, N. (2012). Trying to be something you are not: Masculine performances within a prison setting. *Men and Masculinities, 15*(3), 271–291.

Eckhart, M. (1994). *Selected writings*. Penguin.

7 The Body and Solitary Confinement 199

Edgar, K., O'Donnell, I., & Martin, C. (2003). *Prison violence: The dynamics of conflict, fear and power*. Willan.

Fanon, F. (1961). *The wretched of the earth*. Grove.

Feldman, A. (1991). *Formations of violence: The narrative of the body and political terror in Northern Ireland*. University of Chicago Press.

Foucault, M. (1979). *Discipline and punish*. Random House of Canada.

Goffman, E. (1961). *Asylums: Essays on the social situation of mental patients and other inmates*. Penguin.

Guenther, L. (2013). *Solitary confinement: Social death and its afterlives*. University of Minnesota Press.

Haney, C. (2008). A culture of harm: Taming the dynamics of cruelty in supermax prisons. *Criminal Justice and Behavior, 35*(8), 956–984.

Herman, J. L. (1992). *Trauma and recovery: The aftermath of violence—From domestic abuse to political terror*. Hachette.

Jung, C. G. (1939). *The integration of the personality*. Farrar & Rinehart.

Karup, A. (2016). *The meaning and effect of yoga in prison*. [Unpublished master's thesis]. University of Cambridge.

Keenan, B. (1992). *An evil cradling: The five year ordeal of a hostage*. Hutchinson.

Kerley, K. R., & Copes, H. (2009). 'Keepin' my mind right' identity maintenance and religious social support in the prison context. *International Journal of Offender Therapy and Comparative Criminology, 53*(2), 228–244.

Laws, B., & Crewe, B. (2016). Emotion regulation among male prisoners. *Theoretical Criminology, 20*(4), 529–547. https://doi.org/10.1177/1362480615622532

Laws, B. (2019). The return of the suppressed: Exploring how emotional suppression reappears as violence and pain among male and female prisoners. *Punishment & Society, 21*(5), 560–577.

Laws, B., & Lieber, E. (2020). 'King, Warrior, Magician, Lover': Understanding expressions of care among male prisoners. *European Journal of Criminology*. https://doi.org/1477370819896207

Laws, B. (2021). Segregation seekers: An alternative perspective on the solitary confinement debate. *The British Journal of Criminology, 61*(6), 1452–1468.

Leder, D. (2016). *The distressed body: Rethinking illness, imprisonment, and healing*. University of Chicago Press.

Levine, P. A. (2010). *In an unspoken voice: How the body releases trauma and restores goodness*. North Atlantic Books.

Liebling, A. (1999). Doing research in prison: Breaking the silence? *Theoretical Criminology, 3*(2), 147–173.

Liebling, A. (2014). Postscript: Integrity and emotion in prisons research. *Qualitative Inquiry, 20*(4), 481–486.

Liebling, A. (2015). Description at the edge? I-It/I-Thou relations and action in prisons research. *International Journal for Crime, Justice and Social Democracy, 4*(1), 18–32.

Lock, M. (1993). Cultivating the body: Anthropology and epistemologies of bodily practice and knowledge. *Annual Review of Anthropology, 22*(1), 133–155.

Lozoff, B. (1985). *We're all doing time: A guide for getting free.* Lulu Press, Inc.

Maruna, S., Wilson, L., & Curran, K. (2006). Why God is often found behind bars: Prison conversions and the crisis of self-narrative. *Research in Human Development, 3*(2–3), 161–184.

Moran, D. (2014). Leaving behind the 'total institution'? Teeth, transcarceral spaces and (re)inscription of the formerly incarcerated body. *Gender, Place & Culture, 21*(1), 35–51.

O'Donnell, I. (2014). *Prisoners, solitude, and time.* Oxford University Press.

Scarry, E. (1985). *The body in pain: The making and unmaking of the world.* Oxford University Press.

Sidoli, M. (1996). Farting as a defence against unspeakable dread. *Journal of Analytical Psychology, 41*(2), 165–178.

van der Kolk, B. (2014). *The body keeps the score.* Viking.

Winlow, S., & Hall, S. (2009). Retaliate first: Memory, humiliation and male violence. *Crime, Media, Culture, 5*(3), 285–304.

8

Conclusions

The introduction to this study set out Rustin's (2009) claim about ways of understanding emotions. It will be recalled that Rustin suggests we have understood far more about 'states of feeling' through works of art than from the social sciences (20). Yet, the broader scope of Rustin's argument is important, as rather than a condemnation of emotions research in the social sciences his account reads like a call to action. He explains that the social sciences 'as organised bodies of knowledge' have been influenced by 'a commitment to a new and modern kind of society which would be governed principally by reason' (19), and which therefore lead the subject area away from emotionality. That is to say, Rustin continues, the elevation of reason creates a number of 'implied antitheses' including the relegation of the body to the mind, faith to science, and most importantly for current purposes, emotions to reason (Rustin, 2009: 19). But it is important to note that the social sciences, and keys texts in sociology in particular, were originally formed *in reaction* to capitalistic systems that denied a role for affect, or promoted world views built solely on 'rationality'. It seems more accurate then to describe a process—during the eighteenth-century Scottish Enlightenment, and in later European and American sociological writing in particular—where 'there was ample

© The Author(s), under exclusive license to Springer Nature Switzerland AG 2022   **201**
B. Laws, *Caged Emotions*, Palgrave Studies in Prisons and Penology,
https://doi.org/10.1007/978-3-030-96083-4_8

space for emotion', but that since then 'the category of emotion lost its footing in social explanation' (Barbalet, 2001: 8).

There are strong indications that Rustin's call is being heard. Indeed, this study contributes to a shifting narrative in the social sciences and criminology wherein these classical distinctions and binaries are being disrupted and integrated. Recent waves of scientific research are uncovering the compatibility and interdependence between the head and the heart, as Evans (2002) explains: 'emotions inform our decisions even when we think we are being completely rational' (144), and the most 'intelligent action results from a harmonious blend of emotion and reason' (xii). Reason and emotion are not oppositional poles, rather 'they are intertwined in a collaborative relationship needed for normal functioning' (Sapolsky, 2017: 58). Emotion, then, has an integral role in the social sciences, and is increasingly recognised as moulding 'distinct social configurations, [and] playing an essential part in shaping different ways of life for societies, institutions and individuals in patterned interactions with one another' (Rustin, 2009: 31).

This book resembles a form of 'integration work' in two identifiable ways. First, the focus on 'emotion regulation' reflects an intermingling of both intuitive and conscious processes. That is to say, prisoners were not at the mercy of their emotions. Instead, they exerted a degree of influence over the onset, intensity and expression of their feelings states. As will be further articulated below, detailing this process gives us a deeper understanding of how emotions function in prison and challenges more simplified versions of emotion management in institutional settings.

Second, the rebalancing of emotion and rationality also has significant implications for the treatment of gender.[1] It will be recalled that gender and emotion are also deeply intertwined, and that the elevation of reason and the rejection of sentimentality has been strongly tied to oppositions between masculinity and femininity (Manstead & Fischer, 2000). As Anderson and Smith (2001: 7) surmise: 'detachment, objectivity and rationality have been valued, and implicitly masculinized, while

---

[1] The reverse is also true, and it is more accurate to describe this as a bi-directional relationship. Breakthrough scholarship on gender has drawn significant attention, and revaluation, to issues of emotionality.

engagement, subjectivity, passion and desire have been devalued, and frequently feminized'. In contrast, then, gender was foregrounded in this study, but assumptions and preconceptions about gender that could distort the findings have been avoided (Liebling, 2009). Male and female prisoners have been treated equitably, answering the same questions about their affective states, and have been analysed using the same framework of emotions.

Main Findings

The two studies set out to explore the role of emotion regulation and expression at various different levels of analysis. The following section takes stock of the main findings and, where appropriate, draws thematic connections between them and explains what has been established as knowledge. The reader will not find a fused analysis between the two studies as this has never been the intention of this book. Rather, from this point, there is an attempt to situate the studies within the wider academic literature and explicitly highlight the main contributions. Of particular significance here is the literature on carceral geography and recent studies in the psychology and sociology of imprisonment. Finally, some limitations and future directions of this research are examined.

Destructive Life Experiences and Cycles of Imprisonment

The first substantive chapter revealed the chaotic and damaging pre-prison experiences of the participants. This reinforced findings from systematic studies of prisoner backgrounds (see Leigey & Reed, 2010) and uncovered multiple forms of childhood abuse (emotional, physical, sexual), exploitation and parental neglect. Participants related consistent exposure to domestic violence, drug abuse, suicide and death (of loved ones, friends and family members). They had typically experienced stressful and transient living situations, having being transferred to multiple foster homes, care facilities, schools or spent time living on the street.

Although individual biographies differed, what united them was a general sense of *instability*—as each participant recounted multiple 'destabilizing' or disruptive life events. There was considerable inter-generational 'circularity' in these stories. Many prisoners had close family members who had experienced imprisonment and they often felt estranged from their own children, who expressed anger, confusion, and frustration towards them. For example, children who questioned when their imprisoned parents were coming home, or partners who struggled to juggle the demands of childrearing and living costs along, evoked tremendous feelings of guilt and shame among prisoners. This resonates strongly with recent government reports that emphasise the importance of helping prisoners stabilise their relationships (HMIP, 2016). Lord Farmer (2017: 8) argues that 'good family relationships must be a golden thread running through the processes of all prisons'. It is an uncomfortable finding that the choice to self-isolate, articulated in Part Two of the book, might be influenced by the total absence of any meaningful, or accessible, family relations.

Prisoners' prior experiences could have all sorts of resonances for living in prison: living in 'care' facilities and boarding schools, and early experiences of loneliness and isolation, all provided some exposure to institutional life. These events left lasting emotional scars which shaped emotional orientations while in prison. As Thompson, Hannan, & Miron, (2014: 28) explain, chronic childhood maltreatment has 'lifelong consequences, including increased risk for internalizing problems (e.g., anxiety and depression), externalizing problems (e.g., aggressive behaviour), and emotion dysregulation...[and] can cause hypersensitivity to threat cues and a tendency to respond to non-hostile situations as threatening'. In the prisons context, Grounds (2004) relates how experiences of injustice can cause acute psychological trauma and long-lasting damage. For prisoners in this book, patterns of emotion management were certainly influenced by pre-existing forces and deep traumas that prisoners carried inside. These biographic details of prisoners lives answers, in part, Jamieson and Grounds' (2005: 56) call for research that looks as the context of past experiences to better understand the effects of imprisonment. For many participants, these past emotional difficulties were reflected, perpetuated, and amplified by the prison environment. There are strong linkages here with Easteal (2001: 101) who found that 'an ethos of betrayal is reinforced' in prison because of 'violations of confidentiality' and 'breaches of trust' that echo earlier childhood experiences. By consequence, many prisoners learn that it is better to avoid their feelings, and bury their pain. This finding is reinforced and extended by this thesis, especially in the 'passive' regulation strategies prisoners displayed and the decisions to seek out segregation. Segregation may in some cases provide a comforting, but simultaneously damaging, lopping off of almost all social relations.

The Damage of 'Passive' Regulation

A second important finding is that 'bottling-up' emotion—a 'passive' approach to affect management—was the most common regulation strategy. The distinction between 'passive' and 'active' references the extent to which emotional states were being addressed directly. Over two thirds of the sample spoke about having to block their emotions. This book makes a key contribution by evidencing the pervasiveness of emotional suppression, and the way it applies to a range of specific feeling states. Prisoners were inclined to push down their anger and sadness, but also their joy and elation: it may be recalled that positive emotions also risked attracting the 'wrong' kind of attention. To some extent, bottling was a product of prisoner culture—a finding well documented in wider research (de Viggiani, 2012; Greer, 2002; Jewkes, 2005b)—that hold displays of toughness and emotional restraint in high esteem. However, it was significant that suppression was also a product of the institutional management of emotion. For example, the policies and protocols surrounding ACCT implementation appeared to spotlight rather than support prisoners in need, and often provided unhelpful forms of attention. Further, fears that requesting support would be recorded on prisoners' records, hampering their chances at parole hearings increased the likelihood of withholding. This engendered a feeling of emotional entrapment that was strongly redolent of Crewe's (2011) concept of 'tightness', a modern manifestation of penal power that incites prisoners:

206   B. Laws

> ...to conduct themselves in particular ways...[creating] the sense of not knowing which way to move, for fear of getting things wrong. It conveys the way that power operates both closely and anonymously, working like an invisible harness on the self. It is all-encompassing and invasive, in that it promotes the self-regulation of all aspects of conduct, addressing both the psyche and the body. (522)

This institutional control of emotions provides an important commentary on Sherman's (2003) argument that emotionally intelligent justice should acknowledge the emotions and needs of both offenders and victims. In general, neither of the establishments in this research exemplified this kind of emotional intelligence in their approach to prisoners—most felt isolated, unheard, and cut off from emotional support channels—although Send was more proactive in providing forms of therapy. In the absence of such support channels, seeking out pre-emptive solitary confinement constitutes a way to avoid being embroiled violence.

This study found, however, that the effects of 'caging' one's emotions were almost entirely negative. There was an important relationship between bottling-up emotion and the subsequent loss of control over emotions, including outbursts of violence and dissociated thoughts. Those who went to segregation to avoid difficult situations and feelings were rarely freed from the emotional toll of confinement. Segregation could relieve some fears while simultaneously exacerbate others, such as underlying feelings of anxiety and paranoia. Most prisoners who suppressed their emotions suffered from a kind of 'boomerang' effect, suggesting that emotional suppression had delayed consequences, and failed to provide long-term equanimity. This process is deeply rooted in the damaging and traumatic life experiences of participants before prison. As De Zulueta (1993) argues:

> People who react to stress by carrying on as though nothing has happened dissociate themselves from the reality of their pain, terror or humiliation, but at a price: the self becomes divided and the process of dissociation becomes part of the patient's identity, to be brought back into action when faced with further stress or even situations that are only reminiscent of the original stress. As a result of this repeated dissociative process, the victim becomes emotionally constricted and cannot experience the full range of feelings. (180)

A growing pool of research is highlighting the linkages between unresolved emotion, stress, and the subsequent detrimental effects on health and behaviour. For example, Hawkins (2013) articulates the ways in which unprocessed emotions resurface through the body's endocrine and nervous system, and Maté further argues (2003) that suppression and discharge are inseparable processes caused by the build-up of acute physiological stress. Importantly, then, institutional practices tended to emotionally numb and trigger a population of prisoners who were already highly vulnerable. This seems to confirm Karstedt's (2011: 3) contention that poor acknowledgement of feelings states can lead to 'unrestrained emotions gushing into the arena of criminal justice'.

'Diluting' emotions through distraction was, alongside suppression, a further example of *passive* emotion regulation. Distraction was a common way for prisoners to try to escape unwanted feeling states and rumination. Distraction was achieved through the tranquillising effects of illicit substances or prescribed drugs, or through engaging in a busy routine that left little time for introspection. Indeed, there was an apparent irony that prisoners who appeared most joyful and 'free' from institutional control were those who fully embedded themselves in prison routines (attending programmes, work, and education and undertaking physical exercise). Sparks et al. (1996: 75) explain that routines can be both 'reassuring and consoling' on one hand, while also presenting a 'deadening tedium' on the other. The main finding here was that prisoners who used distraction felt more reassurance than tedium. The nature of solitary confinement, however, does not fit easily into this framework. While establishing a stable routine in segregation could in some ways be easier—removing the threat of other prisoners from the equation—the risks of tedium could be magnified. All of this adds an interesting twist to Crawley's (2011: 258) argument that emotions are central 'to routine operations of social interaction'. Outside of the prisons context, Barbalet (2001: 170) argues that 'emotions are basic to social action and to an understanding of social structures'. This study found that the reverse was also true: in that prison routines helped to regulate emotions, or even that some emotions are best handled in isolation. The important point being made is that emotions appear to be both causes *and* effects: playing a key role in the maintenance of order—and disorder—in prison, but also being evoked by features of the regime. Prisoners who relied on a fixed routine to create emotional order were in a very precarious balance. That is to say, the reliance on routine for distraction was often destabilised by freezes to prisoner movement, the sudden cancellation of activities, finishing courses (creating a new hole in the schedule), or prolonged 'lock-downs'. These disruptions revealed the underlying vulnerabilities that distraction was attempting to mask and suppress. And this perhaps is where rationales for self-segregation can make some sense. To lop off attachment to external activities meant that segregated prisoners had little else that could be taken from them. There was a kind of freedom in their self-reliance which meant they were beyond changes to the prison regime.

Overall, these study findings contrast with Wright, Crewe and Hulley (2017: 12) who argue that suppression provides 'an important and highly adaptive psychic defence mechanism' that 'enables the minimization of painful affects and realities' in prison. The authors argue that bottling is a 'deliberate and pro-active means' to defend against some of the most pernicious challenges of prison life (12)—such as blocking out unwanted thoughts or 'intrusive recollections'—and is therefore a 'useful defensive means' for coping (13). But the evidence here finds less justification for the 'protective potential' of suppression. Rather, it has found that suppression had impacts on other forms of prison behaviour and less positive, long-term effects, on health and well-being. The dependence on drugs, in particular, could have more direct and pronounced side-effects: damaging health, personal relationships and leaving prisoners in debt. There is a closer alignment here with Grounds (2004, 171) who found evidence that prisoners 'learned to deal with emotional pressures and stresses in prison by blocking off painful feelings, avoiding communication, and isolating themselves'. Importantly, Grounds continues, these experiences contribute to 'enduring and disabling personality change…[including] social withdrawal, feelings of emptiness or hopelessness, a chronic feeling of threat, and estrangement' (168).

'Active' Regulation

By contrast, the most effective emotion regulation strategies were 'active' in nature. That is to say, both 'distillation' and 'reappraisal' strategies constituted attempts to engage directly with emotions. Distillation was the attempt to extract and work with the underlying meaning of emotion states. It was most visible in a small number of prisoners who harnessed therapeutic knowledge as a form of self-inquiry, to identify both the causes and consequences of emotion states. A distinction was drawn here between 'distillation' and other activities such as letter-writing, diaries and artwork, which were used to delve into feelings in a more generalised manner to 'externalise' feeling states (which I termed 'processing'). That is, writing about emotions or painting them on canvas was one way of generating affective distance from them. It is certainly true that many of the men in the segregation study were highly introspective: some kept diaries and wrote song lyrics almost compulsively. At best, the attachment and pain of particular feeling states was soothed through such activities, as emotions were reconfigured into something that could be looked at, analysed, and reflected on. As Bluhm (1948: 103) explains, activities based on self-observation allow prisons to turn away from 'passive suffering' to regain active control over their lives. Bluhm further notes a strong, mutually reinforcing 'association between self-observation and self-expression' which constitutes 'a most successful mechanism of survival' (Bluhm, 1948: 103). In line with this, Pennebaker (1997) states that the detrimental health effects of emotional inhibition are relieved by writing about them and additional benefits include enhanced immune function, autonomic activity, muscle tension and long term improvements in mood and well-being. Prisoners in this research who tried to understand, and disentangle, their emotions through writing or art, typically benefitted from a greater ease of self-expression than was previously available to them.

'Reappraisal', adopted by just under a third of prisoners, was an important form of emotional 'alchemy' where unwanted emotions were transformed by reinterpreting the meaning of a given situation. Such findings help to move the discussion of psychological and emotional adaptation in prison beyond the idea that imprisonment constitutes a mere 'deep freeze' (Zamble and Porporino, 1990). Prisoners took control over their emotions in this way by trying to see the 'silver lining' in their personal circumstances. Prison was often recast as a heroic journey and a powerful test of personal resilience. This approach did not attempt to banish uncomfortable emotions and events, but rather sought to accept and modify them. The prisoners who engaged in this strategy appeared to cope better, both physically and psychologically, and were less likely to feel caught up in cycles of negative emotion. The reduction of negative emotions brought about by reappraisal has robust support across a range of psychological literatures (Goldin et al., 2008).

The Fluid-Container Metaphor

These various emotion regulation strategies used by prisoners were brought into relief using the 'fluid-container' metaphor as the basis for a framework of emotion management. The conceptualisation of emotions as fluids (that are 'bottled-up', 'distilled', and 'diluted') resonates with some of the earliest work on prison sociology. For example, Sykes (1954: 79) explains how:

> The pains of imprisonment generate enormous pressure which is translated into behaviour with all the greater vigor because, *like a body of steam under heavy compression* with only a few outlets, the body of prisoners is limited in modes of adaptation' (emphasis added).

The extension of the metaphor in this research offers a clear and intuitive representation of how prisoners regulate emotions, which does not cloud these behaviours in clinical terminology. Furthermore, there was a preliminary attempt to go beyond the descriptive confines of the framework, and explore the extent to which particular emotion regulation strategies (suppression and reframing) were indicative of different patterns of emotional states. Two groups of emotionally 'rigid' and 'flexible' groups were identified based on prisoners' differential perceptions of power, agency and control. This confirms Layder's (2004: 5) argument that there are 'deep-seated associations between power and the emotions' that are 'not simply contingent and haphazard', rather the 'two are to be found in each other's company in every instance…[as] constant companions'.

This first, 'rigid', group of prisoners perceived they had either total responsibility for their feelings, or conversely, no control at all. These prisoners appeared to struggle with their emotions the most, and were most likely to suppress them. By contrast, emotionally flexible prisoners occupied the middle-ground between these poles of control, and generally coped better with the rigors of prison life. These individuals intuited the limits of their agency in prison without succumbing to passivity and embraced a range of active regulation strategies, especially reappraisal. Evans (2002) claims that such pragmatism is the midpoint between emotional extremes, and a signal of emotion intelligence that finds 'balance between emotion and reason in which neither is in control. Emotionally intelligent people know when it is right to control their emotions and when it is right to be controlled by them' (59–60). There are problems in reducing emotion regulation strategies to dichotomies between active and passive, better and worse, rigid and flexible. Indeed, prisoners' motivations for using these strategies were complex and context was critical. For example, although sustained emotional suppression had long-term negative impacts, containing anger was a crucial self-preservation tactic that helped avoid confrontations. However, this research constitutes an attempt to conceptually advance understanding of emotion regulation in prison beyond descriptive categorisations. Following Calverley and Farrall's (2011) lead, if emotional experience and expressivity constitute a fundamental part of the progression into and away from crime, understanding the developmental patterns of prisoners could help further understand this process. It was noteworthy that prisoners who used strategies of emotional reappraisal were most likely to hold positions of responsibility (mentor roles, sought after jobs etc). More broadly, this study contributes to debates about the extent to which prison can be seen as a 'powerful and potentially debilitating social context' with effects that are 'entirely predictable' (Haney, 2005: 86), or whether, by contrast, there are various experiential 'pathways' of prison experiences (O'Donnell, 2014). It appears that many prisoners in this study learned to regulate their emotions in ways that brought a degree of stability to their reality and environment, which challenges arguments claiming total environmental determinism. This supplements Sparks et al. (1996) account that seeks to understand the various factors that lead to the negotiation of order in prison. It will be recalled that although their thesis included no explicit analysis of the role of emotions in establishing order, in a number of places feelings were indirectly introduced into their analysis (1996: 68). Future research could do further develop these ideas by investigating emotional adaptations to imprisonment over time.

Emotions as Social 'Glue'

At the relational level, the first study found that emotions functioned like social glue (Planalp, 1999), binding prisoners to one another, whereas for the segregated men emotions did not create social connection but rather the opposite. But for the former cohort, the principal way that this process manifested was through the social sharing of emotions, enabling prisoners to ventilate their feelings with one another. For most prisoners, there were significant barriers to sharing emotions with officers and family members. In line with Jewkes (2002: 155), 'the fragility and fragmentation of contact with loved ones on the outside [was a] profound source of stress' for prisoners in this study. And although most participants were close to at least one family member, closeness did not always translate to emotional transparency and openness. Indeed, most felt that they had to shelter their difficult feelings from their families and 'put on a brave face'. With a few exceptions, uniformed officers were typically perceived as cold, mechanical and generally unsympathetic to prisoners' emotional needs.

For these reasons, other prisoners were the most reliable group for sharing emotion. Prisoners were able to show empathy for their peers through the mutual experience of imprisonment. Searching for a willing listener, receiving advice, and seeking understanding and compassion helped prisoners alleviate their emotions. These relationships highlighted the importance of emotional reciprocity, which mutually reinforced social bonds between prisoners, increasing intimacy, cooperation and trust. Put short, the emotional dimensions of these interactions had an adhesive function contributing to 'the intimacy and harmony of the relationship' (Fischer & Manstead, 2008: 459).

An important symbol of these affiliations was the re-construction of family groups. This was more pronounced in Send than Ranby, where the prevalence of 'sisters', 'aunties', 'mothers' and 'romantic dyads' was made more explicit through physical and verbal gestures of care. These findings were somewhat analogous to Owen (1998) who argues that interpersonal relationships are the anchors of prison life and the pseudo-family is an essential part of the social order. However, while the women in this study did appear to evidence more frequent displays of emotional cathexis with one another than their male counterparts, these relationships were less pervasive than in Owen's study, indicating that emotion norms are shaped by wider institutional and cultural variables.

Broader displays of care and affection were frequent in both prisons, but they manifested in different ways. In Send, care was typically 'open' and explicit in nature. That is, there were numerous, highly visible, and intimate conversations going on between women all around the prison. Further, the particular intensity of expression conveyed through these interactions (through colourful love letters, and birthday gifts) made it clear that these were affectionate displays. Female prisoners exhibited a form of social communion, pooling together a range of different vocational skills and expertise (hairdressing, cooking, tailoring clothes, card making) to care for their friends. By contrast, in the men's prisons, care was submerged into shared routines and activities undertaken in dyads or small groups. This included playing video games, sports, dominoes, gym workouts, snooker, pool, table tennis. The male prisoners established bonds through competition and displays of skill. Affection was less frequently communicated through explicit verbal commentary. While there were some instances of prisoners expressing a kind of fraternal 'love' for one another, these were relatively isolated occurrences. It was more typical for prisoners to express warmth in a range of non-verbal gestures such as special hand-shakes, high-fives, fist-bumps, and bicep squeezing in the gym. All of this was strongly redolent of Crewe's (2014) argument that men's emotional expressions are often submerged and transmitted in alternative ways.

214 B. Laws

These arguments however do not hold consistently for the segregated men. A few men on the unit suffered precisely because they were being held away from their friends and associates back on the wing. However, most of these men were outside the affective network of relations entirely. In fact, destructive emotions like fear and rage had led them to seek out segregation precisely to escape the anti-social world of imprisonment. While emotion could be cohesive it clearly does not work in a uniform manner.

Contagious Emotions

Outside of close friendship circles and group affiliations, destructive emotions were far more frequent. Indeed, broader interactions between prisoners were often be marked by anger, hostility, frustration and fear. This reflects Grounds' (2004: 170) finding that prisoners adapt by learning to be 'highly aggressive and intimidating as a form of self-protection'. A number of participants described feeling under suspicion, from both officers and other prisoners, which served as a constant reminder that they were mistrusted. This evoked regular sentiments of shame, guilt and anger, directed both internally and towards others. As Gilligan (2003: 1162) argues, 'people resort to violence when they feel they can wipe out shame only by shaming those who they feel shamed them'. This quite accurately describes the reasons for segregation for some of the participants: they felt that had been backed into a corner and humiliated with no alternative but to strike back.

Importantly, these destructive emotions had a contagious quality. In Send, participants explained that sadness and distress were 'absorbed' from others. A number of women complained about prisoners who cast negativity on to them through unsolicited sharing. In these instances emotional resources were being forcibly extracted from prisoners. In Ranby and Whitemoor, anger and violence had a similar kind of affective pull or momentum. There were strong indications here that Randall Collins' conceptualisations of 'ritual interaction' (Collins, 1990) and 'forward panic' (Collins, 2011) applies to particular prison environments. It seemed that prisoners sometimes do 'get pumped up with the emotional strength from participating in the group interaction' (Collins, 1990: 32) in the way that Collins described, and that the 'build-up of tension and fear' contributes to violent incidents in which combatants are 'caught-up in each other's mood' (Collins, 2011: 23). This was often related to the influence of a wider social gaze. Hostile energy and aggression accumulated within the prisoner audience and was seemingly charged into individual prisoners. It is significant that living in segregation units largely removes this social gaze. There was some evidence that violence in Ranby was, in some instances, a direct response to the perception that officers did not provide an adequate level of safety. There are resemblances here with studies of herding communities where the absence of policemen over large areas creates 'cultures of honour':

> Where enforcement of the law is inadequate, it becomes important to defend one's reputation for severity to establish that one is not to be trifled with. Allowing oneself to be pushed around, insulted, or affronted without retaliation amounts to announcing that one is an easy mark. (Cohen & Nisbett, 1994: 552)

There was a recurrent message that other prisoners became targets of hostile emotional energy precisely because there was a lack of viable alternative avenues for channelling difficult feelings. Restrictions on prisoner movement and the enforced proximity to the feeling states of others (in cell sharing situations or on the large wings) catalysed the spread of negative emotion. In this context, Haney's (2005: 86) argument that imprisonment can often be a 'debilitating social context' is hard to deny. The argument set-out in chapter five, that certain environments create particular probabilities of experience—without doing so deterministically— is convincing for these prison settings.

'Liminal' Journeys

Jewkes (2005a) and Turner's (1974) conceptual work on liminality provided a preliminary framework to describe prisoners' experiences of cell spaces. Those who found their cell spaces to be claustrophobic and unsettling were in the midst of a kind liminal upheaval or undergoing a process of transformation. These prisoners were emotionally overwhelmed by the isolation of close confinement experienced a wide repertoire of negative feeling states, especially fear, shame, sadness, frustration and anger. Many of these prisoners were either in the early stages of imprisonment, or were serving very long tariffs.

For prisoners who passed through this liminal upheaval (around two thirds of prisoners in the study), cells functioned more like personal sanctuaries, underscoring the idea that 'a prison cell can become a crucible for spiritual transformation' (O'Donnell, 2014: 162). The extreme isolation of solitary confinement could intensify, and serve as a catalyst for, meditation and religious experiences. The cell was a zone of relative serenity relative to the wider climate of wings and house blocks, where difficult emotions could be explored and disentangled within a safe 'container'. To some extent, cells allowed prisoners to exert a degree of agency over their emotions because they knew that they would have a fixed period of uninterrupted private time every day. Furthermore, prisoners also used their cells to shape their emotions in explicit ways by customising their personal space. This mainly involved modifying tired colour schemes, decorating the walls with pictures, and filling the space with personal artefacts and other 'signifiers of self' (Sloan, 2012: 406). This customisation of space was a way for prisoners to reassert their identities, creating a comfortable and unique sanctuary of their own and elevate their feeling states. Clean, uncluttered cells evoked calmness. Pictures of family members or religious iconography could inspire powerful feelings of love and tenderness.

However, prisoners who were bound into cell-sharing arrangements problematise the notion that participants underwent liminal journeys in a linear manner. That is to say, the main complaints among cell-sharers revolved around a different set of concerns, including the loss of emotional privacy, hygiene and broader fears of contamination from other prisoners. In short, then, the appropriation of liminality here would benefit from refinement. For example, adopting a longitudinal design would allow for comparisons over time and provide a more accurate picture of emotional development. Nonetheless, the use of ideas of liminality in this account highlights important intersections between emotional experience, temporality and space.

Stagnant and Volatile Zones

The wings and house blocks were almost unanimously discussed in negative terms. Prisoners pointed towards indications of physical deterioration and lifelessness that were strongly evocative of Sykes (1954):

> When we examine the physical structure of the prison the most striking feature is, perhaps, its drabness. It has that "institutional" look shared by police stations, hospitals, orphan asylums, and similar public buildings—a Kafka-like atmosphere compounded of naked electric lights, echoing corridors, walls encrusted with the paint of decades, and the stale air of rooms shut up too long'. (7)

In Ranby, the large, factory-like, house blocks appeared to be a kind of assault on the prisoner's soul. These living spaces were homogenous, lonely and anonymous. The experience of these spaces challenges Crawley's (2011: 260) claim that 'emotional interchanges [between officers and staff] cannot be avoided because the degree of intimacy involved in working with prisoners is great'. Studying the emotional dimensions of imprisonment provides an important lens through which to view the new penology (Feeley & Simon, 1992) and the 'culture of control' (Garland, 2001) close up. This analysis reveals that imprisonment increasingly offers an experience of depersonalisation and isolation. Most prisoners in Ranby felt interactions with officers were infrequent and almost completely devoid of intimacy. There was spatial variation however, and the smaller wings in Ranby had integrated design features which 'designed in' and promoted positive social interactions. For example, space was more compartmentalised (there were dedicated servery areas and games rooms) which contributed to a more collaborative atmosphere on these wings. To some extent then, emotions like boredom or joy were driven by environmental features that either created outlets for leisure and communal activities, or alternatively, promoted apathy through their absence.

There were zones in all three prisons that had a 'volatile' quality. The social 'simmering' in these areas indicated that they were always on the precipice of violence. These hostile places shared a number of key attributes that contributed to the high levels of tension. This included high levels of unpredictability, chaos and sensory intensity (noise, and physical density). There were important similarities here with Sparks et al. (1996) who explain the feelings evoked in the absence of a stable routine:

> We are…doomed to trust that the world is sufficiently predictable and solid for us to be able to act capably within it, to develop 'mutual knowledge', and so on. In the absence of such security the actor risks being 'swamped' by anxiety; and for a given individual or group the obverse of routine is the 'critical situation' in which the continuity of the social world is thrown into doubt. (75)

A particularly important variable was the perceived absence of officer supervision in these areas and the lack of natural sightlines. All of these factors coalesced to create spaces that were characterised by difficult emotions, especially: fear, frustration, anger and anxiety. The line route in Ranby was a particularly significant flash point, but was not a fixed 'space' with clearly demarcated boundaries, but rather a sprawling set of transitional spaces. This description closely aligns to Moran's (2011) development of 'liminality' to 'convey the specific spaces of betweenness, where a metaphorical crossing of some spatial and/or temporal threshold takes place' (342). The range of emotions found on the line route substantiates Crewe (2013) call for further analysis of the affective feel of spaces of transition as well as more traditional prison areas. These findings reinforce Layder's (2004) contention that emotions and power are closely entwined. There were high levels of anger and fear in these zones that were indicative of threats to power, status and survival. As Barbalet (2001: 26) puts it: 'A power relationship which results in the dispossession of a participant also leads to their anger'.

'Communitas' and Free Spaces

In sharp contrast to these 'hot spots' there were a range of free spaces that prisoners held in high esteem. Turner's (1974) conceptualisation of 'communitas' was introduced to further understand the commonalities between these different prison zones, especially the ways in which they shared a liberated spirit of openness and inclusivity. These environmental niches (Toch, 1992) functioned as emotional oases, replenishing and soothing prisoners in a tranquil setting away from the harder edges of confinement. Furthermore, because much of the prison environment is experienced as psychologically and spatially 'tight' and presents 'few zones of autonomy…where the reach of power can be escaped' (Crewe, 2011: 522), these spaces were particularly valued. In these areas, institutional control was lighter and there were more relaxed rules about the expression of specific emotions that might have been suppressed in different parts of the prison. Prisoners were also able to channel difficult emotions in these spaces and were most likely to reveal the most authentic versions of themselves in these spaces. Again, Moran's (2011: 347) conceptualisation of liminal space is instructive here. These areas exist:

> …between outside and inside, with prisoners released from their day-to-day prison life, and allowed into a space designed and furnished to feel more like a domestic environment, and visitors in turn allowed to bring in material items from the 'outside' with which to accessorise the experience. (347)

This study develops the line of inquiry set-out by Crewe et al. (2014), explaining in greater detail the mechanisms why emotions can be cathartically released in these spaces. It was the informal, non-punitive, approach of tutors and the 'softer' design features in these spaces helped to create a collegiate, or more professional atmosphere. The recurrent catchphrase that these places did not 'feel like prison' was significant. Overall, these areas reveal what Smoyer and Blankenship (2014: 564) term the 'microgeographies' of imprisonment. That is 'a patchwork of interior spaces' wherein each area has its own 'own unique structure [and] meaning…constructed by physical location, movement, and power, or lack thereof' (564). In these spaces prisoners were able to escape institutional power and assert a degree of their own control: prisoners recovered some degree of power over their emotional expressions.

Forging a Space

The lack of emotional privacy in prison was a significant finding. This was especially apposite for female prisoners who appeared to feel intrusions to privacy more acutely. A distinction was drawn between 'forced exposure' and 'forced spectatorship' in an attempt to disentangle the different features of emotional privacy. While the loss of privacy was explicitly conceived as a physical 'event' (for example, being observed naked by officers) it was compounded by a more diffuse sense of psychological invasiveness. This was highly salient in the therapeutic community in Send where prisoners were coerced to disclose their life histories, traumas and deepest feelings. This recalled Kruttschnitt and Gartner (2005) who describe the enforced expectations of disclosure in treatment settings in some detail. At the affective level, this left prisoners balancing on an emotional tightrope (Greer, 2002), wherein the suppression of affective states and open disclosure were met with psychological scrutiny.

The discussion of privacy presented a window through which to analyse the various ways prisoners used space to increase certain feelings and avoid others. These 'spatial selection' strategies were severely limited by the physical constraints of the prison regime (bars, locks, and concrete walls) and tight living situations (cell-sharing). However, while prisoners did not have complete control over spatiality, they exhibited a degree of bounded agency, forging space for themselves by exploiting gaps in the system, or finding ways to co-opt it. Segregation presents the ultimate achievement of privacy from the gaze and physical threat of other prisoners, though it arguably intensifies the institutional gaze. It would be inaccurate to describe segregation as 'freeing', though it provides a particular kind of liberation from prisoner violence. This alone could be calming, at least temporarily.

Gender Differences and Emotion

As Liebling (2009) notes in her article 'Women in prison prefer legitimacy to sex', preconceptions from academics about what is 'important' to different prisoner groups can mask findings and leave crucial concepts uncovered. By foregrounding gender in a relatively 'neutral' manner in this study, a space for both similarities and distinctions between prisoner emotions has emerged. The first study found clear evidence for some gender concordance at the psychological level (chapter three). This is not to claim that no gender differences emerged. Indeed, social relationships, emotional privacy, and levels of expressivity all revealed important points of contrast.

The most striking distinctions emerged in the domain of relational emotions. First, male and female prisoners had disparate levels of emotional literacy. Women were, on the whole, more emotionally 'fluent' that their male counterparts—the principal differences here were found in the breath and specificity of terminology used to describe emotions and the level of comfort with articulating feelings. It was common in Send to drop-in on 'deep' conversations in public places, and to see women displaying a wide number of emotions together. By contrast, the male prisoners were far more likely to exercise verbal restraint, and express their feelings through actions or understatement. This confirms Deaux's (2000) findings, that women *display* more emotions than men (outside of the prison context) but this does not necessarily relate to differences in the *experience* of emotion. It was argued that this has important implications for power relations in prison. That is, in their small groups and prisoner dyads, the exchange of emotions was indicative of the 'ongoing process of attachment that relates and sustains the human community' (Gilligan, 1992: 156). In this light, it becomes clearer that displays of care and empathy were deeply related to establishing and managing power. Gilligan explains that women can 'equate power with giving and care' (167), and understand 'nurturance as acts of strength' (168). Emotional expression in both prisons functioned like social glue that typically increased levels of intimacy, trust and brought a degree of harmony to these relations. The dynamics of emotions, then, have a lot to say about attempts to establish and maintain order and reveal some of the alternative patterns in which it is achieved.

Second, the atmosphere within friendship groups in the women's prison was more *communal* and collaborative whereas male relationships were defined more by *competition*. Emotions flowed freely in pseudo family units and friendship groups provided in Send, whereas, in Ranby, emotions were typically expressed sub-verbally, being tacitly understood by associates but rarely stated outright. Third, women were generally more likely to *internalise* difficult emotions, whereas men were more likely to *externalise*. This was most apparent in the salient displays of sadness among women that were commensurate to outbursts of anger and physical confrontations among men. Similarly, female prisoners were more inhibited by intense bouts of rumination than their male counterparts. In further support of this claim, the linguistic features of men's accounts, which were less likely to use 'I' and 'me' terms, indicated a tendency towards the 'outward projection' of affective states. Finally, women were more sensitive about cultivating and maintaining their emotional privacy, and seemed more aggrieved when it was breached—through 'pad spins' and beings observed naked—than male prisoners.

Questions remain around the extent to which emotion differences in prison reflect gendered patterns in the wider community. Previous research on prison masculinities has pointed towards an 'intensification' process (see Toch, 1998), whereby aspects of traditional masculine energy are exaggerated, especially traits like dominance, aggression and violence. Yet, the precise impact of gender in shaping prisoners' emotions, and the extent to which the environment magnified gender roles, was hard to identify. That is to say, other factors may have played an equally significant role. For example, these prison regimes had different cultures and operational priorities. Send is a treatment focused institution. Its therapeutic programmes were a significant feature that affected prisoners in both direct and indirect ways, through conversations and stories that circulated around the prison. Indeed, the small number of male participants who had experiences of therapeutic communities in other prisons described similar emotional effects—experiencing group cohesion and affection, and learning about their feelings through others—and were able to speak more extensively about their feelings in ways reminiscent of female prisoners' accounts.

Moreover, it is important not to overemphasise the impact of gender on emotion in the research findings. This was especially clear in relation to the social sharing of emotions. In both prisons, it was frequent to hear that other prisoners were the most common resource for offloading emotions (as opposed to family members and officers). Second, on the whole men and women were found to use an extremely similar suite of emotion regulation strategies. While the wider literature often attributes emotional suppression as the hallmark of maleness (Levant, 1995), and prisons research has emphasised the compulsion for male prisoners to reject all emotions apart from anger (de Viggiani, 2012) this study had found that women articulated similar feeling scripts as men. The fact that women are routinely emotionally controlled and censored in domestic and social worlds in their lives outside prison must account, in part, for these findings. Yet, the existence of these shared narratives suggests that emotion suppression is not the sole province of masculine or feminine conditioning per se and hints at a universal prisoner experience. This is to say, particular emotion regulation strategies are driven and shaped by institutional forces—for example, the management of ACCT plans, and the lack of access to viable outlets for emotion—rather than gender expectations alone. Further, the shared prior experiences of trauma of these men and women, combined with living in a tight, unpredictable, environment made these prisoners particularly susceptible to 'emotional numbing' and dissociating from their feelings (de Zulueta, 1993; Van der Kolk, 2014).

Main Contributions

I do not work toward a grand flourish that might tempt me beyond the boundaries of the material I have been presenting, or might detract from the power (and exceed the limitations) of the observations themselves or what I tried to make of them…We cannot bridge the chasm between the descriptive and the prescriptive without imposing someone's judgment, whether originating from the people in the setting ("What we really need around here …"), from expert opinion ("If these people knew what was good for them …"), or from our own personal assessment ("On the basis of my extensive experience, I strongly recommend …"). There is an implicit evaluative dimension in all description. *The antidote is restraint.* (Wolcott, 2009: 113-114, emphasis added)

224   B. Laws

In the spirit of Wolcott's perspective, this close of this book focuses on the main contributions to knowledge that have been established in this work, rather than a discussion of policy implications. This research contributes to key literatures including the psychology and sociology of prison life and the field of carceral geography. Most explicitly, this thesis attempts to add texture and nuance to accounts of imprisonment that are affectively 'narrow' and emotionally flat. In line with Crewe (2009: 334), who describes prison as a 'place of mirth and warmth as well as misery', the chapters above have attempted to develop the idea that different emotion scripts exist alongside one another in prison. Greater understanding of the prisoner world emerges from trying to understand these various coexisting and sometimes discordant narratives. Prisoners regulate and express their emotions in complex ways. Most prisoners used a combination of different strategies rather than a fixed approach, contingent on the context. That is to say, the social environment and spatial factors shaped emotion responses in meaningful ways. The specific focus on emotions in this process of adaptation responds to Grounds' (2004: 175) critique that studies of adaptation have 'focused on general measures of social adjustment rather than on more subtle, hidden kinds of psychological and emotional disability'. Arguably then, the sustained attention paid to emotion provides a more subtle measurement instrument to help pierce prisoners' inner worlds—though this study is cross-sectional in design and can say less about adaptation over time.

But emotion regulation is also shaped by pre-prison experiences of trauma, violence, neglect and isolation. This book, then, contributes to broader debates about importation and deprivation models of imprisonment: emphasising the importance of integrative approaches that see pre-prison experiences as creating increased susceptibly, or sensitivity, towards particular institutional practices. More specifically, the introduction of psychosocial literature reveals how particular prisoners carry complex traumas inside, in what De Zulueta (1993: 125) terms 'the hidden rage that throbs beneath their defences'. This pain is often triggered by institutional conditions that make certain kinds of emotional expressions more or less permissible. Penalising emotions like anger, joy or sadness effectively tightened and funnelled the repertoire of 'acceptable' feelings that prisoners could display, which in turn leads to both destructive explosions of feelings and emotional numbing. A modern pain of imprisonment is locatable through the form of emotional constriction, which is perhaps a particular consequence of the 'new penology' (Feeley & Simon, 1992) that increasingly isolates and alienates the individual prisoner. Institutional order is achieved, in no small part, through coercively containing prisoners' emotions. Sherman and Strang (2011: 145) claim that 'the primary task of justice is to manage emotions', while Karstedt (2011: 3) maintains that criminal justice systems are at their best when they provide 'mechanisms that are capable of "cooling off" emotions, converting them into more sociable emotions, or channelling them back into reasonable and more standardised patterns of actions and thoughts'. But just as Easteal (2001) found in the prisons context, that expressions of trauma and pain are often interpreted as resistance and non-compliance, a similar case is apparent here with emotions. This study has shown that emotions are often the subject to over-policing and institutional mismanagement that appeared to enflame and catalyse strong emotions. It was found that both sorrow and joy is given little outlet for expression, and that this could have quite destructive consequences. This analysis forms an important dialogue with broader discussions of justice and the 'right' to emotional expression.

This book has been in dialogue with Goffman's (1959) dramaturgical metaphor, that has shaped many of the binary distinctions found in prisons research, including 'inside' and 'outside', 'public' and 'private', 'backstage' and 'frontstage' areas in prison (see Moran, 2015). While Goffman's metaphor is illuminating, focusing the lens squarely on social interactions and impression management is also reductive. Goffman himself openly acknowledged this restrictive focus, noting that 'scaffolds…are to build other things with, and should be erected with an eye to taking them down' (Goffman, 1959: 246). This book has attempted to introduce psychological and spatial perspectives alongside social interactions in a way that tries to move this debate forward. A contention of both studies is that emotions are central to routine operations of social interactions in prison (Crawley, 2011). The various attempts by prisoners to regulate their emotions can be seen as attempts to establish and negotiate order in their environments (see Sparks et al., 1996). Displays of anger and aggression say much about the loss of power and control and the attempts to restore it.

This book has also formed a close dialogue with the carceral geography literature, which develops the knowledge base on imprisonment by shifting the focus from *time* and foregrounding the study of *space* (Morin & Moran, 2015). In so doing, this literature reveals that there is far more to prison space than traditionally conceived. Put simply, there is more spatial texture, differentiation, and fluidity than suggested in the binary distinctions set out above. The conceptualisation of imprisonment in this study has revealed a colourful 'patchwork' of micro climates (Smoyer & Blankenship, 2014) and challenges accounts that present the prison as a grey, undifferentiated monolith. It specifically drives forward the argument of Crewe et al. (2014) that prisons have a distinctive emotional geography. This research, then, contributes to a changing narrative by highlighting the affective dimensions of prison spaces in some detail: saying more about the underlying mechanisms that makes particular prisons zones hostile or cathartic places.

There are important wider linkages here with critical theorisations of prison architecture and spatial practices. At a moment in time when the Ministry of Justice is constructing multiple 'warehouse' style, 'super prisons' across England and Wales, it is important to note that: 'Ugly, bleak, uninspiring buildings give expression to a penal policy that is denuded of hope' (O'Donnell, 2014: 113), and can instil feelings of 'disenchantment' among prisoners (see Jewkes, 2012). The findings in this thesis reinforce the idea that the design and ordering of space shapes the quality of prisoners' relations, levels of isolation, and community spirit. Living in sprawling, often unclean, house blocks was experienced by prisoners as an assault on the soul (Price, 2012), and a commentary on their perceived status as subhuman.

Furthermore, this work resonates with recent critical studies of imprisonment that have attempted to reintegrate emotion into academic debates. These authors have, in different ways, highlighted the emotional complexity of imprisonment (Crawley, 2004; Crewe, 2014; Laws, 2019; Liebling, 2014). More specifically, this has entailed challenging preconceptions and assumptions about prisoner emotion (Liebling, 2009), the over-emphasis of anger and aggression (Laws & Crewe, 2016), and the focus on events over the 'everyday' aspects of prison life (Crawley, 2004). Generally, then, this thesis can be understood as a direct attempt to develop each of these critical ideas to increase our knowledge of prisoners' emotional worlds. Put short, by considering a broader repertoire of emotion states and foregrounding the 'day-to-day' quality of emotions, this research hopes to contribute to a more nuanced understanding of prisoner experiences. As Crawley (2011: 269) argues: 'Emotions…are not merely an "add on" to prison life. On the contrary, the language of the emotions is a central—and very powerful—means by which to communicate what it means to live and work in a prison.' This book affirms this standpoint by showing how studying emotions in prison at different level of analysis provides a valuable link between social structures and individual actors (Barbalet, 2001). The book has revealed how the various pathways of emotional management are influenced deeply by the (anti) social world of the prison and its particular spatial design: emotional suppression and expression is both a product of, and a response to, institutional management.

By focusing on the quotidian we can see how different aspects of imprisonment are connected. As highlighted in several places of this book, solitary confinement does not exist in a vacuum divorced from the context of other kinds of imprisonment. Through bringing these two studies together I hope to make this connection clearer. Prisoners who go to segregation are embroiled in all the kinds of contexts and problems well-articulated in the first study.

Limitations and Future Directions

This book has aimed to centralise emotions in the study of three prisons. To guide this approach, feeling was understood through different frames of analysis—the self, the social, and the spatial. In reality, there are connections and synergies that cut across these conceptual categories. Indeed, as Davidson & Milligan (2004: 524) explain, emotions can be understood as 'as a form of connective tissue' that link a number of different levels of analysis together. The authors further state that 'emotions are understandable—"sensible"—only in the context of particular places. Likewise, place

228   B. Laws

must be felt to make sense' (524). In a similar manner, Simonsen (2013: 18) explains that emotions are always a product (whether directly or indirectly) of forces that 'are essentially *relational*', being 'formed in the intertwining of our "own" bodily flesh with the flesh of the world and with the intercorporeal flesh of humanity'. The division of emotion into three categories this research has merely aspired to orient the findings in a digestible and clarifying manner. Future work could tunnel further inwards to consider the ways in which emotions are embodied, as attempted in Chap. 7. And by contrast, widening out emotionality to consider the ways in which broader political forces and philosophies of punishment shape prisoner affects (such as national increases in sentence lengths).

The extent to which prisoners emotionally adapt to imprisonment has not been wholly reconciled in this book, though the development of the emotion regulation framework beyond descriptive categories was a movement in this direction. In their influential book, *Psychological Survival*, Cohen and Taylor (1972: 105) pose a question that had important ramifications here: 'Would the cumulative result of years of working at something which looked like adaptation, in fact really be a process of learning how to deteriorate?' Such questions have a long history in prisons research, Clemmer (1940: 299) introduced the term 'prisonization' as a 'taking on, in greater or less degree, of the folkways, mores, customs, and general culture of the penitentiary'. At the emotional level, this research reveals the sometimes 'double-edged' nature of adapting to imprisonment and that feelings could be 'institutionally shaped' in the process. On one hand, the most content participants were not passively 'routinized' by the establishment, but rather, appeared to stamp their agency on these daily routines. However, actively co-opting the prison regime in any manner was controversial as some felt that this constituted sacrificing their 'true selves' and losing touch with their outside personas (see Laws 2020). Future research could explore these linkages between institutionalisation and the 'deterioration' of personality, and the broader intersections between emotional regulation and identity. This could involve looking at patterns of emotional development over time through a longitudinal style study.

This book has approached emotion in a broad manner deemed appropriate for explorative research. However, its completion raises questions about the examining specific sets of emotional states such as joy, love and hope. Barbalet (2001: 26) argues that 'it is only particular emotions which people are moved by; emotion in general only exists as an imprecise category of thought'. Equally, future research could delve deeper into the analysis of regulation strategies, and investigate emotion and the micro-climates of prison space. Finally, there are issues surrounding the overall generalisability of these findings. It is well documented that prisons have their own unique histories and institutional cultures, a factor that has implications for emotional dynamics. While only three prisons have been analysed here, it is hoped that the findings will resonate with other similar prison establishments and that the emotions these participants felt and conveyed will transfer, at least partially, to other prisoners' experiences.

References

Anderson, K., & Smith, S. J. (2001). Editorial: Emotional geographies. *Transactions of the Institute of British Geographers, 26*(1), 7–10.

Barbalet, J. M. (2001). *Emotion, social theory, and social structure: A macrosociological approach.* Cambridge University Press.

Bluhm, H. O. (1948). How did they survive? Mechanisms of defense in Nazi concentration camps. *American Journal of Psychotherapy, 2*, 3–32.

Calverley, A., & Farrall, S. (2011). Introduction. In S. Karstedt, I. Loader, & H. Strang (Eds.), *Emotions, crime and justice.* Bloomsbury Publishing.

Clemmer, D. (1940). *The prison community.* Christopher Publishing House.

Cohen, D., & Nisbett, R. E. (1994). Self-protection and the culture of honor: Explaining southern violence. *Personality and Social Psychology Bulletin, 20*(5), 551–567.

Cohen, S., & Taylor, L. (1972). *Psychological survival: The experience of long-term imprisonment.* Penguin.

Collins, R. (1990). Stratification, emotional energy, and the transient emotions. In T. D. Kemper (Ed.), *SUNY series in the sociology of emotions. Research agendas in the sociology of emotions.* State University of New York Press.

Collins, R. (2011). Forward panic and violent atrocities. In S. Karstedt, I. Loader, & H. Strang (Eds.), *Emotions, crime and justice.* Bloomsbury Publishing.

Crawley, E. M. (2004). Emotion and performance: Prison officers and the presentation of self in prisons. *Punishment & Society, 6*(4), 411–427. https://doi.org/10.1177/1462474504046121

Crawley, E. (2011). Managing prisoners, managing emotion: The dynamics of age, culture and identity. *Emotions, crime and justice*, 102–121.

Crewe, B. (2009). *The prisoner society: Power, adaptation and social life in an English prison*. Oxford University Press.

Crewe, B. (2011). Depth, weight, tightness: Revisiting the pains of imprisonment. *Punishment & Society, 13*(5), 509–529. https://doi.org/10.1177/1462474511422172

Crewe, B. (2013). Writing and reading a prison: Making use of prisoner life stories. *Criminal Justice Matters, 91*(1), 20–20. https://doi.org/10.1080/09627251.2013.778750

Crewe, B. (2014). Not looking hard enough: Masculinity, emotion, and prison research. *Qualitative Inquiry, 20*(4), 392–403. https://doi.org/10.1177/1077800413515829

Crewe, B., Warr, J., Bennett, P., & Smith, A. (2014). The emotional geography of prison life. *Theoretical Criminology, 18*(1), 56–74.

Davidson, J., & Milligan, C. (2004). *Embodying emotion, sensing space: Introducing emotional geographies* (November 2014), 37–41. https://doi.org/10.1080/1464936042000317677

De Viggiani, N. (2012). Trying to be something you are not: Masculine performances within a prison setting. *Men and Masculinities, 15*(3), 271–291.

de Zulueta, F. (1993). *From pain to violence: The traumatic roots of destructiveness*. Whurr Publishers.

Deaux, K. (2000). Gender and emotion: Notes from a grateful tourist. In A. Fischer (Ed.), *Gender and emotion: Social psychological perspectives*. University Press.

Evans, D. (2002). *Emotion: The science of sentiment*. University Press.

Easteal, P. (2001). Women in Australian prisons: The cycle of abuse and dysfunctional environments. *The Prison Journal, 81*(1), 87–12.

Farmer, M. (2017). *The importance of strengthening prisoners' family ties to prevent reoffending and reduce intergenerational crime*. Ministry of Justice.

Feeley, M. M., & Simon, J. (1992). The new penology: Notes on the emerging strategy of corrections and its implications. *Criminology, 30*(4), 449–474.

Fischer, A. H., & Manstead, A. S. (2008). Social functions of emotion. In M. Lewis, J. M. Haviland-Jones, & L. F. Barrett (Eds.), *Handbook of emotions* (Vol. 3, pp. 456–468). The Guilford Press.

8 Conclusions 231

Garland, D. (2001). *The culture of control: Crime and social order in contemporary society.* University of Chicago Press.

Gilligan, C. (1992). *In a different voice: Psychological theory and women's development.* Harvard University Press.

Gilligan, J. (2003). Shame, guilt, and violence. *Social Research, 70*(4), 1149–1180.

Goffman, E. (1959). *The presentation of self in everyday life.* Anchor Books.

Goldin, P. R., McRae, K., Ramel, W., & Gross, J. J. (2008). The neural bases of emotion regulation: reappraisal and suppression of negative emotion. *Biological psychiatry, 63*(6), 577–586.

Greer, K. (2002). Walking an emotional tightrope: Managing emotions in a women's prison. *Symbolic Interaction, 25*(1), 117–139. https://doi.org/10.1525/si.2002.25.1.117

Grounds, A. (2004). Psychological consequences of wrongful conviction and imprisonment. *Canadian journal of criminology and criminal justice, 46*(2), 165–182.

Haney, C. (2005). *Death by design: Capital punishment as a social psychological system.* Oxford University Press.

Hawkins, D. R. (2013). *Letting go: The pathway of surrender.* Hay House Inc.

Her Majesty's Inspectorate of Prisons. (2016). *Life in prison contact with families and friends.*

Jamieson, R., & Grounds, A. (2005). Release and adjustment: Perspectives from studies of wrongly convicted and politically motivated prisoners. *The effects of imprisonment, 33*–65.

Jewkes, Y. (2002). *Captive audience: Media, masculinity and power in prisons.* Willian Publishing.

Jewkes, Y. (2005a). Loss, liminality and the life sentence: Managing identity through a disrupted lifecourse. In A. Liebling & S. Maruna (Eds.), *The effects of imprisonment.* Routledge.

Jewkes, Y. (2005b). Men behind bars 'doing' masculinity as an adaptation to imprisonment. *Men and Masculinities, 8*(1), 44–63.

Jewkes, Y. (2012). Aesthetics and anaesthetics: The architecture of incarceration. In L. K. Cheliotis (Ed.), *The arts of imprisonment: Control, resistance and empowerment.* Routledge.

Karstedt, S. (2011). Handle with care: Emotions, crime and justice. Emotions, crime and justice [Onati International Series in Law and Society, Number 1], 1–19.

Kruttschnitt, C., & Gartner, R. (2005). *Marking time in the golden state: Women's imprisonment in California.* University Press.

Laws, B., & Crewe, B. (2016). Emotion regulation among male prisoners. *Theoretical Criminology, 20*(4), 529–547. https://doi.org/10.1177/1362480615622532

Laws, B. (2019). The return of the suppressed: Exploring how emotional suppression reappears as violence and pain among male and female prisoners. *Punishment & Society, 21*(5), 560–577.

Laws, B. (2020). Reimaging 'the Self' in criminology: Transcendence, unconscious states and the limits of narrative criminology. *Theoretical criminology.* https://doi.org/10.1080/1362480620919102

Layder, D. (2004). *Emotion in social life: The lost heart of society.* Sage.

Leigey, M. E., & Reed, K. L. (2010). A woman's life before serving life: Examining the negative pre-incarceration life events of female life-sentenced inmates. *Women & Criminal Justice, 20*(January), 302–322. https://doi.org/10.1080/08974454.2010.512229

Levant, R. F. (1995). *Toward the reconstruction of masculinity: A new psychology of men.* Basic Books.

Liebling, A. (2009). Women in prison prefer legitimacy to sex. *British Society of Criminology Newsletter, 63,* 19–23.

Liebling, A. (2014). Postscript: Integrity and emotion in prisons research. *Qualitative Inquiry, 20*(4), 481–486.

Manstead, A. S. R., & Fischer, A. H. (2000). Emotion regulation in full. *Psychological Inquiry, 11*(3), 188–191.

Maté, G. (2003). *When the body says no: Exploring the stress disease connection.* Wiley & Sons.

Moran, D. (2011). Between outside and inside? Prison visiting rooms as liminal carceral spaces. *GeoJournal, 78*(2), 339–351. https://doi.org/10.1007/s10708-011-9442-6

Moran, D. (2015). *Carceral geography: Spaces and practices of incarceration.* Ashgate.

Morin, K. M., & Moran, D. (Eds.). (2015). *Historical geographies of prisons: Unlocking the usable carceral past.* Routledge.

O'Donnell, I. (2014). *Prisoners, solitude, and time.* Oxford University Press.

Owen, B. A. (1998). *In the mix: Struggle and survival in a women's prison.* SUNY Press.

Pennebaker, J. W. (1997). Writing about emotional experiences as a therapeutic process. *Psychological Science, 8*(3), 162–166. https://doi.org/10.1111/j.14679280.1997.tb00403.x

8 Conclusions   233

Planalp, S. (1999). *Communicating emotion: Social, moral, and cultural processes.* University Press.

Price, T. (2012). *The mythic modern: Architectural expeditions into the spirit.* ORO Editions.

Rustin, M. (2009). The missing dimension: Emotions in the social sciences. In S. D. Sclater, D. W. Jones, H. Price, & C. Yates (Eds.), *Emotion: New psychosocial perspectives.* Palgrave Geography.

Sapolsky, R. M. (2017). *Behave: The biology of humans at our best and worst.* Penguin.

Sherman, L. W. (2003). Reason for emotion: Reinventing justice with theories, innovations, and research—The American Society of Criminology 2002 Presidential Address. *Criminology, 41*(1), 1–38.

Sherman, L., & Strang, H. (2011). Empathy for the devil: Nature and nurture in restorative justice. In *Emotions, crime and justice.* Hart Publishing.

Simonsen, K. (2013). In quest of a new humanism: Embodiment, experience and phenomenology as critical geography. *Progresss in Human Geography, 37*(1), 10–26.

Sloan, J. (2012). 'You can see your face in my floor': Examining the function of cleanliness in an adult male prison. *The Howard Journal of Criminal Justice, 51*(4), 400–410.

Smoyer, A. B., & Blankenship, K. M. (2014). Dealing food: Female drug users' narratives about food in a prison place and implications for their health. *International Journal of Drug Policy, 25*(3), 562–568. https://doi.org/10.1016/j.drugpo.2013.10.013

Sparks, R., Bottoms, A., & Hay, W. (1996). *Prisons and the Problem of Order.* Clarendon Press.

Sykes, G. M. (1954). *The society of captives: A study of a maximum security prison.* Princeton University Press.

Thompson, K. L., Hannan, S. M., & Miron, L. R. (2014). Fight, flight, and freeze: Threat sensitivity and emotion dysregulation in survivors of chronic childhood maltreatment. *Personality and Individual Differences, 69,* 28–32. https://doi.org/10.1016/j.paid.2014.05.005

Toch, H. (1992). *Living in prison: The ecology of survival.* The Free Press.

Toch, H. (1998). Hypermasculinity and prison violence. In L. H. Bowker (Ed.), *Masculinities and violence.* Sage Publications.

Turner, V. W. (1974). *Dramas, fields and metaphors.* Cornell University Press.

van der Kolk, B. (2014). *The body keeps the score.* Viking.

Wright, S., Crewe, B., & Hulley, S. (2017). Suppression, denial, sublimation: Defending against the initial pains of very long life sentences. *Theoretical Criminology, 21*(2), 225–246.

Zamble, E., & Porporino, F. (1990). Coping, imprisonment, and rehabilitation: Some data and their implications. *Criminal Justice and Behavior, 17*(1), 53–70.

Appendix A: Prisoner Artwork

Exploding head

"Whenever people speak of emotions and thoughts they always say I'm up to here with it [points to head]. So I literally did water and a person drowning up to their mouth and they've got the top half of the head missing and it's overflowing ... The whole thing with the head is that there's too much going on and everything is blown up and it's seeping out into the water. And the persons literally gripping onto their skull and they're struggling."

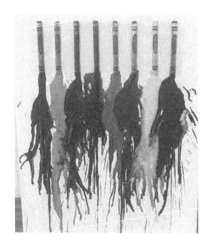

Waxed Emotions

"It is literally how all your emotions can get mixed-up, your dark emotions, the light emotions, the red for the anger, literally whole emotions just getting splattered, they are very channelled at the top ... At the bottom emotions were pouring-out almost making tears from the waxed effects that are coming off of it."

See, Speak, Hear No Evil

"You're not hearing, you're not seeing, you're not getting at what's under the surface. So she [her friend] was trying to cope but I was misinterpreting it. It was just pissing me off, whereas as her friend I should have been more supportive. But this [picture] is about that oblivion of not caring, that perception of not being interested, we do it a lot in prison because we don't look into what is really going on."

Appendix B: Plutchik's Emotion Wheel

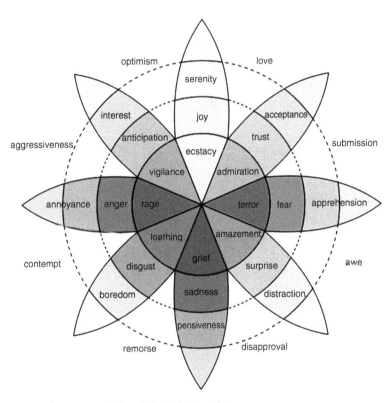

See original image in Plutchik (2001: 349).

© The Author(s), under exclusive license to Springer Nature Switzerland AG 2022
B. Laws, *Caged Emotions*, Palgrave Studies in Prisons and Penology,
https://doi.org/10.1007/978-3-030-96083-4

Pheonix Rising

'What I've realised over time as I've got a thing for phoenixes, I didn't realise what they meant until recently I understood the rising from the ashes kind of thing.'

Interviewer: Do you see yourself as a Phoenix?

'Yes definitely, after this process I have to'

References

Abbott, J. H., & Mailer, N. (1981). *In the belly of the beast: Letters from prison.* Random House.

Abrams, A. I., & Siegel, L. M. (1978). The transcendental meditation program and rehabilitation at Folsom State Prison: A cross-validation study. *Correctional Psychologist, 5*(1), 3–20.

Adey, P. (2008). Airports, mobility and the calculative architecture of affective control. *Geoforum, 39*(1), 438–451.

Alexander, M. G., & Wood, W. (2000). Women, men, and positive emotions: A social role interpretation. In A. Fischer (Ed.), *Gender and emotion: Social psychological perspectives.* Cambridge University Press.

Allen, J. (2006). Ambient power: Berlin's Potsdamer Platz and the seductive logic of public spaces. *Urban Studies, 43*(2), 441–455.

Anderson, E., & McGuire, R. (2010). Inclusive masculinity theory and the gendered politics of men's rugby. *Journal of Gender Studies, 19*(3), 249–261.

Anderson, K., & Smith, S. J. (2001). Editorial: Emotional geographies. *Transactions of the Institute of British Geographers, 26*(1), 7–10.

Asad, T. (1997). Remarks on the anthropology of the body. In S. Coakley (Ed.), *Religion and the body.* Cambridge University Press.

© The Author(s), under exclusive license to Springer Nature Switzerland AG 2022
B. Laws, *Caged Emotions*, Palgrave Studies in Prisons and Penology,
https://doi.org/10.1007/978-3-030-96083-4

References

Atkinson, R., & Flint, J. (2004). Fortress UK? Gated communities, the spatial revolt of the elites and time–space trajectories of segregation. *Housing Studies, 19*(6), 875–892.

Atwood, J. E. (2000). *Too much time: Women in prison.* Phaidon Press.

Auty, K. M., Cope, A., & Liebling, A. (2017). A systematic review and meta-analysis of yoga and mindfulness meditation in prison: Effects on psychological well-being and behavioural functioning. *International Journal of Offender Therapy and Comparative Criminology, 61*(6), 689–710.

Averill, J. R. (1983). Studies on anger and aggression: Implications for theories of emotion. *American Psychologist, 38*(11), 1145.

Baldry, E. (2010). Women in transition: From prison to.... *Current Issues in Criminal Justice, 22,* 253–268.

Barbalet, J. M. (2001). *Emotion, social theory, and social structure: A macrosociological approach.* Cambridge University Press.

Baron-Cohen, S. (2012). *The essential difference: The male and female brain.* Penguin London.

Barsade, S. G. (2002). The ripple effect: Emotional contagion and its influence on group behavior. *Administrative Science Quarterly, 47*(4), 644–675.

Baumeister, R. F., Dale, K., & Sommer, K. L. (1998). Freudian defense mechanisms and empirical findings in modern social psychology: Reaction formation, projection, displacement, undoing, isolation, sublimation, and denial. *Journal of Personality, 66*(6), 1081–1124.

Ben-David, S., & Silfen, P. (1994). In quest of a lost father? Inmates' preferences of staff relation in a psychiatric prison ward. *International Journal of Offender Therapy and Comparative Criminology, 38*(2), 131–139.

Bennett, P. (2010). Security and the maintenance of therapeutic space: A Grendon debate. *Prison Sevice Journal, 187,* 48–187.

Bentham, J. (1791). *Panopticon or the inspection house.* T. Payne Mews Gate.

Berlyne, D. E. (1972). Humor and its kin. In J. H. Goldstein & P. E. McGhee (Eds.), *The psychology references of humor.* Academic Press.

Bettelheim, B. (1943). Individual and mass behavior in extreme situations. *The Journal of Abnormal and Social Psychology, 38*(4), 417–452. https://doi.org/10.1037/h0061208

Bluhm, H. O. (1948). How did they survive? Mechanisms of defense in Nazi concentration camps. *American Journal of Psychotherapy, 2,* 3–32.

Boag, S. (2010). Repression, suppression, and conscious awareness. *Psychoanalytic Psychology, 27*(2), 164–181. https://doi.org/10.1037/a0019416

References 243

Boden, J. M., & Baumeister, R. F. (1997). Repressive coping: Distraction using pleasant thoughts and memories. *Journal of Personality and Social Psychology, 73*, 45–62.

Boden, Z. V., Gibson, S., Owen, G. J., & Benson, O. (2016). Feelings and intersubjectivity in qualitative suicide research. *Qualitative Health Research, 26*(8), 1078–1090. https://doi.org/10.1177/1049732315576709

Bondi, L. (2014). Understanding feelings: Engaging with unconscious communication and embodied knowledge. *Emotion, Space and Society, 10*(1), 44–54. https://doi.org/10.1016/j.emospa.2013.03.009

Bonta, J., & Gendreau, P. (1990). Reexamining the cruel and unusual punishment of prison life. *Law and Human Behavior, 14*(4), 347–372.

Bosworth, M. (1999). *Engendering resistance: Agency and power in women's prisons*. Routledge.

Bosworth, M., & Carrabine, E. (2001). Reassessing resistance race, gender and sexuality in prison. *Punishment & Society, 3*(4), 501–515.

Bosworth, M., & Kaufman, E. (2012). Gender and punishment. In J. Simon & R. Sparks (Eds.), *The Sage handbook of punishment and society*. Sage.

Bosworth, M., Campbell, D., Demby, B., Ferranti, S. M., & Santos, M. (2005). Doing prison research: Views from inside. *Qualitative Inquiry, 11*(2), 249–264.

Bottoms, A. (1999). Interpersonal violence and social order in prisons. In M. Tonry & J. Petersilia (Eds.), *Prisons* (pp. 205–281). University of Chicago Press.

Boyle, J. (1977). *A sense of freedom*. Littlehampton Book Services Ltd.

Bradley, R. G., & Davino, K. M. (2002). Women's perceptions of the prison environment: When prison is 'the safest place I've ever been'. *Psychology of Women Quarterly, 26*(4), 351–359.

Brody, L. R. (1999). *Gender, emotion, and the family*. Harvard University Press.

Brody, L. R. (2000). The socialization of gender differences in emotional expression: Display rules, infant temperament, and differentiation. In A. Fischer (Ed.), *Gender and emotion: Social psychological perspectives*. University Press.

Brown, G. (Ed.). (2019). *Psychoanalytic thinking on the unhoused mind*. Routledge.

Brownmiller, S. (1984). *Femininity*. Hamish Hamilton.

Brzuzy, S., Ault, A., & Segal, E. A. (1997). Conducting qualitative interviews with women survivors of trauma. *Affilia, 12*(1), 76–83. https://doi.org/10.1177/088610999701200105

Burgo, J. (2012). *Why do I do that? Psychological defence mechanisms*. New Rise Press.

244   References

Butler, E. A., & Gross, J. J. (2004). Hiding feelings in social contexts: Out of sight is not out of mind. In P. Philippot & R. S. Feldman (Eds.), *The regulation of emotion*. Lawrence Erlbaum Associates.

Calverley, A., & Farrall, S. (2011). Introduction. In S. Karstedt, I. Loader, & H. Strang (Eds.), *Emotions, crime and justice*. Bloomsbury Publishing.

Campbell, A. (1993). *Out of Control: Men, Women and Aggression*. Pandora.

Cancian, F. M., & Gordon, S. L. (1988). Changing emotion norms in marriage: Love and anger in US women's magazines since 1900. *Gender & Society, 2*(3), 308–342.

Carceral, K. C. (2006). *Prison, Inc: A convict exposes life inside a private prison*. NYU Press.

Carlen, P. (1983). *Women's imprisonment: A study in social control*. Routledge & Kegan Paul.

Carlen, P. (1998). *Sledgehammer: Women's imprisonment at the millennium*. Springer.

Carlen, P. (2013). *Women and punishment*. Willan.

Carpiano, R. M. (2009). Come take a walk with me: The 'Go-Along' interview as a novel method for studying the implications of place for health and well-being. *Health and Place, 15*(1), 263–272. https://doi.org/10.1016/j.healthplace.2008.05.003

Carrabine, E., & Longhurst, B. (1998). Gender and prison organisation: Some comments on masculinities and prison management. *The Howard Journal of Criminal Justice, 37*(2), 161–176.

Casella, J., Ridgeway, J., & Shourd, S. (2016). *Hell is a very small place: Voices from solitary confinement*. New York Press.

Celinska, K. (2013). The role of family in the lives of incarcerated women. *Prison Service Journal, 207*, 23–26.

Chamberlen, A. (2016). Embodying prison pain: Women's experiences of self-injury in prison and the emotions of punishment. *Theoretical Criminology, 20*(2), 205–219.

Chamberlen, A. (2018). *Embodying punishment: Emotions, identities, and lived experiences in women's prisons*. Oxford University Press.

Chesney-Lind, M. (2002). Criminalizing victimization: The unintended consequences of pro-arrest policies for girls and women. *Criminology & Public Policy, 2*(1), 81–90.

Clements, C. B., Althouse, R., Ax, R. K., Magaletta, P. R., Fagan, T. J., & Wormith, J. S. (2007). Systemic issues and correctional outcomes: Expanding the scope of correctional psychology. *Criminal Justice and Behavior, 34*(7), 919–932.

References   245

Clemmer, D. (1940). *The prison community*. Christopher Publishing House.

Cochran, L., & Claspell, E. (1987). The meaning of grief: *A dramaturgical approach to understanding emotion*. Greenwood Press.

Cohen, D., & Nisbett, R. E. (1994). Self-protection and the culture of honor: Explaining southern violence. *Personality and Social Psychology Bulletin, 20*(5), 551–567.

Cohen, S., & Taylor, L. (1972). *Psychological survival: The experience of long-term imprisonment*. Penguin.

Cole, P. M., Dennis, T. A., Smith-Simon, K. E., & Cohen, L. H. (2009). Preschoolers' emotion regulation strategy understanding: Relations with emotion socialization and child self-regulation. *Social Development, 18*(2), 324–352.

Collins, R. (1990). Stratification, emotional energy, and the transient emotions. In T. D. Kemper (Ed.), *SUNY series in the sociology of emotions. Research agendas in the sociology of emotions*. State University of New York Press.

Collins, R. (2011). Forward panic and violent atrocities. In S. Karstedt, I. Loader, & H. Strang (Eds.), *Emotions, crime and justice*. Bloomsbury Publishing.

Collins English Dictionary. (1999). Harper Collins Publishers.

Connell, R. (1987). *Gender and power*. Polity Press.

Cook, F., & Eilkison, M. (1998). *Hard cell*. The Bluecoat Press.

Cowburn, M. (2007). Men researching men in prison: The challenges for pro-feminist research. *The Howard Journal of Criminal Justice, 46*(3), 276–288.

Crawley, E. M. (2004). Emotion and performance: Prison officers and the presentation of self in prisons. *Punishment & Society, 6*(4), 411–427. https://doi.org/10.1177/1462474504046121

Crawley, E. (2011). Managing prisoners, managing emotion: The dynamics of age, culture and identity. *Emotions, crime and justice*, 102–121.

Cressey, D. R., & Galtung, J. (1961). *The prison: Studies in institutional organization and change*. Holt, Rinehart and Winston.

Crewe, B. (2006). Male prisoners' orientations towards female officers in an English prison. *Punishment & Society, 8*(4), 395–421.

Crewe, B. (2009). *The prisoner society: Power, adaptation and social life in an English prison*. Oxford University Press.

Crewe, B. (2011a). Depth, weight, tightness: Revisiting the pains of imprisonment. *Punishment & Society, 13*(5), 509–529.

Crewe, B. (2011b). Soft power in prison: Implications for staff–prisoner relationships, liberty and legitimacy. *European Journal of Criminology, 8*(6), 455–468.

246 References

Crewe, B. (2013). Writing and reading a prison: Making use of prisoner life stories. *Criminal Justice Matters, 91*(1), 20–20. https://doi.org/10.108 0/09627251.2013.778750

Crewe, B. (2014). Not looking hard enough: Masculinity, emotion, and prison research. *Qualitative Inquiry, 20*(4), 392–403. https://doi.org/ 10.1177/1077800413515829

Crewe, B., & Maruna, S. (2006). Self-narratives and ethnographic fieldwork. In D. Hobbs & R. Wright (Eds.), *The Sage handbook of fieldwork*. Sage.

Crewe, B., Warr, J., Bennett, P., & Smith, A. (2014). The emotional geography of prison life. *Theoretical Criminology, 18*(1), 56–74.

Crewe, B., Hulley, S., & Wright, S. (2017a). Swimming with the tide: Adapting to long-term imprisonment. *Justice Quarterly, 34*(3), 517–541. https://doi.org/10.1080/07418825.2016.1190394

Crewe, B., Hulley, S., & Wright, S. (2017b). The gendered pains of life imprisonment. *British Journal of Criminology, 57*(6), 1359–1378.

Crewe, B., Hulley, S., & Wright, S. (2020). *Life imprisonment from young adulthood*. Palgrave Macmillan UK.

Crotty, M. (2003). *The foundations of social research: Meaning and perspective in the research process*. Sage.

Croyle, K. L., & Waltz, J. (2002). Emotional awareness and couples' relationship satisfaction. *Journal of Marital and Family Therapy, 28*(4), 435–444. https://doi.org/10.1111/j.1752-0606.2002.tb00368.x

Csikszentmihalyi, M. (1991). *Flow: The psychology of optimal experience*. Harper Perennial.

Dale, K., & Burrell, G. (2003). An-aesthetics and architecture. In A. Carr & P. Hancock (Eds.), *Art and aesthetics at work*. Palgrave Macmillan.

Damasio, A. R. (1999). *The feeling of what happens: Body and emotion in the making of consciousness*. Houghton Mifflin Harcourt.

Data Protection Act. (1998). *Data Protection Act: Your responsibilities and obligations to data protection*. Information Commissioner's Office.

Davidson, J., & Milligan, C. (2004). *Embodying emotion, sensing space: Introducing emotional geographies* (November 2014), 37–41. https://doi. org/10.1080/1464936042000317677

de Dardel, J. (2013). Resisting 'bare life': Prisoners' agency in the New Prison Culture Era in Columbia. In D. Conlon, N. Gill, & D. Moran (Eds.), *Carceral spaces: Mobility and agency in imprisonment and migrant detention*. Ashgate Publishing Ltd.

References 247

De Viggiani, N. (2012). Trying to be something you are not: Masculine performances within a prison setting. *Men and Masculinities, 15*(3), 271–291.

de Zulueta, F. (1993). *From pain to violence: The traumatic roots of destructiveness.* Whurr Publishers.

Deaux, K. (2000). Gender and emotion: Notes from a grateful tourist. In A. Fischer (Ed.), *Gender and emotion: Social psychological perspectives.* University Press.

Delisi, M., Berg, M. T., & Hochstetler, A. (2004). Gang members, career criminals and prison violence: Further specification of the importation model of inmate behavior. *Criminal Justice Studies, 17*(4), 369–383.

Denborough, D. (2001). Grappling with issues of privilege: A male prison worker's perspective. In D. Sabo, T. Kupers, & W. London (Eds.), *Prison masculinities.* Temple University Press.

Denzin, K. N., & Lincoln, Y. S. (2000). *The Sage handbook of qualitative research.* Sage.

Dirsuweit, T. (1999). Carceral spaces in South Africa: A case study of institutional power, sexuality and transgression in a women's prison. *Geoforum, 30*(1), 71–83.

Djurichkovic, A. (2011). *Art in prisons: A literature review of the philosophies and impacts of visual art programs for correctional populations.* Report for Arts Access Australia. Sidney: UTS ePress.

Douglas, M. (1966/2002). *Purity and danger.* Routledge.

Drake, D. H., & Harvey, J. (2014). Performing the role of ethnographer: Processing and managing the emotional dimensions of prison research. *International Journal of Social Research Methodology, 17*(5), 489–501.

Duncombe, J., & Marsden, D. (1996). Extending the social: A response to Ian Craib. *Sociology, 30,* 155–158.

Easteal, P. (2001). Women in Australian prisons: The cycle of abuse and dysfunctional environments. *The Prison Journal, 81*(1), 87–112.

Eaton, N. R., Keyes, K. M., Krueger, R. F., Balsis, S., Skodol, A. E., Markon, K. E., & Hasin, D. S. (2012). An invariant dimensional liability model of gender differences in mental disorder prevalence: Evidence from a national sample. *Journal of Abnormal Psychology, 121*(1), 282.

Eckhart, M. (1994). *Selected writings.* Penguin.

Edensor, T. (2015). Producing atmospheres at the match: Fan cultures, commercialisation and mood management in English football. *Emotion, Space and Society, 15,* 82–89.

248   References

Edgar, K., O'Donnell, I., & Martin, C. (2003). *Prison violence: The dynamics of conflict, fear and power*. Willan.

Edgar, K., O'Donnell, I., & Martin, C. (2014). *Prison violence: Conflict, power and victimization*. Routledge.

Ehring, T., Tuschen-Caffier, B., Schnülle, J., Fischer, S., & Gross, J. J. (2010). Emotion regulation and vulnerability to depression: Spontaneous versus instructed use of emotion suppression and reappraisal. *Emotion, 10*(4), 563.

Ekman, P. (2007). *Emotions revealed: Recognizing faces and feelings to improve communication and emotional life*. Macmillan.

Ekman, P., & Scherer, K. (1984). Questions about emotion: An Introduction. In K. Scherer & P. Ekman (Eds.), *Approaches to emotion*. Lawrence Erlbaum.

Evans, R. (1982). *The fabrication of virtue: English prison architecture, 1750–1840*. University Press.

Evans, D. (2002). *Emotion: The science of sentiment*. University Press.

Evans, J., & Jones, P. (2011). The walking interview: Methodology, mobility and place. *Applied Geography, 31*(2), 849–858. https://doi.org/10.1016/j.apgeog.2010.09.005

Evans, T., & Wallace, P. (2007). A prison within a prison?: The masculinity narratives of male prisoners. *Men and Masculinities, 10*(4), 484–507. https://doi.org/10.1177/1097184X06291903

Fairweather, L. (2000). Psychological effects of the prison environment. In L. Fairweather & S. McConville (Eds.), *Prison architecture: Policy, design, and experience*. Routledge.

Fanon, F. (1961). *The wretched of the earth*. Grove.

Farmer, M. (2017). *The importance of strengthening prisoners' family ties to prevent reoffending and reduce intergenerational crime*. Ministry of Justice.

Feeley, M. M., & Simon, J. (1992). The new penology: Notes on the emerging strategy of corrections and its implications. *Criminology, 30*(4), 449–474.

Feldman, A. (1991). *Formations of violence: The narrative of the body and political terror in Northern Ireland*. University of Chicago Press.

Ferraro, K. J., & Moe, A. M. (2003). Women's stories of survival and resistance. In B. H. Zaitzow & J. Thomas (Eds.), *Women in prison: Gender and social control*. Lynne Rienner Publishers.

Fiddler, M. (2010). Four walls and what lies within: The meaning of space and place in prisons. *Prison Service Journal, 187*, 3–8.

Fineman, S. (2004). Getting the measure of emotion and the cautionary tale of emotional intelligence. *Human Relations, 57*(6), 719–740. https://doi.org/10.1177/0018726704044953

References   249

Fischer, A. H., & Manstead, A. S. (2000). The relation between gender and emotions in different cultures. *Gender and Emotion: Social Psychological Perspectives, 1*, 71–94.

Fischer, A. H., & Manstead, A. S. (2008). Social functions of emotion. In M. Lewis, J. M. Haviland-Jones, & L. F. Barrett (Eds.), *Handbook of emotions* (Vol. 3, pp. 456–468). The Guilford Press.

Fischer, A. H., Manstead, A. S., Evers, C., Timmers, M., & Valk, G. (2004). Motives and norms underlying emotion regulation. In P. Philippot & R. S. Feldman (Eds.), *The regulation of emotion*. Lawrence Erlbaum Associates.

Fivush, R., & Buckner, J. P. (2000). Gender, sadness, and depression: The development of emotional focus through gendered discourse. In A. Fischer (Ed.), *Gender and emotion: Social psychological perspectives*. University Press.

Folkman, S., & Lazarus, R. S. (1988). Coping as a mediator of emotion. *Journal of Personality and Social Psychology, 54*(3), 466.

Folkman, S., & Moskowitz, J. T. (2000). Stress, positive emotion, and coping. *Current Directions in Psychological Science, 9*(4), 115–118.

Foucault, M. (1977). *Discipline and punish*. Random House of Canada.

Foucault, M. (1979). *Discipline and punish*. Random House of Canada.

Frankl, V. E. (1985). *Man's search for meaning*. Simon and Schuster.

Fredrickson, B., & Levenson, R. W. (1998). Positive emotions speed recovery from the cardiovascular sequelae of negative emotions. *Cognition & Emotion, 12*(2), 191–220.

Frijda, N. H. (1986). *The emotions*. University Press.

Fromm, E. (1964). *The Heart of Man. American Mental Health Foundation*.

Frosh, S. (2003). Psychosocial studies and psychology: Is a critical approach emerging? *Human Relations, 56*(12), 1545–1567.

Gadd, D., & Jefferson, T. (2007). *Psychosocial criminology*. Sage.

Gambetta, D. (2009). *Codes of the underworld: How criminals communicate*. Princeton University Press.

Garland, D. (2001). *The culture of control: Crime and social order in contemporary society*. University of Chicago Press.

Gear, S. (2007). Behind the bars of masculinity: Male rape and homophobia in and about South African men's prisons. *Sexualities, 10*(2), 209–227.

Gelsthorpe, L. (2009). Emotions and contemporary developments in criminology. In S. D. Sclater, D. W. Jones, H. Price, & C. Yates (Eds.), *Emotion: New psychosocial perspectives*. Palgrave Geography.

Gendreau, P., & Bonta, J. (1984). Solitary confinement is not cruel and unusual punishment: People sometimes are. *Canadian Journal of Criminology, 26*(4), 467–478.

250 **References**

Gendreau, P., & Labrecque, R. M. (2018). The effects of administrative segregation. In *The Oxford handbook of prisons and imprisonment* (p. 340). Oxford University Press.

Gendreau, P., & Theriault, Y. (2011). *Bibliotherapy for cynics revisited: Commentary on a one year longitudinal study of the psychological effects of administrative segregation*. Corrections and Mental Health: An Update of the National Institute of Corrections.

Gibbons, J. A. (1997). Struggle and catharsis: Art in women's prisons. *The Journal of Arts Management, Law, and Society, 27*(1), 72–80.

Gifford, R. (2007). The consequences of living in high-rise buildings. *Architectural Science Review, 50*(1), 2–17.

Gillespie, K. (2010). The social life of space: Post-apartheid prisons, and the problem with architectural reform. *Prison Service Journal, 187*, 40–47.

Gilliat-Ray, S. (2011). 'Being there' the experience of shadowing a British Muslim Hospital chaplain. *Qualitative Research, 11*(5), 469–486. https://doi.org/10.1177/1468794111413223

Gilligan, C. (1992). In a different voice: *Psychological theory and women's development*. Harvard University Press.

Gilligan, J. (2003). Shame, guilt, and violence. *Social Research, 70*(4), 1149–1180.

Ginneken, E. F. (2015). Doing well or just doing time? A qualitative study of patterns of psychological adjustment in prison. *The Howard Journal of Crime and Justice, 54*(4), 352–370.

Goffman, E. (1959). *The presentation of self in everyday life*. Anchor Books.

Goffman, E. (1961). *Asylums: Essays on the social situation of mental patients and other inmates*. Aldine Transaction.

Goldie, P. (2003). One's remembered past: Narrative thinking, emotion, and the external perspective. *Philosophical Papers, 32*(3), 301–319.

Goldin, P. R., McRae, K., Ramel, W., & Gross, J. J. (2008). The neural bases of emotion regulation: Reappraisal and suppression of negative emotion. *Biological Psychiatry, 63*(6), 577–586.

Gonzalez, J. (1995). Autotopographies. In G. Braham & M. Driscoll (Eds.), *Prosthetic territories: Politics and Hypertechnologies*. Westview Press.

Goss, J. (1993). The 'magic of the mall': An analysis of form, function, and meaning in the contemporary retail built environment. *Annals of the Association of American Geographers, 83*(1), 18–47.

Grassian, S. (1983). Psychopathological effects of solitary confinement. *American Journal of Psychiatry, 140*(11), 1450–1454.

References   251

Gray, E., Jackson, J., & Farrall, S. (2008). Researching everyday emotions: Towards a multi-disciplinary investigation of the fear of crime. *Journal of Chemical Information and Modeling, 53*, 1689–1699. https://doi.org/10.1017/CBO9781107415324.004

Greer, K. (2002). Walking an emotional tightrope: Managing emotions in a women's prison. *Symbolic Interaction, 25*(1), 117–139. https://doi.org/10.1525/si.2002.25.1.117

Gross, J. J. (2002). Emotion regulation: Affective, cognitive, and social consequences. *Psychophysiology, 39*(3), 281–291.

Gross, J. J. (2008). Emotion regulation. In M. Lewis, J. M. Haviland-Jones, & L. F. Barrett (Eds.), *Handbook of emotions*. Guilford Press.

Gross, J. (2014). Emotion regulation: Conceptual and empirical foundations. In *Handbook of emotion regulation*. Guilford Press.

Grosz, E. A. (1994). *Volatile bodies: Toward a corporeal feminism*. Indiana University Press.

Grounds, A. (2004). Psychological consequences of wrongful conviction and imprisonment. *Canadian journal of criminology and criminal justice, 46*(2), 165–182.

Guenther, L. (2013). *Solitary confinement: Social death and its afterlives*. University of Minnesota Press.

Gullone, E., Jones, T., & Cummins, R. (2000). Coping styles and prison experience as predictors of psychological well-being in male prisoners. *Psychiatry, Psychology and Law, 7*(2), 170–181.

Hairgrove, D. D. (2000). A single unheard voice. In R. Johnson & H. Toch (Eds.), *Crime and punishment inside views*. Roxbury Publishing Company.

Hairston, C. F. (2002). Fathers in prison: Responsible fatherhood and responsible public policies. *Marriage & Family Review, 32*(3–4), 111–135.

Hammersley, M. (2014). Recent radical criticism of interview studies: Any implications for the sociology of education? *British Journal of Sociology of Education, 24*(1), 119–126. https://doi.org/10.1080/0142569032000043650

Hancock, P., & Jewkes, Y. (2011). Architectures of incarceration: The spatial pains of imprisonment. *Punishment & Society, 13*(5), 611–629.

Haney, C. (2003). *The psychological impact of incarceration: Implications for post-prison adjustment*. Papers presented to the 'From Prison to Home' Conference, Washington, DC: January 2002.

Haney, C. (2005). *Death by design: Capital punishment as a social psychological system*. Oxford University Press.

252 References

Haney, C. (2008). A culture of harm: Taming the dynamics of cruelty in supermax prisons. *Criminal Justice and Behavior, 35*(8), 956–984.

Haney, C. (2012). Prison effects in the era of mass incarceration. *The Prison Journal,* 0032885512448604.

Haney, C. (2013). Prison effects in the era of mass incarceration. *The Prison Journal,* 1–24. https://doi.org/10.1177/0032885512448604

Haney, C. (2018). The psychological effects of solitary confinement: A systematic critique. *Crime and Justice, 47*(1), 365–416.

Harber, K. D., & Pennebaker, J. W. (1992). Overcoming traumatic memories. In S. A. Christianson (Ed.), *The handbook of emotion and memory: Research and theory.* Lawrence Erlbaum Associates.

Hareli, S., & Parkinson, B. (2008). What's social about social emotions? *Journal for the Theory of Social Behaviour, 38*(2), 131–156.

Harvey, J. (2005). Crossing the boundary: The transition of young adults into prison. In A. Liebling & S. Maruna (Eds.), *The effects of imprisonment.* Routledge.

Harvey, J. (2007). *Young men in prison: Surviving and adapting to life inside.* Routledge.

Hassine, V., Bernard, T. J., McCleary, R., & Wright, R. A. (1996). *Life without parole: Living in prison today.* Roxbury Publishing Company.

Hatfield, E., & Cacioppo, J. T. (1994). *Emotional contagion.* Cambridge University Press.

Hatfield, E., Cacioppo, J. T., & Rapson, R. L. (1993). Emotional contagion. *Current directions in psychological science, 2*(3), 96–100.

Hawkins, D. R. (2013). *Letting go: The pathway of surrender.* Hay House Inc.

Her Majesty's Inspectorate of Prisons. (2010). *Women in prison, a short thematic review.*

Her Majesty's Inspectorate of Prisons. (2015a). *Report on an unannounced inspection of HMP Send.*

Her Majesty's Inspectorate of Prisons. (2015b). *Report on announced inspection of HMP Ranby.*

Her Majesty's Inspectorate of Prisons. (2016). *Life in prison contact with families and friends.*

Herman, J. L. (1992). *Trauma and recovery: The aftermath of violence—From domestic abuse to political terror.* Hachette.

Hochschild, A. R. (1979). Emotion work, feeling rules, and social structure. *American Journal of Sociology, 85*(3), 551–575. https://doi.org/10.1086/227049

References 253

Hochschild, A. R. (2003). *The managed heart: Commercialization of human feeling*, with a new afterword. University of California Press.

Hoggett, P., & Clarke, S. (2009). *Researching beneath the surface: Psycho-social research methods in practice*. Karnac Books.

Hoke, M., & Pendergrass, T. (2019). *Six by ten: Stories from solitary*. Haymarket Books.

Howe, A. (1994). *Punish and critique: Towards a feminist analysis of penality*. Routledge.

Hrubes, D., Feldman, R. S., Tyler, J. M., & Loggins, K. (2004). Emotion-focused deception: The role of deception in the regulation of emotion. In P. Philippot & R. S. Feldman (Eds.), *The regulation of emotion*. Lawrence Erlbaum Associates.

Independent Monitoring Board. (2016a). *Annual report HMP Ranby* (April 2015), 1–18.

Independent Monitoring Board. (2016b). *Annual report HMP Send* (April 2015), 1–23.

Irwin, J., & Cressey, D. R. (1962). Thieves, convicts and the inmate culture. *Social Problems, 10*(2), 142–155.

Irwin, J., & Owen, B. (2005). Harm and the contemporary prison. In A. Liebling & S. Maruna (Eds.), *The effects of imprisonment*. Routledge.

Jackson, M. (1983). *Prisoners of isolation: Solitary confinement in Canada*. University of Toronto Press.

James, E. (2003). *A life inside: A prisoner's notebook*. Atlantic.

Jamieson, R., & Grounds, A. (2005). Release and adjustment: Perspectives from studies of wrongly convicted and politically motivated prisoners. *The effects of imprisonment*, 33–65.

Jansz, J. (2000). Masculine identity and restrictive emotionality. In A. Fischer (Ed.), *Gender and emotion: Social psychological perspectives*. University Press.

Jewkes, Y. (2002). *Captive audience: Media, masculinity and power in prisons*. Willian Publishing.

Jewkes, Y. (2005a). Loss, liminality and the life sentence: Managing identity through a disrupted lifecourse. In A. Liebling & S. Maruna (Eds.), *The effects of imprisonment*. Routledge.

Jewkes, Y. (2005b). Men behind bars 'doing' masculinity as an adaptation to imprisonment. *Men and Masculinities, 8*(1), 44–63.

Jewkes, Y. (2012a). Aesthetics and anaesthetics: The architecture of incarceration. In L. K. Cheliotis (Ed.), *The arts of imprisonment: Control, resistance and empowerment*. Routledge.

254 References

Jewkes, Y. (2012b). Autoethnography and emotion as intellectual resources: Doing prison research differently. *Qualitative Inquiry, 18*(1), 63–75. https://doi.org/10.1177/1077800411428942

Jewkes, Y. (2013). The aesthetics and anaesthetics of prison architecture. In J. Simon, N. Temple, & R. Tobe (Eds.), *Architecture and justice: Judicial meanings in the public realm.* Ashgate Publishing.

Jewkes, Y. (2014). An introduction to 'doing prison research differently'. *Qualitative Inquiry, 20*(4), 387–391. https://doi.org/10.1177/1077800413515828

Jewkes, Y., & Johnston, H. (2007). The evolution of prison architecture. In Y. Jewkes, B. Crewe, & J. Bennett (Eds.), *Handbook on prisons.* Willan.

Jiang, S., & Winfree, L. T. (2006). Social support, gender, and inmate adjustment to prison life insights from a national sample. *The Prison Journal, 86*(1), 32–55.

John, O. P., & Gross, J. J. (2004). Healthy and unhealthy emotion regulation: Personality processes, individual differences, and life span development. *Journal of Personality, 72*(6), 1301–1334.

Johnson, R. (1987). *Hard time: Understanding and reforming the prison.* Brooks/Cole Publishing.

Johnson, L. M. (2008). A place for art in prison: Art as a tool for rehabilitation and management. *Southwest Journal of Criminal Justice, 5*(2), 100–120.

Johnston, R. (1973). *The human cage: A brief history of prison architecture.* Walker.

Johnston, N. B. (2000). *Forms of constraint: A history of prison architecture.* University of Illinois Press.

Jones, R. S., & Schmid, T. J. (2000). *Doing time: Prison experience and identity among first-time inmates.* Jai Press.

Jones, R. S., & Schmid, T. J. (2003). Parallels in the prison experiences of women and men. In B. H. Zaitzow & J. Thomas (Eds.), *Women in prison: Gender and social control.* Lynne Rienner Publishers.

Jose-Kampfner, C. (1990). Coming to terms with existential death: An analysis of women's adaptation to life in prison. *Social Justice, 17*(40), 110–125.

Jourard, S. M. (1974). Some lethal aspects of the male role. In J. H. Pleck & J. Sawyer (Eds.), *Men and masculinity.* Prentice Hall.

Jung, C. G. (1939). *The integration of the personality.* Farrar & Rinehart.

Karp, D. R. (2010). Unlocking men, unmasking masculinities: Doing men's work in prison. *The Journal of Men's Studies, 18*(1), 63–83.

Karstedt, S. (2011). Handle with care: Emotions, crime and justice. Emotions, crime and justice [Onati International Series in Law and Society, Number 1], 1–19.

Karup, A. (2016). *The meaning and effect of yoga in prison.* [Unpublished master's thesis]. University of Cambridge.

Keenan, B. (1992). *An evil cradling: The five year ordeal of a hostage*. Hutchinson.

Kerley, K. R., & Copes, H. (2009). 'Keepin' my mind right' identity maintenance and religious social support in the prison context. *International Journal of Offender Therapy and Comparative Criminology, 53*(2), 228–244.

Kiesling, S. F. (2005). Homosocial desire in men's talk: Balancing and re-creating cultural discourses of masculinity. *Language in Society, 34*(05), 695–726.

King, R. D., & McDermott, K. (1995). *The state of our prisons*. Clarendon Press.

Knight, C. (2014). *Emotional literacy in criminal justice: Professional practice with offenders*. Springer.

Kolind, T., & Bjønness, J. (2019). 'The right way to be a woman': Negotiating femininity in a prison-based drug treatment programme. *Punishment & Society, 21*(1), 107–124.

Kovecses, Z. (2000). *Metaphor and emotion: Language, culture and body in human feeling*. University Press.

Kraftl, P., & Adey, P. (2008). Architecture/affect/inhabitation: Geographies of being-in buildings. *Annals of the Association of American Geographers, 98*(1), 213–231.

Kruttschnitt, C., & Gartner, R. (2005). *Marking time in the golden state: Women's imprisonment in California*. University Press.

Kupers, T. A. (2005). Toxic masculinity as a barrier to mental health treatment in prison. *Journal of Clinical Psychology, 61*(6), 713–724.

Kupers, T. (2008). Prison and the decimation of pro-social life skills . In A. Ojeda (Ed.), *Psychological torture: Phenomenology, psychiatry, neurobiology and ethics: Vol. 5*. Trauma and disaster and psychology (G. Reyes, Series Ed.). Praeger.

Kusenbach, M. (2003). Street phenomenology. *Ethnography, 4*(3), 455–485. https://doi.org/10.1177/146613810343007

Laursen, J., & Laws, B. (2017). Honour and respect in Danish prisons: Contesting 'cognitive distortions' in cognitive-behavioural programmes. *Punishment & Society, 19*(1), 74–95. https://doi.org/10.1177/1462474516649175

Laws, B. (2014). *Fronting, masking and emotion release: An exploration of prisoners' emotional management strategies*. Howard League for Penal Reform. Online Publication.

Laws, B. (2019). The return of the suppressed: Exploring how emotional suppression reappears as violence and pain among male and female prisoners. *Punishment & Society, 21*(5), 560–577.

Laws, B. (2020). Reimaging 'the Self' in criminology: Transcendence, unconscious states and the limits of narrative criminology. *Theoretical criminology*. https://doi.org/10.1080/1362480620919102

256 References

Laws, B. (2021). Segregation seekers: An alternative perspective on the solitary confinement debate. *The British Journal of Criminology, 61*(6), 1452–1468.

Laws, B., & Crewe, B. (2016). Emotion regulation among male prisoners. *Theoretical Criminology, 20*(4), 529–547. https://doi.org/10.1177/1362480615622532

Laws, B., & Lieber, E. (2020). 'King, Warrior, Magician, Lover': Understanding expressions of care among male prisoners. *European Journal of Criminology*. https://doi.org/1477370819896207

Layder, D. (1998). *Sociological practice: Linking theory and social research*. Sage Publications.

Layder, D. (2004). *Emotion in social life: The lost heart of society*. Sage.

Leder, D. (2016). *The distressed body: Rethinking illness, imprisonment, and healing*. University of Chicago Press.

Lees, L., & Baxter, R. (2011). A 'building event' of fear: Thinking through the geography of architecture. *Social & Cultural Geography, 12*(2), 107–122.

Leigey, M. E., & Reed, K. L. (2010). A woman's life before serving life: Examining the negative pre-incarceration life events of female life-sentenced inmates. *Women & Criminal Justice, 20*(January), 302–322. https://doi.org/10.1080/08974454.2010.512229

Levant, R. F. (1995). *Toward the reconstruction of masculinity: A new psychology of men*. Basic Books.

Levine, P. A. (2010). *In an unspoken voice: How the body releases trauma and restores goodness*. North Atlantic Books.

Lewis, H. B. (1971). Shame and guilt in neurosis. *Psychoanalytic Review, 58*(3), 419.

Liebling, A. (1992). *Suicides in prison*. Routledge.

Liebling, A. (1999). Doing research in prison: Breaking the silence? *Theoretical Criminology, 3*(2), 147–173.

Liebling, A. (1999b). Prison suicide and prisoner coping. *Crime and Justice, 26*, 283–359.

Liebling, A. (2001a). Suicides in prison: Ten years on. *Age, 30*(30), 16–30.

Liebling, A. (2001b). Whose side are we on? Theory, practice and allegiances in prisons research. *British Journal of Criminology, 41*(3), 472–484.

Liebling, A. (2007). Prison suicide and its prevention. In Y. Jewkes, B. Crewe, & J. Bennett (Eds.), *Handbook on prisons*. Routledge.

Liebling, A. (2009). Women in prison prefer legitimacy to sex. *British Society of Criminology Newsletter, 63*, 19–23.

Liebling, A. (2014). Postscript: Integrity and emotion in prisons research. *Qualitative Inquiry, 20*(4), 481–486.

Liebling, A. (2015). Description at the edge? I-It/I-Thou relations and action in prisons research. *International Journal for Crime, Justice and Social Democracy, 4*(1), 18–32.

Liebling, A., & Arnold, H. (2005). *Prisons and their moral performance: A study of values, quality, and prison life.*

Liebling, A., & Maruna, S. (Eds.). (2013). *The effects of imprisonment*. Routledge.

Liebling, A., & Straub, C. (2012). Identity challenges and the risks of radicalisation in high security custody. *Prison Service Journal, 203*, 15–22.

Liebling, A., Laws, B., Lieber, E., Auty, K., Schmidt, B. E., Crewe, B., … Morey, M. (2019). Are hope and possibility achievable in prison? *The Howard Journal of Crime and Justice, 58*(1), 104–126.

Lincoln, Y. S., & Guba, E. G. (2000). Paradigmatic controversies, contradictions, and emerging confluences. In K. N. Denzin & Y. S. Lincoln (Eds.), *The Sage handbook of qualitative research*. Sage.

Lock, M. (1993). Cultivating the body: Anthropology and epistemologies of bodily practice and knowledge. *Annual Review of Anthropology, 22*(1), 133–155.

Loftus, E. F. (2005). Planting misinformation in the human mind: A 30-year investigation of the malleability of memory. *Learning & Memory, 12*(4), 361–366. https://doi.org/10.1101/lm.94705

Long, D. (1987). Working with men who batter. In M. E. Scher, M. E. Stevens, G. E. Good, & G. A. Eichenfield (Eds.), *Handbook of counseling & psychotherapy with men*. Sage Publications, Inc.

Long, C. R., & Averill, J. R. (2003). Solitude: An exploration of benefits of being alone. *Journal for the Theory of Social Behaviour, 33*(1), 21–44.

Lozoff, B. (1985). *We're all doing time: A guide for getting free*. Lulu Press, Inc.

Lutz, C. A. (1990). Engendered emotion: Gender, power and the rhetoric of emotional control in American discourse. In C. A. Lutz & L. Abu-Luhod (Eds.), *Language and the politics of emotion*. University Press.

Mandaraka-Sheppard, A. (1986). *Coping with the self in prison: inmates' self image and its relations with behaviour in prison*. The dynamics of aggres.

Mandela, N. (1969). *Letter to daughters Zeni and Zindzi*. Published Online. http://www.abc.net.au/news/specials/nelson-mandela/2013-12-06/nelson-Mandela-letters/2900788

Manstead, A. S. R., & Fischer, A. H. (2000). Emotion regulation in full. *Psychological Inquiry, 11*(3), 188–191.

References

Martin, L. L., & Mitchelson, M. L. (2009). Geographies of detention and imprisonment: Interrogating spatial practices of confinement, discipline, law, and state power. *Geography Compass, 3*(1), 459–477.

Maruna, S. (2001). *Making good: How ex-convicts reform and rebuild their lives.* American Psychological Association.

Maruna, S., Wilson, L., & Curran, K. (2006). Why God is often found behind bars: Prison conversions and the crisis of self-narrative. *Research in Human Development, 3*(2–3), 161–184.

Massumi, B. (2002). *Parables for the virtual: Movement, affect, sensation.* Duke University Press.

Maté, G. (2003). *When the body says no: Exploring the stress disease connection.* Wiley & Sons.

Maté, G. (2011). *When the body says no: The cost of hidden stress.* Vintage Canada.

McConville, S. (2000). The architectural realization of penal ideas. In L. Fairweather & S. McConville (Eds.), *Prison architecture: Policy, design, and experience.* Routledge.

McCorkle, R. C. (1992). Personal precautions to violence in prison. *Criminal Justice and Behavior, 19*(2), 160–173.

McCreaddie, M., & Wiggins, S. (2008). The purpose and function of humour in health, health care and nursing: A narrative review. *Journal of Advanced Nursing, 61*(6), 584–595.

Medlicott, D. (1999). Surviving in the time machine suicidal prisoners and the pains of prison time. *Time & Society, 8*(2–3), 211–230.

Medlicott, D. (2001). *Surviving the prison place: Narratives of suicidal prisoners.* Ashgate.

Merriam, B. (1998). To find a voice: Art therapy in a women's prison. *Women & Therapy, 21*(1), 157–171.

Messerschmidt, J. (1993). *Masculinities and crime: Critique and reconceptualization of theory.* Rowman & Littlefield.

Messerschmidt, J. (2001). Masculinities, crime, and prison. In D. Sabo, T. Kupers, & W. London (Eds.), *Prison masculinities.* Temple University Press.

Meyer, J. C. (2000). Humor as a double-edged sword: Four functions of humor in communication. *Communication Theory, 10*(3), 310–331.

Minister, P., & David, H. (2016). *MoJ Press Release,* 10–12.

Moloney, K. P., van den Bergh, B. J., & Moller, L. F. (2009). Women in prison: The central issues of gender characteristics and trauma history. *Public Health, 123*(6), 426–430.

References 259

Moran, D. (2011). Between outside and inside? Prison visiting rooms as liminal carceral spaces. *GeoJournal, 78*(2), 339–351. https://doi.org/10.1007/s10708-011-9442-6

Moran, D. (2014). Leaving behind the 'total institution'? Teeth, transcarceral spaces and (re)inscription of the formerly incarcerated body. *Gender, Place & Culture, 21*(1), 35–51.

Moran, D. (2015). *Carceral geography: Spaces and practices of incarceration*. Ashgate.

Moran, D., Pallot, J., & Piacentini, L. (2009). Lipstick, lace, and longing: Constructions of femininity inside a Russian prison. *Environment and Planning D: Society and Space, 27*, 700–720.

Moran, D., Conlon, D., & Gill, N. (2013a). *Carceral spaces: Mobility and agency in imprisonment and migrant detention*. Ashgate Publishing.

Moran, D., Pallot, J., & Piacentini, L. (2013b). Privacy in penal space: Women's imprisonment in Russia. *Geoforum, 47*, 138–146.

Morash, M., & Schram, P. J. (2002). *The prison experience: Special issues of women in prison*. Waveland Press.

Morgan, R. D., Gendreau, P., Smith, P., Gray, A. L., Labrecque, R. M., MacLean, N., Van Horn, S. A., Bolanos, A. D., Batastini, A. B., & Mills, J. F. (2016). Quantitative syntheses of the effects of administrative segregation on inmates' well-being. *Psychology, Public Policy, and Law, 22*(4), 439.

Morin, K. M. (2016). The late-modern American jail: Epistemologies of space and violence. *The Geographical Journal, 182*(1), 38–48.

Morin, K. M., & Moran, D. (Eds.). (2015). *Historical geographies of prisons: Unlocking the usable carceral past*. Routledge.

Morreall, J. (1983). *Taking laughter seriously*. SUNY Press.

Newton, C. (1994). Gender theory and prison sociology: Using theories of masculinities to interpret the sociology of prisons for men. *The Howard Journal of Criminal Justice, 33*(3), 193–202.

Nielsen, M. M. (2011). On humour in prison. *European Journal of Criminology, 8*(6), 500–514.

Nietzsche, F. (1889/1990). *Twilight of the idols*. Penguin Classics.

O'Donnell, I. (2014). *Prisoners, solitude, and time*. Oxford University Press.

O'Keefe, M. L., Klebe, K. J., Stucker, A., Sturm, K., & Leggett, W. (2010). *One Year Longitudinal Study of the Psychological Effects of Administrative Segregation*. Colorado Department of Corrections, Office of Planning and Analysis.

Owen, B. A. (1998). *In the mix: Struggle and survival in a women's prison*. SUNY Press.

260   References

Pace, T. W., Negi, L. T., Adame, D. D., Cole, S. P., Sivilli, T. I., Brown, T. D., ... Raison, C. L. (2009). Effect of compassion meditation on neuroendocrine, innate immune and behavioral responses to psychosocial stress. *Psychoneuroendocrinology, 34*(1), 87–98.

Peay, J. (2010). *Mental health and crime.* Routledge-Cavendish.

Pendergrass, T., & Hoke, M., eds. (2018). *Six by Ten: Stories from Solitary.* Haymarket Books.

Pennebaker, J. W. (1997). Writing about emotional experiences as a therapeutic process. *Psychological Science, 8*(3), 162–166. https://doi.org/10.1111/j.14679280.1997.tb00403.x

Philippot, P., & Feldman, R. S. (2004). *The regulation of emotion.* Lawrence Erlbaum Associates.

Philo, C., & Parr, H. (2000). Institutional geographies: Introductory remarks. *Geoforum, 31*(4), 513–521.

Pile, S. (2010). Emotions and affect in recent human geography. *Transactions of the Institute of British Geographers, 35*(1), 5–20.

Planalp, S. (1999). *Communicating emotion: Social, moral, and cultural processes.* University Press.

Pleck, J. H. (1981). *The myth of masculinity.* MIT Press.

Plutchik, R. (2001). The nature of emotions. *American Scientist, 89*(4), 344–350.

Polletta, F. (1999). 'Free spaces' in collective action. *Theory and Society, 28*(1), 1–38.

Price, T. (2012). *The mythic modern: Architectural expeditions into the spirit.* ORO Editions.

Quinlan, E. (2008). Conspicuous invisibility: Shadowing as a data collection strategy. *Qualitative Inquiry, 18*(8), 1480–1499.

Ricciardelli, R., Maier, K., & Hannah-Moffat, K. (2015). Strategic masculinities: Vulnerabilities, risk and the production of prison masculinities. *Theoretical Criminology, 19*(4), 491–513.

Rimé, B. (2007). Interpersonal emotion regulation. In J. J. Gross (Ed.), *Handbook of emotion regulation.* Guilford Press.

Rose, G., Degen, M., & Basdas, B. (2010). More on 'big things': Building events and feelings. *Transactions of the Institute of British Geographers, 35*(3), 334–349.

Rotter, J. B. (1966). Generalized expectancies for internal versus external control of reinforcement. *Psychological Monographs: General and Applied, 80*(1), 1.

Rucker, L. (2005). Yoga and restorative justice in prison: An experience of 'response-ability to harms'. *Contemporary Justice Review, 8*(1), 107–120.

Rustin, M. (2009). The missing dimension: Emotions in the social sciences. In S. D. Sclater, D. W. Jones, H. Price, & C. Yates (Eds.), *Emotion: New psychosocial perspectives*. Palgrave Geography.

Sabo, D. (2001). Doing time, doing masculinity: Sports and prison. In D. Sabo, T. Kupers, & W. London (Eds.), *Prison masculinities*. Temple University Press.

Sabo, D., Kupers, T., & London, W. (2001). *Prison masculinities*. Temple University Press.

Salmela, M. (2005). What is emotional authenticity? *Journal for the Theory of Social Behaviour, 35*(3), 209–230.

Sandelowski, M. (1995). Sample size in qualitative research. *Research in Nursing & Health, 18*(2), 179–183.

Sapolsky, R. M. (2017). *Behave: The biology of humans at our best and worst*. Penguin.

Scarry, E. (1985). *The body in pain: The making and unmaking of the world*. Oxford University Press.

Scase, R. (1999). *Britain towards 2010*. Economic Research Council.

Scheff, T. J. (1979). *Catharsis in healing, ritual, and drama*. University of California Press.

Scheff, T. J., & Retzinger, S. M. (1991). *Emotions and violence: Shame and rage in destructive conflicts*. iUniverse.

Schmid, T. J., & Jones, R. S. (1991). Suspended identity: Identity transformation in a maximum security prison. *Symbolic Interaction, 14*(4), 415–432.

Schwartz, B. (1972). Deprivation of privacy as a functional prerequisite: the case of the prison. *J. Crim. L. Criminology & Police Sci., 63*, 229.

Scraton, P., Sim, J., & Skidmore, P. (1991). *Prisons under protest*. Open University Press.

Segal, L. (1990). *Slow motion: Changing masculinities, changing men*. Rutgers University Press.

Seymour, J. F. (1980). *Niches in prison: Adaptation and environment in correctional institutions*. State University of New York at Albany.

Shalev, S. (2018). Can any good come out of isolation? Probably not. *Prison Service Journal, 236*, 11–16.

Shalev, S., & Edgar, K. (2015). Deep custody: Segregation units and close supervision centres in England and Wales. *London: Conquest Litho, 93*, 14.

Sherman, L. W. (2003). Reason for emotion: Reinventing justice with theories, innovations, and research—The American Society of Criminology 2002 Presidential Address. *Criminology, 41*(1), 1–38.

262 References

Sherman, L., & Strang, H. (2011). Empathy for the devil: Nature and nurture in restorative justice. In *Emotions, crime and justice*. Hart Publishing.

Sibley, D., & van Hoven, B. (2009). The contamination of personal space: Boundary construction in a prison environment. *Area, 41*(2), 198–206. https://doi.org/10.1111/j.1475-4762.2008.00855.x

Sidoli, M. (1996). Farting as a defence against unspeakable dread. *Journal of Analytical Psychology, 41*(2), 165–178.

Sim, J. (1994). Tougher than the rest? Men in prison. In T. Newburn & B. Stanko (Eds.), *Just boys doing the business*. Routledge.

Simonsen, K. (2013). In quest of a new humanism: Embodiment, experience and phenomenology as critical geography. *Progress in Human Geography, 37*(1), 10–26.

Simpson, J., & Weiner, E. S. (1989). *Oxford English dictionary online*. Clarendon Press.

Skogstad, P., Deane, F., & Cusack, J. (2009). Men and prison: Gender role conflict and help seeking. In Z. D. Buchholz & S. K. Boyce (Eds.), *Masculinity: Gender roles, characteristics and coping*. Nova Science Publishers.

Sloan, J. (2012). 'You can see your face in my floor': Examining the function of cleanliness in an adult male prison. *The Howard Journal of Criminal Justice, 51*(4), 400–410.

Smith, P. S. (2006). The effects of solitary confinement on prison inmates: A brief history and review of the literature. *Crime and Justice, 34*(1), 441–528.

Smith, C. (2015). *To flourish or destruct: A personalist theory of human goods, motivations, failure, and evil*. University of Chicago Press.

Smoyer, A. B., & Blankenship, K. M. (2014). Dealing food: Female drug users' narratives about food in a prison place and implications for their health. *International Journal of Drug Policy, 25*(3), 562–568. https://doi.org/10.1016/j.drugpo.2013.10.013

Soulliere, D. (2009). Televisualizing the male prisoner exploring masculinity is Oz. In Z. D. Buchholz & S. K. Boyce (Eds.), *Masculinity: Gender roles, characteristics and coping*. Nova Science Publishers.

Sparks, R., Bottoms, A., & Hay, W. (1996). *Prisons and the Problem of Order*. Clarendon Press.

Spens, I. (1994). *Architecture of incarceration*. Academy Editions.

Spradley, J. P. (1979). *The ethnographic interview*. Holt, Rinehart and Winston.

Stanghellini, G., & Rosfort, R. (2013). *Emotions and personhood: Exploring fragility-making sense of vulnerability*. University Press.

Stebbins, R. A. (2001). *Exploratory research in the social sciences*. Sage.

References   263

Steiner, C. (2003). *Emotional literacy: Intelligence with a heart*. Personhood Press.

Sturdy, A. (2003). Knowing the unknowable? A discussion of methodological and theoretical issues in emotion research and organizational studies. *Organization, 10*(1), 81–105.

Sturdy, A. (2008). Emotion research. *The SAGE dictionary of qualitative management research*. https://doi.org/10.4135/9780857020109

Suedfeld, P., Ramirez, C., Deaton, J., & Baker-Brown, G. (1982). Reactions and attributes of prisoners in solitary confinement. *Criminal Justice and Behavior, 9*(3), 303–340.

Suter, J. M., Byrne, M. K., Byrne, S., Howells, K., & Day, A. (2002). Anger in prisoners: Women are different from men. *Personality and Individual differences, 32*(6), 1087–1100.

Sykes, G. M. (1954). *The society of captives: A study of a maximum security prison*. Princeton University Press.

Sykes, G. M. (1958). *The society of captives. In The Society of Captives*. Princeton University Press.

Sykes, G. (1978). *Criminology*. Harcourt Brace Jovanovich.

Tait, S. (2011). A typology of prison officer approaches to care. *European Journal of Criminology, 8*(6), 440–454.

Tangney, J. P., Wagner, P., Fletcher, C., & Gramzow, R. (1992). Shamed into anger? The relation of shame and guilt to anger and self-reported aggression. *Journal of Personality and Social Psychology, 62*(4), 669.

Taylor, S. E. (1989). *Positive illusions: Creative self-deception and the healthy mind*. Basic Books.

Teplin, L. A., Abram, K. M., & McClelland, G. M. (1996). Prevalence of psychiatric disorders among incarcerated women: I. Pretrial jail detainees. *Archives of General Psychiatry, 53*(6), 505–512.

Thoits, P. A. (1990). Emotional deviance: Research agendas. In T. D. Kemper (Ed.), *Research agendas in the sociology of emotions*. State University of New York Press.

Thomas, J. (2003). Gendered control in prisons: The difference difference makes. In B. H. Zaitzow & J. Thomas (Eds.), *Women in prison: Gender and social control*. Lynne Rienner Publishers.

Thompson, K. L., Hannan, S. M., & Miron, L. R. (2014). Fight, flight, and freeze: Threat sensitivity and emotion dysregulation in survivors of chronic childhood maltreatment. *Personality and Individual Differences, 69*, 28–32. https://doi.org/10.1016/j.paid.2014.05.005

References

Tice, D. M., Baumeister, R. F., & Zhang, L. (2004). The role of emotion in self-regulation: Differing roles of positive and negative emotion. In P. Philippot & R. S. Feldman (Eds.), *The regulation of emotion*. Lawrence Erlbaum Associates.

Toch, H. (1992). *Living in prison: The ecology of survival*. The Free Press.

Toch, H. (1998). Hypermasculinity and prison violence. In L. H. Bowker (Ed.), *Masculinities and violence*. Sage Publications.

Townsend, S. S. M., Kim, H. S., & Mesquita, B. (2013). Are you feeling what I'm feeling? Emotional similarity buffers stress. *Social Psychological and Personality Science, 5*(5), 526–533. https://doi.org/10.1177/1948550613511499

Tschumi, B. (1996). *Architecture and disjunction*. MIT press.

Turner, V. W. (1974). *Dramas, fields and metaphors*. Cornell University Press.

Ugelvik, T. (2014). Prison ethnography as lived experience: Notes from the diaries of a beginner let loose in Oslo prison. *Qualitative Inquiry, 20*(4), 471–480. https://doi.org/10.1177/1077800413516272

Valera, P., & Kates-Benman, C. L. (2016). Exploring the use of special housing units by men released from New York correctional facilities: A small mixed-methods study. *American Journal of Men's Health, 10*(6), 466–473.

van Hoven, B. (2011). 'We were just testing what kind of man you are'—Negotiating masculinities in a New Mexico prison. *Justice Spatiale—Spatial Justice, 3*, 1–12.

van Hoven, B., & Sibley, D. (2008). 'Just duck': The role of vision in the production of prison space. *Environment and Planning D: Society and Space, 26*, 1001–1017.

van der Kolk, B. (2014). *The body keeps the score*. Viking.

Van der Kolk, B. (2014). *The body keeps the score: Mind, brain and body in the transformation of trauma*. Penguin UK.

Vince, R. (2018). Segregation—Creating a new norm. *Prison Service Journal, 236*, 17–26.

Walker, N. (1987). The unwanted effects of long-term imprisonment. In A. E. Bottoms & R. Light (Eds.), *Problems of long-term imprisonment*. Gower.

Walker, S., & Worrall, A. (2000). Life as a woman: The gendered pains of indeterminate imprisonment. *Prison Service Journal, 132*, 27–37.

Wallace, B. A. (2009). *Contemplative science: Where Buddhism and neuroscience converge*. Columbia University Press.

Walton, C., Coyle, A., & Lyons, E. (2004). Death and football: An analysis of men's talk about emotions. *British Journal of Social Psychology, 43*(3), 401–416.

Wilde, O. (2010). *De Profundis*. Modern Library.

Winlow, S., & Hall, S. (2009). Retaliate first: Memory, humiliation and male violence. *Crime, Media, Culture, 5*(3), 285–304.

Wolcott, H. F. (1990). *Writing up qualitative research*. Sage Publications.

Wolcott, H. F. (1999). *Ethnography: A way of seeing*. Rowman Altamira.

Wormith, J. S. (1984). The controversy over the effects of long-term incarceration. *Canadian Journal of Criminology, 26*, 423.

Wright, S., Crewe, B., & Hulley, S. (2017). Suppression, denial, sublimation: Defending against the initial pains of very long life sentences. *Theoretical Criminology, 21*(2), 225–246.

Wyner, R. (2003). *From the inside: Dispatches from a women's prison*. Aurum Pr Ltd.

Yanos, P. T., & Hopper, K. (2008). On 'false, collusive objectification': Becoming attuned to self-censorship, performance and interviewer biases in qualitative interviewing. *International Journal of Social Research Methodology, 11*(3), 229–237.

Zaitzow, B. H., & Thomas, J. (2003). *Women in prison: Gender and social control*. Lynne Rienner Publishers.

Zamble, E., & Porporino, F. (1990). Coping, imprisonment, and rehabilitation: Some data and their implications. *Criminal Justice and Behavior, 17*(1), 53–70.

Zhang, Z., Spicer, A., & Hancock, P. (2008). Tales of hyper-organizational space: The work of JG Ballard. *Organization, 15*(6), 889–910.

Index[1]

A

Absorption, 108, 168
Abuse
  emotional, 203
  physical, 17, 203
  sexual, 203
Adaptation, 56, 167, 181, 209, 210, 212, 224, 228
  to cell, 115
Addiction, 20, 124, 188
Affect, 7, 15, 28, 39, 50, 84, 108, 115, 142, 197, 201, 205, 208
Aggression, 4, 9, 14, 18, 28, 40, 49, 55, 88, 90–92, 94–99, 109, 143, 144, 172, 215, 222, 226
Alchemy and emotion transformation, 38–42

Anger, 4, 7, 9, 10, 13, 22, 29–32, 42, 44, 46, 49, 55, 60, 64, 66, 70, 85, 86, 88, 94–96, 99, 100, 109, 112, 115, 119, 123, 124, 128, 136, 139, 145, 163, 204, 205, 211, 214, 216, 218, 222–226, 237
Anxiety, 4, 31, 34, 35, 40, 95, 112, 114, 118, 119, 123, 126, 127, 132, 133, 162, 183, 197, 204, 206, 218
Artwork, 8, 46, 47, 75, 94, 129, 174, 195, 209

B

Bentham, J., 107, 180

---

[1] Note: Page numbers followed by 'n' refer to notes.

© The Author(s), under exclusive license to Springer Nature Switzerland AG 2022
B. Laws, *Caged Emotions*, Palgrave Studies in Prisons and Penology,
https://doi.org/10.1007/978-3-030-96083-4

268 Index

Body/bodies
  damaged, 153, 175,
    182–187, 197
  embodiment, 153
  exercising the, 187
  maintaining, 186–191
  scars, 153, 180–183
Body waste, *see* Dirty protest
Boredom, 36, 37, 88, 91, 98, 112,
  143, 217

C

Calverley, A., 5, 50, 52, 53, 211
Canteen, 73, 80, 84, 187
Carlen, P., 29, 95, 99, 100, 188
Cell
  as claustrophobic, 108,
    112–115, 215
  as sanctuary, 108, 115–119
Chaplaincy, 130, 131
Children, 16, 67, 68, 74n3, 81, 95,
  112, 132, 133, 135, 204
Classrooms, 109
Cohen, S., 36, 42, 47, 56, 228
Collins, R., 91, 102, 214, 215
Contagious emotions,
  85–91, 214–215
Control, 6, 9, 11, 13, 19, 26,
  32–34, 36, 42, 47, 50–55,
  51n9, 59, 60, 66, 86, 95,
  97–101, 109, 116, 119, 123,
  127, 129, 140, 141, 144, 145,
  159, 167, 174, 180, 186, 192,
  206, 207, 209–211, 219,
  220, 226
Cooking, 79, 80, 84, 187, 213
Coping, 34n6, 52, 56, 186, 188,
  189, 192, 208

Crewe, B., 5, 10, 15, 18, 19, 29, 52,
  54, 56, 79, 81, 94, 96, 102,
  107–109, 115, 124, 132, 135,
  145, 146, 162, 180, 182, 183,
  186, 187, 194, 205, 208, 213,
  218, 219, 224, 226, 227
Csikszentmihalyi, M., 130

D

Damaged bodies, 153, 181–186
Denial, 42, 44, 115, 138, 197
Depression, 4, 37, 94, 112, 204
Desistance, 5, 50, 52
Destructive emotions, 66, 92,
  110, 214
Diluting emotions, *see* Emotion
  management
Dining room, 96, 109, 122, 124,
  125, 127, 128, 143
Dirty protest, 153, 181, 189–191
Distilling emotions, *see* Emotion
  management
Drugs, 16, 28, 30–32, 30n4, 36, 37,
  74n3, 91, 100, 110n1, 124,
  161, 168, 203, 207, 208

E

Edgar, K., 90, 156, 160, 170,
  173, 185
Emotion management, 9, 14, 35–38,
  202, 204, 207, 210
Emotions
  contagious, 85–91, 214–215
  destructive, 66, 92, 110, 214
  embodied emotions, 4, 190,
    194, 228
  flexibility, 49–54, 62

losing control of, 33, 34

management of, 9, 14, 38, 87, 101, 102, 108, 110, 145, 202, 204, 205, 210, 223, 227

methodological complexity of, 5, 27

rigidity, 49–54

theory of, 107

Empathy, 72–75, 74n3, 93, 98–100, 183, 212, 221

Explosions of emotion, 33, 225

Expression, 5, 6, 28–31, 47–49, 60, 75, 79, 81, 85, 92–95, 99, 101, 108, 109, 118, 120, 124, 129, 132, 139, 146, 185, 202, 203, 213, 219, 221, 224–227

Fear, 7, 9, 10, 22, 31, 32, 34, 40, 42, 43, 45, 60, 68, 73, 77, 89–91, 96, 100, 102, 109, 113, 118, 124, 128, 139, 143–146, 151, 165–167, 173, 184, 187, 188, 190, 193, 205, 206, 214–216, 218

Female prisoners, 21, 29, 31, 48, 73, 75, 79, 80, 92, 93, 98, 102, 120, 203, 213, 220–222

Fighting, 18, 19, 40, 82, 127, 163

Forward panic, 91, 214

Foucault, M, 107, 180

Freedom, 11, 44, 118, 129, 132, 144, 208

Frustration, 13, 22, 32, 42, 49, 54, 64, 66, 88, 89, 94, 109, 112, 119, 139, 144, 163, 170–172, 181, 184, 204, 214, 216, 218

Gangs, 17, 18, 22, 96, 165, 173

Gaze (institutional), 191, 220

Gender
differences in experience of imprisonment, 212
similarities, 221

God, 31, 64, 168, 169, 188, 192, 193, 195

Goffman, E., 101, 108, 128, 129, 146, 180, 183, 188, 225

Gratitude, 40, 77, 130

Guilt, 50, 68, 69, 95, 111, 132, 133, 204, 214

Gym, 37, 49, 82, 84, 93, 109, 129–131, 186, 187, 213

Hair salon, 129, 131

Happiness, 30, 42, 110, 132, 193

Healthcare, 159

Hope, 3, 37, 40, 50, 56, 96, 169, 175, 193, 226, 227, 229

Hunger strike, 188

Identity, 18, 19, 101, 109, 111, 113, 117, 118, 131, 133, 139, 169, 183, 187, 192, 194, 198, 206, 216, 228

Imprisonment, 4–8, 10, 11, 13–15, 25–49, 54–56, 62, 65–67, 80, 85, 88, 92, 95, 96, 100, 102, 107, 111, 115, 118, 147, 152, 153, 156, 162–164, 175, 180, 181, 186–188, 192, 198, 203–228

270 Index

Institutionalisation, 146, 167, 174,
195, 228
Isolation, 141, 142, 151,
156, 167–169
damaging effects of, 142, 151
lesser evil, 153, 174, 197
seeking out, 152, 153
segregation unit, 152, 153,
175, 190
solitary confinement, 151–153,
156, 157, 159, 175, 197, 216

J

Jewkes, Y., 5, 10, 28, 37, 46, 55, 81,
107, 108, 111, 112, 115, 117,
118, 121, 122, 146, 205, 212,
215, 226

K

Koran, 193, 194

L

Leder, D., 184, 191
Library, 80, 86, 109, 140
Liebling, A, 4, 33, 33n5, 62, 63, 86,
94–96, 98, 101, 115, 167,
181, 196, 198, 203, 211,
220, 226
Life before prison, 14
Life sentence, 40
Liminal spaces, 111, 112, 115, 219
Loneliness, 158, 204
Love, 3, 4, 17, 28, 63, 67, 72,
79, 81, 83, 84, 111, 118,
132, 133, 189, 193, 213,
216, 228

M

Madness, 33
Maruna, S, 115, 192
Masculinity, 4, 22, 29, 97, 202, 222
Meaning, 6, 42, 46, 77, 79, 101,
107, 113, 139, 168, 183, 192,
194, 209, 219
Medication, 31
Meditation, 39, 192–194, 216
Monastic, 169
Mood, 38, 39, 42, 46, 60, 77, 84,
88, 91, 95, 102, 117, 121,
194, 209, 215
Motivation, 9, 26, 153,
155–175, 211
for segregation, 152,
153, 155–175
Music, 30, 46, 47, 84, 114, 129,
141, 190, 193
Muslim prisoners, 163, 165, 166
fear of, 165

N

Nature, 15, 32, 35, 72, 77, 79, 82,
93, 97, 125, 128, 131, 139,
144, 146, 151, 153, 158, 172,
180, 190, 193, 207, 209,
213, 228
Noise (sensory intrusion),
119, 122, 189

O

O'Donnell, I., 35, 45, 56, 68, 90,
120, 123, 141, 147, 157,
159, 168, 173, 197, 211,
216, 226
Odour, 190, 191

Index   271

P

Panic attack, 86, 133, 145
Panopticon, 180
Positive emotions, 7, 31, 67, 205
Positivity, 84, 116, 134
Power, 11, 29, 59, 60, 62, 66,
    98–101, 107, 109, 180, 190,
    193, 195, 205, 206, 210, 211,
    218, 219, 221, 223, 226
Prayer, 193, 194
Progression (of the sentence),
    170, 171, 175
Psychologists, 71, 138, 139
PTSD, 21, 31

R

Regret, 185
Relationships
    family, 203
    prisoners, 4, 17, 59, 73
Resistance, 11, 135, 158, 186, 225
Rumination, 42, 47, 54, 113,
    207, 222

S

Safety, 18, 89, 124, 128, 131,
    165–168, 184, 215
Security, 6, 37, 45, 113, 118, 126,
    128, 129, 153, 163, 171, 218
Segregation unit, 6, 152, 153,
    155, 156, 160, 163, 165, 169,
    171, 173–175, 179,
    185, 189–191
Self-harm/Self-injury, 29n3, 33, 34,
    34n6, 64, 94, 123, 180, 183

Sexual abuse, 203
Silence, 120, 141, 172, 190
Solitary confinement, 6, 10, 147,
    151–153, 156–159, 162, 173,
    175, 179–198, 206, 207,
    216, 227
Solitude, *see* Isolation
Sparks, R., 98, 126, 146, 168, 207,
    212, 218, 225
Spatial selection, 110, 143–145, 220
Spirituality, 189, 192, 194
Staff members, 62, 66, 130,
    135, 146
Suicide, 20, 21, 29n3, 31, 33, 33n5,
    49, 91, 115, 123, 166, 203
Supermax prisons, 175
Survival, 13, 42, 56, 186, 189,
    209, 218

T

Tattoos, 183
Therapeutic community, 71, 124,
    136, 136n6, 137, 139,
    220, 222
Therapeutic spaces, 71,
    109, 136–140
Therapy, 100, 136, 137, 139, 140,
    166, 206
Torture, 157, 181, 196
Trauma, 8, 14, 17–21, 34, 49, 55,
    76, 96, 181, 184, 190, 197,
    204, 220, 223–225

V

Victim, 34, 137, 206

272　Index

Violence
　retaliatory, 166
Visit halls, 109, 132–136

Writing, 4, 29, 45, 47, 56, 132,
　168, 184, 196, 197,
　201, 209

Worst of the worst, 185

Yoga, 194

CPSIA information can be obtained
at www.ICGtesting.com
Printed in the USA
LVHW082056070522
718180LV00004B/145